THE COLOMBO FAMILY

A History of New York's Colombo Mafia Family

ANDY PETEPIECE

Tellwell Talent
www.tellwell.ca

ISBN
978-0-2288-2661-3 (Paperback)
978-0-2288-2662-0 (eBook)

Acknowledgments

To Patti
My Best Friend

To Our Best Friends
Dook, Boomer, Tanner, and Digger

Introduction

Thanks for purchasing this book. It is the history of New York's Colombo crime Family from the early 1920s to the present day. In an attempt to avoid confusion, I have called the organization the Colombo Family, although that label did not come into use until the late 1960s.

Details on the Colombo Family are sparse for the first twenty-some years. No one understood the Mafia back then, plus informers and turncoat witnesses were rare. From the time of the famous 1957 National Meeting of La Cosa Nostra at Apalachin, New York, much more evidence became available. As we moved into the 1980s, turncoats were becoming very common, plus we have had the luxury of many transcripts from F.B.I. electronic surveillance of the bad guys.

My advanced apologies for the endless names and dates. They are simply unavoidable. The good news is that there is no exam once you have finished going through the book, so there is no need to memorize anything. (Big smile)

In specific chapters, I tell the story of hood A from start to finish. Then I go back in time to outline the significant events of hood B. I hope this style makes it easier to follow the lives of the top characters.

At no point do I claim that my book contains all the significant details in this Family's history. Nor do I profess to have the "true" story of each incident. This is my present understanding of the Colombo Family history.

I trust you will find a few interesting stories in this book by the time you are finished

Notes

NOTE ONE:

A simplified explanation of RICO.

RICO stands for Racketeer Influenced and Corrupt Organizations Act. Congress passed it in 1970.

The Act allows increased criminal penalties for acts performed as part of an ongoing criminal enterprise.

For this book, the ongoing criminal enterprise is the Colombo crime Family.

To convict someone under RICO, the government must show that the person is a member or Associate of the criminal enterprise.

Then the feds must show that the crimes were committed to maintain or enhance his position in the enterprise.

RICO conspiracy is the planning of the Act (s). For example, you are planning a murder ordered by the Boss.

Substantive RICO is the performance of the Act (s). For example, carrying out the murder ordered by the Boss.

The government must prove the accused committed at least two criminal acts to win a conviction for RICO or RICO conspiracy.

It has to be at least two criminal acts to prove there was a "pattern of racketeering."

Thirty-five crimes are considered "predicate acts" for RICO. They include such things as murder, murder conspiracy, extortion, drug dealing, etc.

RICO VS. NON-RICO

If a jury convicts a person of extortion on his behalf, he might get a sentence of five years. However, if the government proved that the person committed two acts of extortion on behalf of his crime Family, a RICO conviction, the sentence could be twenty years.

NOTE TWO:

The government can use the RICO law in civil cases. The most famous example was the government's very successful effort to purge the Teamster Union of Mafia control.

NOTE THREE:

I capitalize on Family when it refers to the Mafia organization. When writing about a person's blood family, I don't use a capital. I also use capitals on Boss, Underboss, Consigliere, Capo, Soldier, and Associate simply because I like the way it looks.

NOTE FOUR:

The proper name for the Italian American Mafia is Cosa Nostra. I use La Cosa Nostra (L.C. N) because that is the label commonly used by the F.B.I. and the court system.

NOTE FIVE:

The term "made guy" or the verb "made" means the Boss formally inducted the person into La Cosa Nostra. "Wiseguy" means the same thing.

Table of Contents

Appendix B
A list of the Gallo crew from 1962.

Appendix C
A well-researched discussion of the Joey Gallo murder, along with criticisms of the Frank Sheeran version of the hit.

Appendix D
A detailed diagram illustrating the Joey Gallo murder scene.

Appendix E
The original New York Police Department's shooting diagram of the Joey Gallo murder.

Appendix F
A leadership chart of the Colombo Family from the F.B.I.

Appendix G
A summary of an F.B.I. bugged conversation by Buffalo Boss Stefano Magaddino concerning Joe Magliocco and the Colombo Family.

Appendix H
A second summary of an F.B.I. bugged conversation by Buffalo Boss Stefano Magaddino concerning Joe Magliocco and the Colombo Family.

CHAPTER ONE

A Typical Mafia Family

Around the turn of the twentieth century, millions of honest Italians immigrated to the United States, seeking a new and more prosperous life. They and the following generations would contribute significantly to America and would become an essential part of its fabric. Unfortunately, a group of men who decided, whether by choice or circumstance, to follow their own rules and not those of their new country also arrived. It would be these men who would begin to form the outlines of Mafia Families.

Most immigrants from Sicily would have at least heard whispers of that island's secret society now known as the Sicilian Mafia. Others, from the southern Italian province of Calabria, would be vaguely familiar with the 'Ndrangheta which is better recognized today as the Calabrian Mafia. Residents of Naples would be aware of the Camorra, another secret society.

New arrivals initially tend to live together in enclaves of their kind. The Italians who flooded into America were no different. In major cities, there were groupings of Sicilians, Calabrians, and Neopolitans. Not surprisingly, the initial outlines of the Mafia Families that developed did so along these lines as well. However, this exclusivity would not last long in America.

Gradually, in its formal membership, a blending took place that created a unique American Mafia. Among those who swore a blood oath of allegiance to La Cosa Nostra were: adult males from all regions of Italy, young men born in Italy but raised in America, and also Italian-American males born of Italian parents. This mixture would continue for a hundred years, but

---

gradually the majority of the membership would be Italian-Americans, born of Italian-American parents. It was a natural evolution as the waves of Italian immigrants ended as World War One began in 1914.

From about 1900 to 1963, law-abiding Americans had only the vaguest idea about Italian-American organized crime. What they did know was tainted by racism and myth.

In the early decades of the twentieth century, there was little incentive for the politicians and the various arms of the judiciary to tackle crime in the Italian enclaves. Few of those in positions of power understood the language and customs of these latest newcomers. Furthermore, for many of the new Americans, experience suggested that the police might not be trustworthy. Sadly, in that era, many municipal forces were plagued with officers who owed their positions to politics and corruption. Additionally, social factors such as poverty would play a role in the emergence of youth gangs, which were the training grounds for many future Mafia hoods. With these conditions, it is not surprising that the emerging Mafia Families grew without much hindrance.

The three main Italian criminal groups all had strict codes of secrecy, so it wasn't a surprise that the developing Italian-American families incorporated this critical rule. Their members and Associates would not talk about their organization. As a result, there was much confusion about the existence of the Mafia.

Consequently, for the first half of the twentieth century, vague terms such as "The Black Hand" or "Mafia" were bandied about when significant criminal activity erupted in the Italian enclaves. During the era of Prohibition (1920-1933), there were gangs of every ethnic makeup. Generic terms such as "Syndicate" came into use to signify the obviously "organized" criminal associations. Ironically, it was during this very period that the American Mafia came into its own.

KEFAUVER

The Kefauver Hearings (1950-1951) brought the concept of a national Italian-American criminal organization called the Mafia to the public's attention. Senator Estes Kefauver (Tennessee) headed the Special Committee to Investigate Organized Crime in Interstate Commerce. It held hearings in 14 cities and concluded with a report implying "the Mafia," was a foreign entity working within the United States. It would take decades to dispel this notion of an alien invasion and lay the blame on homegrown problems. However, after a brief flurry of excitement, the "Mafia" problem was pushed into the background by the furor over the fear of communist infiltration into major sectors of American life.

APALACHIN

On November 14, 1957, the spotlight focused on the Mafia. On that day, near the tiny New York State town of Apalachin, fifty-some mobsters were gathered at the estate of Joseph Barbara to discuss La Cosa Nostra's business. State Troopers Edgar Croswell and Vincent Vasisko, along with the Bureau of Alcohol and Tobacco agents Kenneth Brown and Arthur Ruston, drove into Barbara's driveway and caused a panic amongst the gangsters gathered there. Roadblocks were set up, and eventually, authorities identified 58 hoods. This event captured the imagination of the American public as days of headlines followed across the nation.

Investigations, hearings, grand juries, and court cases resulted from the Apalachin discovery. The Bureau of Narcotics emerged as the best-informed unit. The files contained the names of many of the key players in La Cosa Nostra. They had an excellent understanding of the structure that bound the various groups together. On the other hand, J. Edgar Hoover and his F.B.I. looked foolish. They had little to offer in the way of intelligence on the gathered hoods. The F.B.I. responded by immediately focusing on La Cosa Nostra.

In 1959 the F.B.I. had listening devices secreted in two significant meeting places of the Chicago Mafia Family. Agents overheard boss Sam Giancanna discuss meeting with the "Commission." This organization was a group of seven major Mafia Bosses who met to sort out inter-family disputes and set primary policy for all the Families. From this information, the F.B.I. began using the term "The Criminal Commission et al." to refer to the Mafia.

LA COSA NOSTRA

In September of 1961, informant Greg Scarpa told his F.B.I. handler that the name of his organization was "La Causa Nostra." Despite this information, the F.B.I. continued to use the label "The Criminal Commission et al." until an internal memo from Director Hoover on January 16, 1963, ordered the various offices to change the name to "La Causa Nostra." On April 23, 1963, another F.B.I. document suggested the term should be "Cosa Nostra" instead of "Causa." By July 1, 1963, the New York Office of the F.B.I. was using "La Cosa Nostra" but also included its variations; "Cosa Nostra," "La Causa Nostra," "Causa Nostra," "causa nostra," and "Onorata Societa."

Finally, on August 12, 1963, a semblance of order was brought to the matter. The information from the informant in September 1961 and from other sources was incorrect. From this point on, the F.B.I. used "La Cosa Nostra" and its acronym "L.C.N." to signify what we call the American Mafia. Throughout this book, I use these terms interchangeably.

THE FORMAL STRUCTURE OF A MAFIA FAMILY

At the top of the pyramid-shaped structure of a Mafia Family sits the Boss. Some other terms used by Mafia members for this position are "father" and "representante." His rule is dictatorial, but smarter leaders always considered the political implications of their major decisions. This talent would often come into play when he was selecting his various officers and approving new inductions into the Family.

Like most influential leaders, the Boss of a Mafia Family attracts a lot of attention. Consequently, names like Capone, Luciano, and Gotti are known to many of the general public. On the downside, being well known makes a Boss a prime target of law enforcement, and many have ended their lives behind bars.

Being the Boss also means that all the other members of the Family pay you tribute in one form or another. This monetary success creates envy amongst some of the underlings, and numerous heads of Families have gone down in a blaze of gunfire. The October 25, 1957 murder of Albert Anastasia, the December 16, 1985, whacking of Paul Castellano, are two notable examples.

The Boss gets to pick his second in command called the Underboss. This person's role varies with each Family, but in simple terms, he often handles many of the day-to-day problems that arise. Holding this position does not automatically mean that you are next in line for the top slot.

Another high-level position is the Consigliere. Originally this person was to act as a bridge between the leaders of the Family and its Soldiers. He was to advise Family members on various matters, but in reality, the Consigliere probably did not buck the Boss on too many issues. There are some instances of the Consigliere being an active member of a Family. In the case of the Colombo organization, there were two examples of the Consigliere running murder squads.

The last layer of the administration is the Capos, who are selected by the Boss. These are the street leaders of crews of Soldiers and Associates who do the dirty work. Holding this position means excellent prestige amongst the street people, and it is often very lucrative in that those on the rungs below

are supposed to cut the Capo in on their monetary successes. Of course, the Capo then has to kick a portion upstairs to the Boss.

Soldiers make up the most numerous and lowest level of formal members of La Cosa Nostra. For Italian-American criminals, it is a tremendous honor to be accepted into the organization, and it isn't long before everyone on the street knows of this elevation.

INDUCTION AND RULES

Most new Soldiers go through a formal ceremony when they are "made." Although variations exist, the recruit has a bit of blood drawn from his finger by the use of a pin. The dripping blood symbolizes his rebirth into the Family. Secondly, the Boss lights a wallet-sized picture of a saint (or tissue paper) on fire. The inductee juggles it between his hands to prevent any blistering of the skin. As he does so, he repeats a pledge never to betray members of the organization. The new member would then formally meet everyone present. Afterward, the Boss quickly outlines the basic rules of La Cosa Nostra.

All members are supposed to obey any order they may receive from a person in higher authority within the Family. They are not to speak of the Family business or even the existence of the organization to outsiders. Inductees, when introducing a made member to another, use the term "friend of ours" or "amico nostra." This secret method of introduction has become academic, as the F.B.I.'s intelligence has been on top of Family membership lists for decades.

ASSOCIATES

People who regularly engage in criminal activity with members of La Cosa Nostra are called Associates by law enforcement. Some of these men are eligible for future induction due to their Italian-American heritage. Others will never become members because they don't meet that criterion. People of a wide range of ethnic backgrounds have been mob Associates. Over the last 15 years or so, the first category of Associates has started to become known as "wannabes" by law enforcement and the media. Both groups of Associates are vital to the functioning of a La Cosa Nostra Family, including the Colombos.

Albert Gallo, the father of the infamous Joseph "Crazy Joey" Gallo, was a mob Associate. He took part in his son's activities, especially during the Gallo brother's revolt against their Mafia boss, Joseph Profaci, in the early sixties. Chapter Six details this rebellion.

When his sons and their allies holed up on Brooklyn's President Street in 1961, Pappa Gallo moved in to cook for the boys despite the danger. This active participation came back to haunt the elder Gallo. On November 15, 1961, the Immigration and Naturalization Service attempted to have Albert Gallo deported, but he won a delay. Two years later, Gallo pled guilty to a fraud charge involving an attempt by his son Larry to obtain a bank loan. By making himself an active Associate, Albert Gallo became a legitimate target of law enforcement and the Gallo enemies.

Ruby Stein was a more influential mob Associate than Albert "Pappa" Gallo. Along with Jiggs Forlano, Stein was active in gambling and its accompanying loansharking. Forlano was the muscle behind the mathematically inclined Stein. The latter was considered a prime money-maker. Unfortunately for Stein, he lent money to various members of the infamous "Westies" in the late 1970s.

On May 5, 1977, Ruby Stein's career as a mob Associate came to a grisly end. At a Westies, hangout called the 596 Club, Daniel "Danny" Grillo, William "Billy" Beattie, and Richard "Richie" Ryan shot Stein. His corpse was dragged into the washroom and cut up into pieces. Making money for the mob didn't save Stein from lunatics.

While not a money-maker like Stein, Gallo Associate Robert "Bobby B" Boriello was a mob wannabe on the rise. He was friendly with Steven "Stevie" Gallo, a nephew of Joseph "Crazy Joe" Gallo, which brought him into the thick of the action at a young age. Gallo turncoat Peter "The Greek" Diapoulos identified Boriello as part of the hit teams of Joseph "Crazy Joe" Gallo.

Two decades later, Boriello was still in the midst of the action, this time as a Soldier in the Gambino Family run by his buddy John "The Dapper Don" Gotti. On April 13, 1991, Boriello's life long dance with death caught up to him when he was gunned down. He had gone from a wannabe to a made man, but he had also ended up quite dead.

BLOOD FAMILIES

Like all of us, Mafia guys are the product of two biological parents, and most have a slew of brothers, sisters, aunts, uncles, cousins, wives, in-laws and kids. This blood clan would be sure to gather at baptisms, weddings, and burials. For some blood families, the funerals came far too soon for some of its members.

Mafia relatives not involved in the "life" were supposed to be strictly off-limits to any threats and violence. This rule was another Mafia myth.

On July 10, 1934, Kansas City Mafia Boss John Lazia was alighting from his car in front of a hotel when a gunman opened fire on him with a machine gun. Now anyone who has had any experience with a machine gun of that era will instantly know that we are not talking about a precision instrument. Sitting in the car as Lazia came under fire was his wife, a certified non-combatant. By sheer luck, she avoided injury by the stream of bullets that killed her husband. Mrs. Lazia would not be the only Mafia blood family member to be involved in Mafia violence despite the rules.

Girlfriends or "gummares" do not receive the same theoretical protection given to blood relatives who are not involved with La Cosa Nostra. A case in point involves Anthony "Nino" Colombo, the father of Joseph Colombo. For some reason, the higher powers in the Family decided that Anthony Colombo had to die. Rumors suggested that the senior Colombo had committed the unforgivable sin of fooling around with the wife of another wiseguy. This mistake may have been correct, but one must be careful of accepting the street talk as gospel. Often, mob leaders will paint their victims with a black brush to "justify" their murder. Sometimes, the real reason has to do with money and greed, which don't appear too noble. In any event, when Anthony Colombo was found garroted in the back of his Pontiac two-door on February 6, 1939, joining him in death under the oilskin tablecloth was Christina Oliveri. Whatever her offense, if any, she didn't deserve this kind of end.

Then there was the case of the morons from either the Pittsburgh or Cleveland Family who took out Youngstown's Charles "Cadillac Charlie" Cavallaro. This man was a veteran mobster who was fully aware of the hazards of the life he had chosen. It wouldn't have crossed his mind that he was putting his two young sons in danger when he started his vehicle on November 23, 1962. The ensuing explosion tore up Charlie and his most youthful boy. By a fluke, his second son survived the disaster. This insanity happened at Cavallaro's home, and his wife was the first witness to the bomb's horrible results. So much for the sanctity of the innocent.

One Mafia wife blurred the lines between non-combatant blood family members and those that were involved and thus legitimate targets. Colombo turncoat Lawrence Mazza testified during a 1994 trial that the wife of Capo Theodore "Teddy" Persico did just that. She came out of the Persico house carrying a bag that contained a Mac-10 machine pistol, and its silencer. The Persico crew was going out hunting for rival Capo Pasquale "Paddy" Amato. They thought they would have better luck with a silenced automatic weapon.

Mafia wives also sometimes have to carry things besides guns. Take the first wife of Colombo hood Michael Franzese for example. Her husband had a series of legal problems that must have taken a toll. Then Franzese started running around with a dancer.

To add humiliation to that mess, you only have to consider how Franzese protected his family financially. He claims he set up a large fund that would support them in high style just by using the interest. The problem was that this money was the product of his illegal scams. Furthermore, Franzese says he gave this money to lawyers who ended up stealing it.

Michael Franzese's attention remained focused on himself and his new love. Meanwhile, his first family lived under the threat of eviction from their residence. Franzese cashed in on his criminal notoriety by writing a book called, *Quitting the Mob* (1992). He further humiliated his first wife by detailing his romance with the dancer.

Being a blood relative of a Mafia member or Associate carries a heavy burden. Most likely, you will have to suffer through numerous court cases in which your loved one's freedom is at stake. Along the way, there will be many financial ups and downs as his career ricochets from success to failure. Add on top of this the constant fear that the next time he leaves, it may be the last time you see him alive. Things get worse if he decides, under legal pressure, to become a turncoat. Now you are isolated from your friends, and sometimes you have to pick up and leave, moving to a new town where you don't know anyone. Now big money stops. Hubby will have to earn an honest living, and your lifestyle will fall considerably. Factor in the anger he is feeling at his bad luck and a happy camper you don't have. Best of luck!

CHAPTER TWO

The Early Years

Villabate is a town in the Sicilian province of Palermo that should not be confused with the capital city of the same name. Joseph Profaci was born there on October 1, 1897. About a year later, on June 29, 1898, Joseph Magliocco came into this world. They would be friends, brothers-in-law, and Mafia partners for the rest of their lives.

Magliocco would be the first to move to the United States. It is unclear why his father Giovanni and mother Carmela packed up their five kids and headed west, but we can make some educated guesses. The Magliocco family left the port of Palermo on April 9, 1914. During this period, tensions were rising rapidly in Europe as World War One approached. Italy's alliances with England and other countries meant she was involved. Perhaps the Maglioccos were anticipating the worst and seized the opportunity to take their family to a safer location. Maybe they emigrated in the hopes of improving their standard of living. Whatever the reason, the entire Magliocco family was going to the United States to join the eldest son Angelo who was already living in Brooklyn.

In the harbor in Palermo, the Magliocco family trudged up the gangplank of a two-year-old passenger ship named the Taormina. It had been built in the shipyards of Glasgow, Scotland, and was now doing runs between the Mediterranean and New York City. This vessel could carry 2,680 passengers but only 60 in first class. The vast majority of the passengers, some 2,500 occupied the third class areas in the lower decks. That is where the Maglioccos bedded down.

On April 22, 1914, the Taormina and the Maglioccos arrived in New York harbor. Like millions of other arrivals, the family had to go through immigration on Ellis Island, and it is from these records that we get a glimpse of their situation. Father Giovanni indicated to officials that none of his family could read or write. Mr. Magliocco likely meant that his family wasn't able to read and write in English.

The senior Magliocco went on to tell the agents that they had a minimum of $250, were all in good health, had never been in America before, and intended to stay and seek citizenship. They next made their way over to Brooklyn to the residence of their son Angelo at 462 Canal Street.

Joseph Profaci did not make the long voyage over the Atlantic until 1921. World War One had broken out in 1914 and lasted till November 11, 1918. During this conflict, Italy was on the side of the Allies against Germany. Young Profaci served for a time in the Italian army, but it is not clear whether he saw any action. Upon his release, Profaci began having legal problems, including an arrest for rape and a conviction for forgery. He then probably decided that he might have a better future in the United States.

Unlike Magliocco, Profaci made the Atlantic trip without any of his family with him. Profaci personally paid his second-class fare and boarded the vessel Providence in Palermo harbor. This ship was similar in size to the one that carried the Maglioccos seven years earlier. Built-in 1915, the Providence could hold 2,240 paying passengers with 140 in first class, 250 in second, and 1,850 of them down in the third class areas. The on-ship doctor took care of illnesses and completed immigration forms. The ship left Palermo harbor on August 24, 1921.

On September 4, 1921, Profaci was answering questions and going through medical checks on Ellis Island. Profaci indicated that he could read and write in Italian, was in good health, and had never been in America before. He intended to stay permanently, obtain American citizenship, and he was going to bunk down at a cousin's place on Elizabeth Street in New York City. Profaci further stated that he had never been in prison, nor had he received welfare. He also answered "no" to the standard questions such as, was he an anarchist, a polygamist, or did he intend to overthrow the government by the use of violence.

Little did the immigration officers know that they were admitting a man who would become one of the most powerful Mafia Bosses of the century. Nor did Profaci understand that some of his answers would come back to haunt him more than thirty years later.

Profaci made sure to complete his naturalization responsibilities and became an American citizen on September 27, 1927. Joseph Magliocco was naturalized a year earlier on August 5, 1926.

Somehow Profaci managed to put himself at or near the top of what was to become an enduring criminal organization. Intelligence gathered years later, indicated that Profaci headed the Italian lottery in significant sections of Brooklyn during the late 1920s.

Twenty years later, on January 11 of 1948, a major New York gambling operation of Profaci was busted. The police arrested his brother Salvatore and others. Prosecutors estimated that this enterprise sometimes had a gross of $100,000 per week. The point is that Profaci's Mafia Family was heavily involved in gambling from at least the 1920s onward.

Most likely, another key ingredient in the rise of both Profaci and Magliocco was Prohibition. Millions of people still wanted to drink, and there were plenty of characters and gangs willing to flout the law to satisfy the public's desires. Profaci and Magliocco seized the opportunity, and their fortunes quickly rose.

Many Sicilian enclaves were home to supposedly benevolent societies whose aim was to improve the circumstances of all Sicilians. Unfortunately, over the years, mobsters recognized the value of a ready-made, legitimate organization for political and illegal purposes. Controlling segments of these organizations became vital to many Mafia Bosses and those aspiring to such heights.

1928 CLEVELAND MEETING

Profaci, Magliocco, and other Mafia members met in Cleveland, Ohio, at the Statler Hotel on December 5, 1928. The purpose of the gathering remains unclear. It would be reasonable to assume it had something to do with Prohibition. The ramifications of the July 1, 1928 murder of Frankie Yale probably were in play as well.

The presence of Profaci and Magliocco at this famous event is beyond question. Cleveland Police raided the hotel and took twenty-some men in for questioning. According to the information included with their mugs shots, the police arrested Profaci and Magliocco on December 6, 1928. They laid a charge of being a suspicious person against the two. The same fate befell the other hoods who had been caught up in the raid.

The information described Profaci as being five feet, six inches, and weighing 178 pounds. Magliocco was considerably heavier at 236 pounds with a height of five feet eight inches. According to the reports, their complexions were dark. Magliocco's eyes were listed as medium chestnut in color, whereas Profaci's were dark chestnut. Both men were well dressed in suits and ties, which must have been a change for the police who would usually be booking men in much cheaper clothing.

Profaci also had a leg injury for which he was using a cane. A group picture of fourteen of the men showed Profaci sitting in a wheelchair, which must have been provided by the police force.

Harvey Aronson, in his book, *The Killing of Joey Gallo* (1973), claimed that a boiler explosion injured Profaci. This incident supposedly took place after the Cleveland fiasco while he was on an ocean voyage from the west coast of the U.S.A. back to New York. The pictures and reports of Profaci's injury existing while in Cleveland rules out the Aronson version. Profaci had injured his knee in an auto accident in 1928, which accounts for his use of the wheelchair.

It has been very tempting for some writers to label Profaci as a Mafia Boss at this point in his career, and they may be correct. However, a closer examination would suggest he might have not yet attained the pinnacle of the Family at the time of the Cleveland meeting.

Although there was a large delegation from Chicago at the Statler Hotel, big Boss Alphonse Capone was not apprehended. Why he was absent is unclear. Some theories suggest that his non-Sicilian heritage may have played a role.

Vincenzo Mangano certainly was present, and there are pictures and fingerprints to prove it. Later Mangano became a long time Boss of the Gambino Family. In 1928, Mangano was still three years away from sitting on that Family's throne.

The absence of known Mafia Bosses at this Cleveland gathering is puzzling. Perhaps it suggests that Profaci had not yet ascended the throne of his own Mafia Family based in Brooklyn and Staten Island. There is no conclusive evidence to settle the issue. However, the puzzle is academic since he did become Boss within a short period. Joseph Bonanno, in "*A Man of Honor* (1983)", placed Joseph Profaci in the top seat by 1930. The leadership picture in the four other New York Mafia organizations is clearer.

After more than a decade of turmoil in what we now know as the Genovese Family, Joseph "Joe the Boss" Masseria had settled in as Boss. Then, just as it is now, the Genovese Family was considered the biggest and most powerful Mafia group. Masseria wasn't hesitant to use that strength.

The Gambinos were also large and powerful. Boss Salvatore "Tata" D'Aquila, a rival of Masseria, had been murdered (October 11, 1928) just before the disastrous Cleveland meeting. Manfredi "Al" Mineo, who was considered an ally of Masseria, had taken his place.

Gaetano "Tommy" Reina was the leader of what we now call the Lucchese Family. Masseria and Mineo were just not too sure about the friendship of Reina, especially if trouble broke out. This uncertainty would prove to be deadly for Reina. His interests in the ice business also had to be a temptation for Masseria.

Nicola "Cola" Shiro was in nominal charge of the Family we now call the Bonannos. Reportedly he was an aging man who was a figurehead for Buffalo Boss Stefano Magaddino, who used to head up this group before fleeing legal problems. Sitting in the wings was the very ambitious and devious Salvatore Maranzano, who chaffed at his lack of power in the Family.

THE CASTELLAMMARESE WAR

A series of tensions between Mafia groups led to the Castellammarese War of 1930-1931. Thanks to the writings or testimony of Mafia members, Joe Bonanno, Joe Valachi, and Nicole Gentile, we have a good understanding of the conflict. Newspaper accounts and official records help fill in the blanks.

In Chicago, Alphonse "Al" Capone was battling with Joseph Aiello, Boss of a local Mafia Family composed mainly of men of Sicilian background. Each side began looking for allies in an attempt to increase their power. This political maneuvering spread the conflict far beyond the city limits of Chicago.

The Mafia Bosses of Detroit and Buffalo supported Aiello because of their shared heritage and established friendships. Capone was connected to Joseph "Joe the Boss" Masseria of New York. He had begun his criminal career in New York and was acquainted with Masseria Family members. Capone needed Masseria's support. He might be able to prevent Aiello's friends in Detroit, Buffalo, and New York from aiding his cause.

Joe Bonanno penned a one-sided history of the Castellammarese War. According to Bonanno, Masseria demanded that the heads of the four other New York Families publicly express their support of him. Part of the reason for this demand was to prevent any New York Family from aiding Aiello. It is also reasonable to speculate that Masseria was seizing an opportunity to assert public dominance over the heads of the four other New York Families. Control of certain rackets would be a critical factor in his decision as well. This Masseria action shifted the focus and the resulting bulk of the fighting to the Big Apple.

After initial uncertainty, the tide slowly began to turn against Masseria. Some of his Capos secretly sought peace terms with the opposition forces led by Salvatore Maranzano of the Bonanno Family. (Former Bonanno boss Nicola Shiro had faded into the background when events escalated to the shooting phase.)

His men killed Masseria on April 15, 1931. Five months later, the apparent victor, Salvatore Maranzano, was surprised and murdered in his New York office on September 10, 1931. The theory on his killing is that the Bosses of the other Families had agreed that they would be better off with a consensus type of leadership rather than the autocratic Maranzano.

THE COMMISSION

From the chaos of the Castellammarese War emerged a system that all hoped would bring some sense of stability and safety to life in La Cosa Nostra. The victors wanted to make it more difficult for rebels to shoot their way to the top of a Family. This peace format ended up being called "The Commission."

Seven of the major La Cosa Nostra Bosses would meet periodically to settle interfamily disputes, set broad policy, and approve the selection of new Bosses. They would also accept the induction of new members to control the growth rate of the Families. The Commission would maintain a balance of strength between the groups.

Joseph Profaci, the Boss of a powerful New York Family, could not be ignored. He and the four other New York Bosses had positions at the Commission table. Also seated were the Bosses of Buffalo and Chicago. This configuration would last until 1961.

Profaci became the first unofficial secretary of the Commission. According to Joseph Bonanno, it would be Profaci's job to contact the Commission members when there was a need for a meeting. There was little fear of being interrupted by police officials, many of who had no idea who these guys were anyway.

The sitting La Cosa Nostra Bosses ratified the idea of a Commission in late 1931. It was also decided to have a National Meeting of all the Bosses every five years. These gatherings were a further attempt to provide a mechanism to prevent another outbreak of war amongst Families. One of its primary functions would be to ratify the members of the Commission, who would thus be serving five-year terms. The truth of the matter is that the meetings became a rubber stamp for the seven Families who had the original seats. At the 1956 National Meeting, it was decided to add the Bosses of Detroit and Philadelphia beginning in 1961.

With his appointment to the powerful Commission, Profaci was firmly entrenched as a significant Mafia leader. His extensive blood and marriage family ties were used to ensure a continuation of his reign.

PROFACI'S BLOOD FAMILY

Before the Castellammarese War, on April 29, 1928, Joseph Profaci had cemented his ties with friend Joseph Magliocco by marrying Magliocco's older sister Ninfa. The ceremony took place at Our Lady of Peace Church at 522 Carroll Street in Brooklyn.

The marriage application listed Profaci's home address as 279 Bay 11th Street in Brooklyn and the same address for Ninfa. However, this was the residence of the Maglioccos, so the first residence of the newlyweds is unclear. They eventually moved to a large two-story brick home with a two-car garage seated on a big lot at 8863 15th Avenue in Bath Beach, Brooklyn. The residence was only a few blocks from the address listed on the marriage certificate.

Profaci's wealth, from both legal and illegal businesses, allowed him to also purchase a 328-acre farm in Hightstown, New Jersey, in 1931. It had a 30-room house with a private chapel and even a runway for light airplanes. Some have claimed the estate once belonged to President Teddy A Roosevelt. That is incorrect for the late President never owned property in N.J. A Roosevelt family did possess the place at one time, but it was neither the President nor his relatives.

Joseph Profaci, like so many Mafia leaders of the era, made sure to induct blood relatives into his crime Family. There were several reasons for this. First of all, it gave the relative a form of prestige amongst other Mafia members and those aware of Mafia life. Secondly, it created a blanket of protection around the relative, which significantly increased their chances of being successful in a particular type of business. Third, by making blood relatives members of the Mafia Family, the Boss was also providing himself with assured loyalty from at least these persons. For the same reason, they were often promoted to positions of authority and thus power, which made a coup less likely.

One of Joseph Profaci's key men was his younger brother Salvatore. Most of what we know about him comes from the writing of his daughter Rosalie in her book" *Mafia Marriage* (1990)" and from Gaye Talese in, *"Honor Thy Father* (1971)." Joseph Profaci's F.B.I. file was useful, as well.

Salvatore had illegally entered the United States in 1926, by way of Canada, with the help of Joseph Bonanno and Stefano Magaddino, both of whom would become famous names in the Mafia. In 1934, Salvatore married a niece of Joseph Magliocco. She had been living with the childless Underboss and his wife. Both her parents had died years before. The couple eventually took up residence at 8215, 14th Avenue in Bensonhurst, Brooklyn. In an unknown year, probably before he was married, Salvatore became a made member of La Cosa Nostra but outwardly strove to maintain the facade of a successful businessman.

From her writings, it is clear that Rosalie dearly loved her father despite the fact he was very strict with her, especially in terms of dating. A similar picture is painted by Talese, who had close connections to both Rosalie and her mother. He relates a scene where Mrs. Profaci reminisced about how loving and kind her husband was. But she recalled an incident during Rosalie's high school years when she permitted Rosalie to attend a dance with an older date. Rosalie's father returned home unexpectedly. That put a quick end to any chance that his daughter would be attending any social function without his approval.

Salvatore Profaci was involved in running several businesses, including the P.L.S. Suit and Coat Company, at 45 Clark Street in Newburgh, New York. A version of this concern had come into existence in 1936 with Salvatore's brother Frank as a critical player. Another firm, at least on paper, was spun off the original in 1941 with a slight name change. According to Rosalie, this enterprise made uniforms during World War Two and then raincoats afterward. Then, in 1948, it began making women's dresses but formally shut down a year later. However, in 1950, it was revived to produce men's clothing and continued in this vein through at least 1952.

Rosalie's father also was a principal in a shoe manufacturing concern and had a variety of real estate holdings, including his New Jersey farm. A 1957 F.B.I., investigation also revealed that his brother Joseph owned a New York olive oil company in which Salvatore had an interest. Additionally, Salvatore Profaci was a management agent for the P. Zaccaro Company of New York City.

Salvatore Profaci participated in the gambling rackets, according to Bill Bonanno. He also revealed that Profaci was a Capo. His daughter Rosalie admitted that her dad was probably engaged in gambling, but this was a simple undertaking. She is conveniently forgetting the police payoffs and loansharking that invariably accompany gambling controlled by the Mafia.

Salvatore Profaci also had the benefit of being known as a long-time friend of powerful Mafia Boss Joseph Bonanno. Bonanno had helped Salvatore's illegal entry into the United States, and the two became very close friends. Salvatore served as an usher at Bonanno's November 15, 1931 wedding.

Whatever influences Salvatore Profaci had within his brother's Mafia Family ended in 1954. A tragic boat accident, at a marina at Point Pleasant, NJ, severely burned the 51-year-old Profaci. He lingered for a time in the hospital but finally succumbed, leaving a widow and five children.

Bill Bonanno wrote that thousands attended Profaci's wake. The large crowd was probably more a reflection of the status of Joseph Profaci than that of the late Salvatore. After the accident, Mrs. Profaci and her brood moved back to Brooklyn from Cornwall, New York, where they had been living for the last few years. They took up residence on Brooklyn's Bay 10th Street in a home that backed up on that of Joseph Profaci at 8863 15th Avenue. Profaci cut a door in his garage to create a direct route between the two properties. From that point until his death in June 1962, he became the head of his brother's family.

The union of Joseph Profaci and Ninfa Magliocco, mentioned above, would eventually produce six children, four boys, and two girls. Three of these offspring would be involved in the life of La Cosa Nostra well into their senior years.

Salvatore Profaci, the eldest son, born on May 18, 1936, was inducted into La Cosa Nostra during his father's reign and would eventually rise to the position of Capo after Joseph Profaci's death in 1962. Salvatore had the unique experience of being caught by F.B.I. bugs discussing Mafia affairs in two different locations thirty years apart.

If nothing else, these events proved his long-standing participation in La Cosa Nostra. On December 20, 1985, a judge sentenced Salvatore to four years for defrauding A&P of approximately $500,000. At the time, he was supposedly acting as their garbage consultant. The federal prison doors opened for Profaci on September 9, 1988, and to no one's surprise was right back into the Mafia life.

With these blood allies and other loyalists, powerful La Cosa Nostra boss Joseph Profaci appeared secure in his personal, business, and Mafia milieu.

CHAPTER THREE

Living the Good Life

There was no question that Joseph Profaci was making money in the years from 1930 onwards. The real discussion was the source of the majority of his income. It was probably a combination of legitimate dollars and the rackets.

It would have been nice if Profaci had to file honest tax returns on both his rackets income and that of his business enterprises. Unfortunately for us, he did neither, so we are left to speculate as to his take-home pay from government hearings and FBI investigations. Incomplete as these materials may be, at least they give us some idea of the financial position of this New York Mafia Boss.

When Joseph Profaci arrived in the United States, in 1921, he claimed to be a "merchant" on his immigration forms that were filled out on Ellis Island. That seems to be a good description of the path Profaci and Underboss Joseph Magliocco took, at least openly, when they established themselves in their new country.

Most of the Italian immigrants loved to continue the traditions of their homeland. Men with an entrepreneurial streak were quick to see opportunities in these desires, and they began to provide various commodities, including food, to the new Americans. Profaci was one of these men, and he began to specialize in the importation of olive oil, a staple of the Italian diet.

OLIVE OIL

Unlike most people in business, Profaci had a built-in advantage to grow his company. What merchant in Profaci territory was not going to stock his shelves with a product pushed by the local Mafia Boss? Having friends amongst other mob leaders such as Joseph Bonanno and Vincent Mangano meant that Profaci had an edge in their territory as well.

This good fortune was not restricted to New York City either. Profaci had friends, relatives, and Mafia acquaintances across the country and could quickly introduce his products on an extensive geographical scale. He began to be called the "biggest importer of olive oil in America," although I've never seen any figures to back up that claim.

In sworn testimony in 1950, Profaci stated he owned the Mama Mia Importing Company. Before 1936 this company was called Mama Mia Oil Company. According to a later statement by Profaci, $300,000 in cash, brought from Sicily by a Profaci sister, was injected into the company in the years 1937, 1938, and 1939. The finances of this business would attract lots of attention in the future.

Other Profaci enterprises included the Santuzza Oil Company and the Sunshine Oil Company. During this period, Profaci also headed a real estate firm operating under the name of Maniapro Realty Corporation and was suspected of holding interests in a variety of other concerns.

Like many businesspeople, Profaci had the use of a company-owned car. But there was a catch to even this mundane detail. On November 27, 1957, the FBI did a spot check on Profaci's Brooklyn home and noted the presence of a 1957 Chrysler Windsor. Its license plate number revealed that it should have been a 1957 Chevy owned by the Carmela Mia Packing Company. Profaci did have a 57 Chevy, registered to himself, but it had its correct tags. The purpose of this deception is unclear. Perhaps it was an attempt to be more anonymous, or maybe it was some tax scam. Whatever the reason, this little ploy reveals a bit of the character of the Mafia Boss.

LEGITIMATE ALCOHOL

Profaci's Underboss, Joseph Magliocco, was also very successful in "legitimate" business. From 1918 through 1926, he ran some small grocery stores then became involved in the olive oil and cheese business. The then-popular beer brands Stegmaier, Fitzgerald, and Blatz, were distributed by Magliocco's Sunland Company. Under the umbrella of Ward Trading,

Magliocco controlled several other businesses, including Arrow Linen and 181 Lawrence Avenue Realty Corporation.

Antonio "Nino" Magliocco, a brother of Joseph and a reputed member of the crime Family, opened Peerless Importers in 1943. It still distributes wine and spirits in both New York and Connecticut. By 2001 it had sales estimated to be around $710 million and employed 1,200 people. Forbes Magazine listed it as one of America's top 500 companies. There is no suggestion the company is "mobbed up."

The above gives just a glimpse of the "legitimate" enterprises of both Profaci and Magliocco. No one ever really had a clear picture of the facts of ownership of these and several other companies which at times appeared to be in their orbit. The extent of illegal money that may have been used to fuel the growth of these companies is unknown. However, the reputation of these two Mafia leaders was a double-edged sword. Before 1950, the fear factor would have helped obtain markets for their various products. Later, the allegations of Mafia connections would cause endless legal problems for Profaci, Magliocco, and their offspring.

ILLEGAL INCOME

Prohibition was "the" key factor in the growth of organized crime. It also made individuals very rich, Profaci, and Magliocco being among these men. But Prohibition ended in 1933, so the two had to turn to or return to or perhaps more correctly, concentrate on other illegal enterprises to keep the tax-free money flowing in.

Gambling was the critical income producer for most Mafia Families, including the one headed by Joseph Profaci. Before the explosion of sports betting, numbers were the main game in town.

Numbers is a simple betting game in which the player picks a three-digit number from 000 to 999. On a winning wager of $1, the player would get $600, a 600-to-1 payoff. The Italian Lottery was a generally accepted label. The majority of the action took place in Italian enclaves. Eventually, his gambling racket expanded outward, but care was taken not to intrude on the territories of other Mafia Families.

It is impossible to make a reasonable estimation of the gambling income that came Profaci's way. However, it had to be huge to make a profit while paying salaries and bribes to corrupt police and politicians.

The companion to gaming is loansharking. In simple terms, it is the lending of money at exorbitant interest rates. The Mafia hood giving out the loan doesn't want the principal back quickly. It's the weekly interest that produces the big dollars. We can safely assume that many Capos passed money up to Profaci and Magliocco from their loansharking operations. The two leaders would lend their money to the Capos and thus were loanshark's loanshark. They couldn't lose!

Other illegal enterprises would include: extortion, union racketeering, fraud, fencing stolen property, and on and on. The list would be endless, but they all produced money that was moved upward in the chain of command. An educated guess would be that Profaci and Magliocco quickly made more money illegally than in their "legitimate" enterprises. It is also reasonable to assume that Profaci used some of this "dirty money" to finance some of his social responsibilities.

WEDDINGS

In North America, the general custom has been that the bride's parents host and pay for the wedding of their daughters. For the rich, it is often an opportunity to display their wealth through an extremely expensive reception. Joseph Profaci demonstrated his financial status when he married off his two daughters in the late 1940s and early 1950s. Unlike the affairs of "ordinary" rich people, Profaci's main concern was to impress those from the other La Cosa Nostra Families from around the nation.

Profaci's eldest daughter, Carmella, had met and fallen in love with Anthony Joseph Tocco from Detroit. The Toccos were royalty, at least in Mafia circles. The father of the groom, William "Black Bill" Tocco, had been a friend and ally of Detroit Boss Joseph Zerilli from childhood. Their faction had battled to the top of the Detroit Family in the 1920s. At the time of the marriage, William Tocco was a senior Capo in the Detroit Family. A Mafia induction ceremony for his son Anthony Joseph had probably already taken place.

Carmella's sister, Rosalie Profaci, also fell for a Detroit mobster. Her choice was Anthony Joseph Zerilli, son of that city's Boss Joseph Zerilli. Anthony had been inducted into La Cosa Nostra and would rise towards the top as the decades passed.

It would have been custom for Joseph Profaci to have held a dinner with the extended families of the bride and groom before the wedding. He did that when his niece Rosalie was engaged to Salvatore "Bill" Bonanno.

Both Profaci daughter weddings were held, in separate years, at Brooklyn's St. Bernadette Church, the Profaci family's place of worship. Only a few hundred guests could squeeze into the building for the marriage vows, but there would be room for everyone at the reception.

Rosalie's party took place at New York's Commodore Hotel, which was attached to Grand Central Station in Manhattan. (Today it is called the Grand Hyatt and should not be confused with another Commodore Hotel just down the street.) It was a prestigious place due to its size and location. Some critics were not too impressed with its interior calling it "pedestrian." That didn't seem to bother Joseph Profaci or his daughter, however.

We don't have the complete guest lists from either of the weddings. A police report states that there were eight hundred guests at the June 4, 1955 reception of Carmella Profaci at New York's Biltmore Hotel. It was a small Mafia wedding compared to that of Josephine Tocco, Carmella's new sister-in-law. One thousand five hundred guests sat down to dinner and entertainment at that event. When Carmella's cousin (not her sister), Rosalie Profaci, married Salvatore "Bill" Bonanno in 1956, there were a reported 3,000 people invited to the reception.

The Profaci sisters would also have been the recipients of a large amount of cash from their guests. It would have been placed in envelopes and given to the bride and groom during the reception. Rosalie Bonanno wrote that she and her husband received around $100,000, so we can assume that at least half that amount went to the Profaci sisters at their receptions. It was a significant amount of money to start a marriage.

VIOLENCE

While these marriage vows spoke of new beginnings, there were no escaping violent endings in the Mafia milieu. There were some murders from 1939 onward that had a Profaci connection.

On February 6, 1939, Anthony "Nino" Colombo, father of future Boss Joseph Colombo, was found strangled in the back of his Pontiac two-door. Lying beside Colombo was Christina Oliveri, reportedly Colombo's girlfriend. An oil tablecloth covered the bodies which suggest they were killed in some house and later dumped in the backseat of the car.

It is unclear whether Anthony Colombo was a member or an Associate of the Colombo Family. Whatever the truth of the matter, the Anthony Colombo killing would not have caused Profaci any loss of sleep. Being a religious man, he might have tossed and turned over the murder of the married Oliveri, mother of two children. Some speculated that she was the "property" of some other Mafioso and thus a valid target according to the laws of La Cosa Nostra.

In 1935, Vincenzo Troia angered the leaders of his Newark, New Jersey organization. Accordingly, they whacked him out on August 22 and claimed that it was justifiable because he was making an unauthorized attempt to seize

control of the Family. Most likely, the Commission, which included Profaci, approved this hit.

Gaspare D'Amico was considered by some to be the Boss of the same Newark, New Jersey Family that Troia was trying to take over. On February 22, 1937, D'Amico barely survived an assassination attempt and decided his best course of action was to flee to Italy. Information in FBI files suggests that Joseph Profaci was behind this shooting. The police never arrested him on this matter, and little evidence exists to back up the allegation.

Philadelphia Boss John "Big Nose" Avena was mowed down by machine-gun fire from a passing car on August 17, 1936. Years later, Avena's son, Salvatore, would become entangled in a business dispute with powerful Associates of the Genovese Family. Salvatore Arena would call upon Salvatore Profaci, son of Joseph Profaci, to help him with the potentially deadly problem. The marriage of two of their children connected the men.

Marriage also makes the killing of Detroit's Joseph Tocco of interest to our look at Joseph Profaci. Tocco was a victim of Detroit's very violent gang wars that had begun well before Prohibition. Twenty years later, a daughter of Profaci married a nephew of the departed Joseph Tocco.

Profaci's fellow Commission member, Frank Nitti, Boss of the Chicago Family, committed suicide on March 19, 1943, after being indicted the day before for significant extortion of the movie industry. The reasons behind his action remain murky. Theories include his reasonable fear of prison and concern that he would be held responsible for the indictments.

Gaetano "Tommy" Gagliano was an original Commission member and headed what we now call the Lucchese Family. Like Profaci, Gagliano had interests in the garment industry, but the two were able to co-exist without too much difficulty. Profaci lost an ally when Gagliano died in 1951. Underboss Lucchese succeeded him but was not similarly disposed towards Profaci.

One of Profaci's closest friends was Vincent Mangano, Boss of the Gambino Family. According to Joseph Bonanno, he, Profaci, Mangano, and Magliocco would often get together to socialize and tighten the bonds between their three Mafia Families. On April 19, 1951, Mangano lost out in a power struggle with his Underboss Albert Anastasia and disappeared. His brother met a similar fate, but authorities found his body. While a personal loss to Profaci, the Gambino Family remained an ally as Anastasia needed Profaci's support.

Willie Moretti was an influential Mafia figure in New Jersey. Frank Costello appointed him Underboss when he took over the Family. That occurred when it became clear that Charles "Lucky" Luciano would not be able to return to the streets of New York. Moretti had three severe problems as the 1950s unfolded. First of all, he had begun to like the attention that he received from the press after appearing before a Congressional hearing. Then it appeared Moretti's mind was deteriorating due to a physical illness. Moretti probably also relished being noticed just as John Gotti would nearly forty years later.

Note:
The coroner's report on Moretti stated there was no sign of brain damage.

Moretti's main problem was the ambitions of Capo Vito Genovese. The latter had been Luciano's original Underboss but had to flee to Italy to avoid a murder investigation. He was forcibly returned to the United States in 1944 to face the murder trial, but the judge directed a verdict of not guilty. Genovese immediately set his sights on the leadership of his Family, and Moretti was in the way.

Deviously, Genovese began complaining about Moretti's lack of self-control, and the Commission had to agree. Moretti was gunned down on October 4, 1951, and Genovese immediately moved into his position. His continuing ambition would create high tension within the Commission and thus for Profaci.

Like everyone else in life, Joseph Profaci faced numerous problems as the years passed. His reputation as a mobster caused some, but others were brought on by his greed.

PROBLEMS

Not content with the legitimate profits, Profaci tampered with his olive oil by "adulterating and misbranding" it. The Food and Drug Administration charged him with this offense in 1949. The result was a $12,000 fine, a suspended sentence, and a years' probation. Future events would prove that the Mafia Boss didn't learn his lesson from this incident.

Olive oil was the least of Profaci's problems in 1951. A year earlier, on May 3, 1950, the United States Senate authorized the formation of The Special Committee to Investigate Organized Crime in Interstate Commerce. The chairman was Senator Estes Kefauver (Tennessee). Commonly called the Kefauver Committee, its five senators visited fourteen cities and invited hundreds of witnesses, including Joseph Profaci.

Profaci appeared before the Kefauver Committee on February 14, 1951, and contrary to legend testified about many aspects of his life. The mob Boss gave his proper place and date of his birth, along with the fact that he had become a citizen in September of 1927. Profaci went on to give his place of residence and then testified that he owned a New Jersey farm in Hightstown.

His 1928 arrest in Cleveland was a topic of discussion. When asked why he was in Cleveland, Profaci replied, "To expand my business...to open up territory...because there was some friend of my father told me they had a friend over there and he says they need me there in Cleveland." Profaci wasn't fooling anyone with that answer.

The Kefauver Committee's final report stated that there was a nation-wide crime syndicate known as the Mafia. Some hoods such as Profaci became prime targets, in no small part due to their new notoriety.

On April 29, 1954, United States Attorney General Herbert Brownell Jr. announced that Profaci was a racketeer. He went on to explain that the government would take steps to take away his citizenship and deport him to Italy. The allegation was that Profaci had lied on his 1927 application for naturalization by failing to disclose his arrest record in Italy.

The government's deportation efforts against Profaci poked along. They were still in a state of limbo when he faced another round of bad publicity in late 1957. Chapter Four will cover these events.

PROFACI AND THE IRS

It wasn't just the immigration arm of the federal government that was interested in Profaci. The IRS charged Profaci for income tax evasion in 1952. A few surprises emerged when they tried to seize his assets.

Before the IRS could take his prized New Jersey estate, a company foreclosed on it. They claimed Profaci hadn't met his mortgage payments, and thus it was no longer a Profaci asset that the government could grab. The IRS seized his Brooklyn house. But when it was put up for auction, a company purchased it and promptly rented it back to Profaci. His family continued to live there till he died in 1962. Others, connected to Profaci, bought the remaining seized properties. Even his nephew Salvatore purchased two parcels of land for meager prices. What this meant was that Profaci could legally claim that he liquidated all his assets to meet the taxes. It was a joke, and everyone knew it.

Profaci did lose the Mama Mia Packing Company to the tax people. But that wasn't such a significant loss since he formed the Carmela Mia Packing Company with Adriano Liberato installed as president. Liberato had been the sales manager of Mama Mia before the government seized it. Profaci would claim to be just an employee of this firm, and the IRS was not able to prove otherwise. A similar story happened with Profaci's realty company. A "new" enterprise called Rosalie Properties emerged after the IRS grabbed the limited assets of Maniapro Realty.

For some reason that never became clear, the government dropped the criminal tax charges against Profaci. Early in the 1960s, the FBI would look into rumors that bribery played a role in this good fortune for the mob Boss. It appears that a mob informant was the source of these stories. Whatever the case, nothing came of the subsequent investigation.

Despite a marshal's sale of some of his visible assets, Profaci, his wife, and two of his companies still had considerable debts to the IRS. Individually, Profaci owed $321,304.36; he and his wife jointly were still in hock for $18,249.90. Mama Mia Packing owed a whopping $959,036, while Maniapro Realty Corporation's tax debt was $186,316.88. Profaci avoided meeting most of these obligations by keeping his name out of the new companies that he formed. The Boss claimed he was simply an employee and kept his salary at a level below that which the IRS could garnishee it.

Despite having to liquidate all his public assets to meet his tax obligations, Joseph Profaci never skipped a beat. He continued to use his home and the New Jersey estate. Florida vacations were typical, as were the late model automobiles he drove. Most people would like to have tax problems like this!

As 1956 approached Joseph Profaci, and Joseph Magliocco were sitting securely atop their crime Family and were living the life of the rich and reasonably well unknown. Unfortunately for these two Mafia leaders, their good luck was about to change.

Profaci spent the years from late 1921 to early 1925 unsuccessfully running a grocery store in Chicago.

CHAPTER FOUR

Don't Go, Joe!

As had been agreed back in 1931, the Bosses of the various La Cosa Nostra Families were to gather every five years for a National Meeting. From the testimony of Joseph Valachi and the writing of Joseph Bonanno, we know that the 1931 meeting took place in Chicago but are basically without substantial evidence about the locations of the 1936 and 1941 conventions.

From Joseph Bonanno's autobiography, *A Man of Honor* (1983), we are aware that the 1946 event took place, but not the location. However, there is an indication that the convention happened in Havana, Cuba, or perhaps nearby Florida.

Salvatore "Lucky" Luciano made a clandestine trip from his exile in Italy and arrived in Cuba in approximately October of 1946. The former Boss of the Genovese Family probably wanted to be in attendance, or near the National Meeting of the Mafia Bosses. We have nothing to indicate that Profaci and Magliocco flew to Cuba for any reason.

A National Meeting of La Cosa Nostra and a Commission meeting are two different things. The former happened every five years, while the Commission could meet at any time. Thanks to Joseph Bonanno's *A Man of Honor* (1983), we have a couple of glimpses of Joseph Profaci taking part in life or death decisions by the Commission.

MURDERING MORETTI

In early 1951, tensions within the Gambino Family were high. Boss Vincent Mangano was at odds with his ambitious Underboss Albert Anastasia. Both were casting about for allies as the conflict moved from cold to hot. In April, some group arranged the disappearance of Vincent Mangano and the murder of his brother Philip. Bonanno would have us believe that although things were coming to a head, the Commission did not approve the killings ahead of time. That statement seems to fly in the face of the purpose of the Commission.

Bonanno claimed that the loss of their good friend saddened both he and Profaci. However, there was nothing they could do about it. Anastasia claimed self-defence at a Commission meeting following the Manganos' deaths. Frank Costello, Boss of the Genovese Family, supported Anastasia.

If Bonanno's version is truthful, it means that Profaci and Bonanno were sitting on a board of directors that had no control over its members. It was a Commission that did not sanction Anastasia for breaking one of the fundamental rules of La Cosa Nostra. It's either that or Bonanno was lying about the Commission not sanctioning the hits. If he was lying, that means our subject, Joseph Profaci, took part in the betrayal of one of his dearest friends. That says a lot about his character. Whatever the real story is, Profaci comes across poorly.

We have no real idea where and on what exact date the 1951 National Meeting took place. Fortunately, we do have some information about the next convention in 1956.

1956 NATIONAL MEETING

On October 18, 1956, Bonanno Underboss Carmen "Lilo" Galante was leaving the Binghamton area on Route 17 when New York State Trooper F.W. Leibe stopped him for speeding. Further investigation revealed that Galante and others with criminal records had been booked into various Binghamton area hotels/motels on October 17 and 18. In 1983, Joseph Bonanno confirmed that the 1956 National Meeting of La Cosa Nostra took place at the Apalachin estate of Joseph Barbara.

On July 9 and 10 of 1956, both Profaci and Magliocco were registered at the Arlington Hotel in Binghamton along with Joseph Barbara. Perhaps this was in preparation for the October convention, but it could merely have been regular mob business as well. No proof exists that Profaci and Magaddino were at the 1956 Mafia gathering. There is evidence that strongly suggests they were.

Mafia Bosses voted to retain Profaci as a member of the seven-man Commission for the next five years. Also returned to their seats were: Joseph Bonanno, Tommy Lucchese, Frank Costello, and Albert Anastasia from the New York Families. Stefano Magaddino of Buffalo and Anthony Accardo of Chicago were the other two members.

It was also decided, in 1956, that the Commission would be expanded to nine members starting in 1961. It appeared that sitting Philadelphia Boss Joseph Ida would be one of the newcomers, but by 1961, Angelo Bruno had replaced the retired Ida as Philadelphia leader. The ninth spot was to go to Detroit's Joseph Zerilli, which it did five years later.

Affairs of La Cosa Nostra must have seemed to be going well as Profaci and Magliocco drove away from Barbara's estate. Things wouldn't unfold as happily the next time they gathered around Barbara's BBQ!

MORE VIOLENCE

In 1957 the world of the New York La Cosa Nostra was a mess. Neither the successful 1956 National Meeting nor the presence of the Commission was able to prevent the public outbreak of violence. The Mafia boys' greed, ambition, suspicions, and stupidity were going to change them from a secret society into a very public one.

Vito Genovese was not happy in his secondary position in the Genovese Family. When prosecutor Thomas Dewey won a conviction of Charles "Lucky" Luciano in 1936, the throne should have gone to Genovese. But Vito had been mixed up in a small-time murder and had to flee to Italy. He was returned to the United States in 1946 to face trial for that killing, but the judge gave a directed verdict of acquittal when the government's case proved inadequate. Genovese returned to action in his Family, but it was as a Capo to Boss Frank Costello and Underboss Willie Moretti.

With Moretti's murder in 1951, Genovese moved into the second slot but retained higher ambitions. After getting his ducks in order in the spring of 1957, Genovese ordered Soldier Vincent "Chin" Gigante to murder Costello, which he attempted on May 2, 1957. Although Gigante only succeeded in wounding Costello, Genovese's plan worked because Costello, having no stomach for warfare, quietly retired and left the top slot to Genovese.

Profaci and Magliocco watched the killing continue on June 17, 1957. Frank Scalise, one of the powers in the Gambino Family, entered a Bronx store to purchase fruit. Two gunmen killed him and escaped. For decades afterward, it was claimed that Anastasia ordered the death of Scalise for "selling" memberships in his La Cosa Nostra Family. That sounds more like a justification to hide a power grab to me.

What we do know about the Scalise hit is that street talk attributed the shooting to Vincent "Jimmy Jerome" Squillante, a close aide to Anastasia. Probably, Anastasia, had Scalise taken out because he did not trust his loyalty. However, we don't know the real reason.

There wasn't much mystery about the next domino that fell. Albert Anastasia, Boss of what we now call the Gambino Family, had been at odds with Vito Genovese for an extended period. According to Joseph Bonanno, Anastasia had come to Joseph Profaci and himself, seeking their blessing for the first strike against Genovese. The two Mafia leaders refused this "permission" and urged Anastasia to seek an accord with Genovese. This suggestion would turn out to be fatal advice.

On October 25, 1957, Anastasia was sitting in his favorite barber chair in the Park Sheridan Hotel. Next to him sat the man suspected of killing Frank Scalise, Vincent "Jimmy Jerome" Squillante. Suddenly, two men entered the shop and opened up on Anastasia with .38 and .32 caliber pistols killing the feared mob Boss.

I am confident it was carried out under the auspices of Anastasia's Underboss Carlo Gambino and his aide Joseph "Joe the Blonde" Biondo. According to noted Mafia expert Jerry Capeci, the two shooters were Gambino Associates Stephen "Stevie Coogan" Grammauta and Arnold "Witty" Wittenburg. They were under the direction of Soldier Stephen Armone. His brother Joseph "Joe Piney" Armone would later become Underboss and then Consigliere during the reign of John Gotti in the late 1980s.

I do not accept the long-held belief that a crew in the Colombo Family under Lawrence "Larry" Gallo murdered Anastasia. First of all, the mob protocol dictated that the victim's own Mafia Family should carry out his murder. The Gallo crew was not part of the Gambino group. Secondly, there is no proof that the Gallos did the hit. The only evidence that they were involved was from one of their Associates. Sidney Slater said that Joseph Gallo, indicating four companions, stated, "You can call us the barbershop quintet." That's the total of the evidence that the Gallos did the shooting. The information about the real killers places the Gallo claim in the "bragging" category.

APALACHIN 1957

The rash of shootings in New York created uncertainty in the world of La Cosa Nostra. Commission members were involved, and they were supposed to be the peace and deal makers for the rest of the Mafia Families. For this reason, and there were other secondary concerns, significant players on the Commission called for a National Meeting for mid-November 1957.

Mafia leaders gathered for National Meetings every five years. The last one took place in October of 1956. Those who called this out of sequence gathering felt the issues were important enough to bring in Bosses and their aides from around the country. It would prove to be a mistake.

The leading Mafia Bosses planned the National Meeting at Apalachin on November 14, 1957, at least two weeks ahead of time. On November 5, 1957, Barbara drove over to Amour and Company in Binghamton and placed an order for $432.81 worth of meats to be picked up on November 13. That amount would be the approximate equivalent of $3900 in 2019. It would buy a lot of meat.

Sergeant Edgar Croswell of the New York State Troopers was long suspicious of Joseph Barbara due to his past criminal record and associations. The accidental discovery of Barbara's son making a block of motel reservations aroused the curiosity of Croswell and his partner Vasisko.

Around noon the next day, November 14, 1957, Croswell and Vasisko, accompanied by two agents of the Bureau of Alcohol and Tobacco, drove up to the estate of Barbara just outside Apalachin, New York. A group of men observed the officers as they were taking down plate numbers of some of the parked vehicles. The four lawmen left and drove down the one road leading from Barbara's estate.

Not exactly sure what they were up against, the officers set up a roadblock and called for reinforcements. A commercial truck left the estate, drove through the barricade, returned to Barbara's, and then drove through the barrier once again without being stopped. The officers let the following car pass as one of them recognized the driver.

State Troopers stopped the next vehicle and identified the four occupants. They were then allowed to leave. A decision was then made to take all those who were stopped down to the local New York State Trooper station in Vestal. The plan was to identify the men with some semblance of order. Other troopers were sent out to round up the dozen or so men who were seen running into the woods.

Joseph Profaci was among those identified at the trooper station after being stopped in a vehicle. Profaci had left the estate in a 1957 Oldsmobile driven by Patsy Monachino. Also in the car were Patsy's brother Sam and Anthony "Guv" Guarnieri. All three were members of Barbara's Mafia Family.

Joseph Magliocco was also brought to the Vestal office and formally identified. It is humorous to imagine the huge Magliocco setting off into the woods on foot. However, it is unclear where the troopers initially detained him.

The fiasco at Apalachin brought on days of headlines and articles as well as years of hearings, grand juries, court cases, and endless appeals. No matter how you cut it, Apalachin was a mess for La Cosa Nostra.

APALACHIN INQUIRIES

On December 12, 1957, the Joint Legislative Committee on Government Operations for New York State began public hearings related to the Apalachin affair. The Committee was trying to determine what the Apalachin meeting was about and who its participants were.

Additionally, the Committee was to evaluate the effectiveness of state and local law authorities in combating this "invisible government" and whether the laws were adequate in dealing with this menace. Accordingly, the Committee called many witnesses from both sides of the law.

One of the first casualties of the BBQ was Salvatore Tornabe, a member of the Colombo Family. He was a salesman for Magliocco's Sunland Beverages but acted as a gopher for his Mafia Family. According to a note found in his possession, Tornabe had several tasks to perform the week of the gathering. His first responsibility was to meet with Carmine Galante. Later Tornabe was to pick up two Bosses at Newark Airport. He then drove Frank Zito (Springfield) and James Colletti (Denver) to Apalachin.

Tornabe appeared before the New York State Joint Legislative Committee on December 21, 1957. He refused to answer all the questions. His stress levels were probably very high. On December 30, he keeled over and died.

A Director of the Bureau of Narcotics, John Cusak, told the Committee that the Apalachin BBQ was a meeting of the "Mafia." In 1957, with little public knowledge of this organization, his declarations were frightening for it brought on fears of a sinister foreign directed entity, perhaps trying to overthrow the legitimate government. In other words, a threat like that of the feared communists! In hindsight, we know this was a significant exaggeration. But the fears have to be evaluated in the context of the times.

For the Bureau of Narcotics, Joseph Profaci and Joseph Magliocco were significant players in the Mafia and thus had to be associated with the evil of narcotics. Both were listed as Associates of Charles "Lucky" Luciano, then living in Italy and considered to be a mastermind behind the thriving heroin trade. In fact, during a 1949 raid on the Rome apartment of Luciano, Magliocco's name was found among the notes and address books seized from the former Mafia Boss. That this connection necessarily meant that Profaci and Magliocco were involved in the heroin trade seems to be a stretch.

PROFACI SUBPOENAED

The New York State Temporary Commission of Investigation, appointed by the governor, also investigated the Apalachin affair. They called Joseph Profaci as a witness during their public hearings in January 1959. But he was released after complaining that his lawyer was not available and that he was ill. On January 27, 1959, Profaci returned to testify and gave his name, address, age, marital status, his wife's name, the number of children he had, and their names. He refused to give details about his children's personal lives and also took the Fifth Amendment about all matters concerning the Apalachin meeting.

After much wrangling, the Committee conferred immunity upon Profaci. This immunity meant he could no longer use the protection of the Fifth Amendment. Profaci then went through the time-consuming steps of refusing to answer each specific question then relenting after he was formally ordered to do so. From this emerged Profaci's version of the reasons behind his presence at Barbara's estate.

Profaci claimed that he was just an employee of the Carmela Mia Packing Company. He had met Joseph Barbara, in the early 1950s through Adriano Liberato, the President of Carmela Mia since 1954. Profaci testified that he felt obliged to carry on business as usual after Liberato died on November 4. Consequently, he planned to go to the Binghamton, New York area to collect monies owed to Carmela Mia Packing by various merchants from that district.

Being unable to drive due to a deformed knee, Profaci asked his brother-in-law, Joseph Magliocco, to do that chore. The two men left Brooklyn around 4 PM on November 13, 1957, and after getting lost, arrived in Endicott (near Apalachin) around 8:30 or 9:00 PM. The next day, since Barbara's bottling plant was in Endicott, the men decided they might as well say hello. After phoning the plant, someone told them Barbara was at his Apalachin home, and the two Mafiosi agreed to travel there.

The two men drove to the Barbara estate in nearby Apalachin, New York. Profaci stated that Magliocco remained in the car while he made a brief visit to the ailing Barbara. Sometime after 1 PM, Profaci left and was stopped by the New York State Troopers at a roadblock. After five minutes, Profaci claims he was released, and he and Magliocco drove to Wilkes Barrie, Pennsylvania, where they spent the night of November 14, 1957. The next day they drove back to Brooklyn.

No one believed Profaci's story of ending up in Endicott because he and Magliocco had become lost. State Police evidence showed that they stopped a vehicle driven by Barbara soldier Patsy Monachino. His passengers were Profaci and two other men. Troopers later stopped Magliocco, who had fled on foot.

On the Federal level, Joseph Profaci was in demand by various committees, grand juries, and agencies. Among these was the Senate "Select Committee on Improper Activities in the Labor or Management Field," which was formed in January of 1957 after other investigations revealed questionable relations between local unions and racketeers. However, when the Apalachin affair became headline news, the Committee redirected its inquiries to include a look into the Mafia gathering. Senator John McClellan called several Apalachin detainees, including Profaci. Other than more unwelcome publicity, this appearance only inconvenienced Profaci.

The FBI also wanted to speak to Profaci about Apalachin and consequently interviewed him on March 24, 1958. Now well experienced in being interviewed, Profaci calmly stuck to his story about his presence in Apalachin being social. He denied any knowledge of a "convention," and the agents learned nothing for their efforts.

On October 8, 1958, Profaci appeared before a two-day hearing concerning his immigration status. Two months later, on December 9, 1958, Judge Walter Brachhausen ordered Profaci deported for lying on his immigration forms. Fortunately for Profaci, this order was overturned on appeal on January 12, 1960.

PROFACI INDICTED

A year before this victory, on May 13, 1959, Profaci and Magliocco were among 27 men who were indicted by a Federal Grand Jury in the Southern District of New York. The authorities cited both men for conspiracy to obstruct justice for not telling the true nature of the Apalachin gathering. After a New York trial, a jury convicted Profaci, Magliocco, and nineteen other hoods. On January 13, 1960, Judge Irving Kaufman sentenced Profaci and his Underboss to five years imprisonment.

For a time, these sentences caused consternation in the Profaci and Magliocco households and muted joy amongst the Profaci Soldiers who were not happy with their leadership. However, on November 18, 1960, an appeal overturned the convictions of Profaci, Magliocco, and nineteen others, releasing all of them from ongoing or pending prison sentences.

CHAPTER FIVE

Profaci's Mafia Life

INCREASING ATTENTION

Without personally knowing Profaci and Magliocco, it is impossible to understand their thinking process. We have to make some assumptions based on their actions and the writings of people who did know them. Rosalie Bonanno, a niece to both men, Salvatore "Bill" Bonanno, an acquaintance and ally of the two, and Joseph Bonanno, a contemporary of the two mob leaders, were well acquainted with the two mobsters. Additional information comes from informers, police, and the files of the FBI and the Bureau of Narcotics.

Joseph Profaci liked to stand out from the crowd but only in the context of a very successful legitimate businessman and patron of the church. Rosalie Bonanno, in her book *Mafia Marriage* (1990), described Profaci as, "a flamboyant man who smoked big cigars, drove big, black Cadillacs...". He was a generous contributor to his church, and he sought and received the friendship of various parish priests, which also made him stand out from the crowd. Furthermore, the sheer size and location of his daughters' weddings also guaranteed attention. I think it is fair to conclude that Joseph Profaci wanted to be known as a leading citizen amongst those not in or associated with La Cosa Nostra.

Numerous stories about Joseph Profaci recounted the daring of some thieves who reportedly broke into his New Jersey estate. They drew a mustache and nipples on one of the religious statues in his private chapel. Rosalie Bonanno, Profaci's niece, revealed the real story in her book, *Mafia Marriage* (1990). She said it was an inside job done by some of the Profaci kids who were acting silly. So much for the fearless burglars.

Unlike many leading Mafia figures, Joseph Profaci did not have an extensive criminal record in the United States. I discussed the circumstances of his 1928 arrest in Cleveland in Chapter 2, which ended in a quick not guilty verdict for Profaci. This incident had a brief flurry of interest but was quickly forgotten, especially in the Italian enclaves. In 1934, he had been questioned about the murder of a small-time hood named Ferdinand Boccia but was released. Very little publicity resulted from this event.

The 1950-1951 Kefauver Hearings were a different matter. They were a national forum that did attract continued media attention across the nation. Profaci was a guest and surprisingly, testified about several personal details including his place of birth, residences, and his business interests.

However, these were small stories and did not capture the attention of the general public, although they must have been embarrassing to his family. It was common for articles to have been removed from the newspapers in her household, according to Rosalie Profaci. No doubt, the missing pieces had to do with her uncle's underworld activities and may very well have been the two mentioned above.

Profaci's FBI file shows another effect of the bad publicity coming to Profaci from the Kefauver Hearings. The FBI obtained the tags of different cars parked in front of Profaci's home. From the license plates, law enforcement discovered some of Profaci's Associates. There were no reports before the Kefauver affair.

Knowing that Mafia hoods like Joseph Profaci liked to maintain an air of respectability, FBI agents would use this to pry Mafiosi for information. What follows is a Gambino Soldier, Michael Scandifia, telling his Capo, Peter Ferraro, what FBI agents said to him while searching for some other mob Associates. "We don't want to go to Petey Pumps (Ferraro), we don't want to embarrass him with his daughter." Yeah right!

The Apalachin fiasco of late 1957 set off a firestorm of publicity. It made headlines around the nation, and the Profaci name was right there for everyone to see. This time the attention was not short-lived. There were numerous hearings, grand jury appearances to be made, licensing bodies to appear before, and so on. Each one produced its own story about these mysterious men and their frightening power.

Besides the publicity, Profaci and Magliocco now came under the direct scrutiny of the FBI. They both became targets of investigations, including background checks of their criminal records, businesses, family members, and Associates. The FBI conducted surveillance and squeezed informants for further information. With Profaci, the New York office of the FBI even sought permission from Hoover to open Profaci's mail. Washington approved on December 16, 1957, as long as it didn't end up embarrassing the FBI, which meant Director J. Edgar Hoover.

In Chapter Three, I discussed the difficulties Joseph Profaci had with the Food and Drug Administration. Not only was he convicted of mislabeling his Santucci bulk olive oil product in 1950, but also he had a repeat performance in 1952. Whether he was tampering with the oils on other occasions is unknown. Defenders of Profaci might suggest that these charges were simply harassment by the Federal Government because they could not catch the mob leader on more severe charges. There may very well be truth to this theory, but most people would find it hard to have sympathy for someone who was messing with things they ate.

The attention Profaci received during the Kefauver Hearings led to questions about the legality of his citizenship. Despite a public announcement, in April 1954, that steps would be taken to begin denaturalization against Profaci, little happened. The publicity after the discovery of the November 1957 Apalachin meeting revived the effort. Assistant United States Attorney Margaret Milius (EDNY) said she was going to ask Federal Judge Mortimer Byers to set a trial date for this matter.

Chapter Three discussed Profaci's tax problems. They dragged on until his death in 1962. But that didn't seem to bother the Boss for his expensive lifestyle continued unabated, and he made no serious effort to resolve the matter. Nevertheless, this problem led to continued scrutiny from the authorities who were anxious to pin just about any offense on the elusive Mafia leader.

The FBI investigated rumors, in November of 1957 that Profaci was getting illegal payments from Vitale Brothers Incorporated, a Brooklyn garment industry concern. The belief was that Profaci influenced the International Ladies Garment Workers Union, Local 89, which allowed Vitale Brothers to operate outside some of the union's rules. Despite the investigation, Assistant United States Attorney William Lynch decided, on October 14, 1958, that there wasn't enough evidence to prosecute the case as it then stood.

Being a friend of Joseph Profaci had its difficulties after the Apalachin affair. New York Police Commissioner Kennedy suspended the pistol permits of three men who had been character witnesses for Profaci in various legal proceedings. A fourth man who had supported Underboss Joseph Magliocco also lost his license.

Joseph Magliocco was also having some problems with an arm of the New York State government. The State Liquor Authority regulated his beer distribution enterprise, Sunland Beverages. Magliocco's consorting with people with criminal records at Apalachin made him vulnerable to their censorship. The result was that the Authority did not renew Sunland Beverages' license when it expired on June 30, 1958. That decision had to have been a financial blow to Magliocco. As late as January 23, 1961, a confidential informant told the FBI that Magliocco was still trying to have the license for Sunland returned to the business.

Profaci's Mafia territory included the Red Hook section of Brooklyn. It bordered on most of that borough's docks, which were long dominated by the International Longshoremen's Association and La Cosa Nostra. Despite Profaci's presence, pier action belonged to the Gambino Family. But in the 1950s, it was not at all clear to authorities that there was a Mafia, let alone five distinct Families in the New York area.

There was rampant corruption, extortion, thievery, bribery, and similar crimes choking the vitality of what should have been a booming, honest industry on the docks. In yet another attempt to clean up the mess, Governor Thomas Dewey ordered the New York State Crime Commission to launch an investigation.

The New Jersey Law Enforcement Council commenced a similar undertaking. Since Profaci was a significant hoodlum in Brooklyn, he became a prime target. From these investigations came, in August of 1953, the still-active Waterfront Commission whose mandate was and is to keep crime off the docks of the New York-New Jersey Harbor. While the investigations turned out to be a minor inconvenience to Profaci, it had to have added to his stress level.

PROFACI MEMBERS

A Mafia Boss can't use trades, free agency, and the draft to ensure that he has a balance of experience and youth in his Family. In pro sports, the potential recruit has been scouted and evaluated by experts before the draft, but busts still occur. Often this player hangs around for a year or two then begins a journey through the league as a perennial backup player.

In La Cosa Nostra, a similar "scouting" of the potential recruit takes place as he labors as an Associate. His chances of being inducted go way up if he can consistently earn money. But there are instances when the Boss has to do favors. He might feel compelled to enlist the son of a long-time Capo or the cousin of one of his favorite Soldiers. Whatever the cause, La Cosa Nostra ends up with its share of troublemakers and deadbeats, despite its vaunted reputation for recruitment.

Some of Profaci's men were recruited during Prohibition when it was tough not to turn a dollar. A man with few brains but a good shot was needed during that period but became a liability after 1933. Then, in the peace process that resulted because of the Castellammarese War, membership was frozen at existing levels, and a Family could only induct new members when someone died. Many of the Soldiers were in their twenties or thirties; Mother Nature was not going to be taking a significant toll for another thirty years. Thus the Boss was stuck with what he had, and sometimes what he had wasn't very good.

A similar situation happened when promotions were required. A mob Family was a loose amalgamation of a bunch of mini-gangs, each having developed their leadership. When a Capo died, a Boss usually appointed the new leader from among the existing crew, and often it was a relative of the previous leader. It was not smart to "parachute" a new man into the leadership of a team that he hadn't developed in, although it did happen occasionally.

From the beginning of his reign in the late 20s, Joseph Profaci had surrounded himself with men whom he believed he could count on to be loyal. With Profaci, as with many other Bosses, that meant relatives and close friends. Joseph Magliocco, his Underboss, was a long-time friend and his brother-in-law. The Boss never had to worry about a coup coming from his second-in-command.

Profaci also turned to kin for some of the Capo positions. His brother Salvatore was elevated to the leader of a crew early in Joseph's reign since many of the leaders were young during Prohibition. Salvatore was a key Capo by the early 1950s. His death, due to an accident, must have been both a personal and professional loss for Profaci.

Frank Profaci was a younger brother who we know was a Capo by the early 60s, if not before. It is not clear if he earned his stripes after the death of Salvatore or if he had developed his crew along the way.

Ambrosio Magliocco, older brother of Joseph, was made a Capo at some point and continued in that slot into the 1960s. Another sibling, Antonio, was listed as a member of the Family as late as 1980.

Charles "The Sidge" LoCicero, was a top Profaci Capo, and he may even have been Consigliere at one point. Like so many in the Family, LoCicero had worked his way up in the gambling and loansharking rackets. His "legitimate" business was the Florentine Furniture Company, which, not surprisingly, had tax problems, much like some of the enterprises owned by Profaci. In LoCicero's case, a fortunate fire broke out and destroyed all his company's records.

At one point, someone fired fifteen shots into Locicero, but he survived. LoCicero had a lot of personal experience, his lengthy criminal record attested to that. In Chapter Seven, I'll tell you about a famous incident in which LoCascio played a mediator role.

Sebastiano "Buster" Aloi was another senior Capo whose main activity was running a profitable gambling and loansharking ring. Of course, members of his crew had their fingers in every other kind of racket imaginable from extortion to labor racketeering. He was sending an excellent package of money up the line to Magliocco and Profaci regularly. Aloi also had friends outside the Family, including one with Carlo Gambino, who became Boss of the Gambino Family in 1957. This friendship would be influential in later affairs.

Towards the end of Profaci's reign, John "Sonny" Franzese was a rising star in the Family. Profaci promoted him to Capo but was very suspicious of his ambitions. According to Dary Matera, co-author of *Quitting the Mob* (1992), Franzese's home base in the 40s and 50s was the Jackson Heights section of Queen's. Franzese is worth mentioning at this point, for he had the potential to become a contender for Profaci's throne in the future.

By the end of 1959, the best estimates are that the Colombo Family had about ten Capos, one hundred and twenty Soldiers, and at least a similar number of Associates. It was a small Family with an active nucleus of Profaci supporters. Although it had aging leadership, the future appeared bright to the Profaci loyalists. They were wrong!

There is always unrest lying just beneath the surface in Mafia Families. In each Family, there is usually a man of high ambition and little restraint. Once inducted, the young man begins to be a bit more politically astute. He knows his superiors won't hesitate to kill him if the offense is high enough.

To maintain control, a transparent chain of command must exist. Everyone must obey orders from a superior without question. However, there are endless disputes in which the right or wrong is less clear. For example, two members from two different crews might get in an argument over the splitting of spoils from some hijacking. In theory, a superior is supposed to settle the dispute at a sit-down. Inevitably, one of the adversaries leaves the table angry inside despite having accepted the decision by the superior. This anger is just waiting for a chance for revenge. It's the power of his superiors that makes the Soldier swallow his pride.

It's not only Associates, Soldiers, and Capos who are subject to sit-downs. The Commission often had to settle disputes between Families. Profaci was an original member in 1931. For decades its dominant faction included Profaci. This state of affairs was coming to an end as the 1960s approached.

PROFACI'S FRIENDS AND FOES

One of the main political changes that affected Profaci negatively was the rise of Carlo Gambino to the top of the Family that would bear his name. Before Gambino, Vincenzo Mangano had led the Family from 1931 through to his disappearance in 1951. Albert Anastasia then took over. He was the one behind the Mangano vanishing act. Fortunately for Profaci, Anastasia kept the Family headed in a direction that coincided with the thinking of Profaci and his other allies.

That all changed in October of 1957 when Anastasia was taken out by a coup involving his Underboss, Carlo Gambino, who was backed by Bosses Tommy Lucchese and Vito Genovese.

Suddenly, the balance of power on the Commission was tipping away from Profaci and Joseph Bonanno. This shift was a signal to malcontents within their Families that a change at the top might very well be possible.

Profaci had to observe rival Boss Vito Genovese. As tough as any mobster, Genovese also was extraordinarily ambitious and wouldn't hesitate to use force if diplomacy didn't get him his way. Therefore, it must have been with great pleasure that Profaci learned that Genovese had become entangled in a massive heroin conspiracy. A jury convicted him on April 11, 1959. A week later, a judge handed Genovese a fifteen-year sentence and a $20,000 fine. Profaci's grin must have been from ear to ear.

Profaci's growing concern about the Gambino and Lucchese Families must have tempered the excellent news about Genovese. As mentioned previously, Tommy Lucchese had helped Carlo Gambino gain the throne of that Family by backing a coup against sitting Boss Albert Anastasia. The marriage of Lucchese's daughter Frances to Gambino's son Thomas strengthened those bonds. Profaci was well aware that the joining of these two Families meant difficulties for him in the future.

There was some other positive news, however. Back in 1956, the National Meeting of La Cosa Nostra had decided to add two new members to the Commission starting in 1961. Joseph Zerilli, Profaci's friend and relative through marriage, was firmly established as Boss of Detroit, and that Family would have one of the new seats. Zerilli would be supportive of the veteran Profaci and help counter-balance the growing power of Lucchese and Gambino.

A closer look at the future Commission make-up for 1961 would temper Profaci's happiness about the elevation of Zerilli. Philadelphia also was to get a seat on the Commission. But a change had taken place in that city. The publicity generated by the Apalachin fiasco had shaken Philly Boss Joe Ida. He soon abdicated and returned to Italy. After a short period of uncertainty, the Commission recognized Angelo Bruno as the new Boss. He was a friend and business partner of Carlo Gambino and thus would offset the vote of Detroit's Joseph Zerilli. Profaci was no further ahead in his political power.

One of Profaci's most significant problems was his friend and ally, Joseph Bonanno. After being caught at Apalachin on November 14, 1957, Bonanno began an era where he would disappear from view for extended periods. These Houdini acts were a tactical move to avoid various subpoenas from grand juries, hearings, and other arms of state and federal governments. It also allowed Bonanno to steer clear of fellow Mafiosi and some of the problems that arose at higher levels of La Cosa Nostra. This tactic might have worked in the short term, but strategically, it was a disaster for Bonanno and his friends.

Profaci's alliance with Bonanno meant that Profaci would be losing the firm support of Commission member Stefano Magaddino of Buffalo. The bad blood that existed between Magaddino and Bonanno impacted Profaci's relationships with the Buffalo Boss. Bonanno's enemies looked upon any friend of Bonanno with suspicion. Thus Profaci and his Underboss Joseph Magliocco were losing support by remaining allied with Bonanno. In hindsight, it would have been better for both men to have forged new alliances as Bonanno began a long slide from power.

Besides moving away from Bonanno, Profaci probably should have expanded the circle of those holding power within his Family. Through 1959 Profaci had kept control in the hands of blood family members. While this was a tried and true method of not only holding onto power, it was also a policy which created frustration and unrest just beneath the surface. Profaci and Magliocco chose to ignore these dangers as the 1950s ended, or perhaps they were just too preoccupied with other problems to even consider what would become their downfall.

Profaci would not be the first, nor the last Mafia leader to miss the signals that all was not well within his empire. And to be fair, in December of 1959, the chances of open opposition to Profaci seemed remote.

It was clear that legal problems hampered Profaci. His main difficulty in this area was his conviction for obstruction of justice for failing to explain why he and others had gathered at the estate of Joseph Barbara on November 14, 1957. Another concern was the ongoing efforts of the federal government to deport Profaci. For those who wished to see Profaci dethroned, and these were members and rival Bosses, the scales of justice seemed to be the best bet to make their wishes come true as 1960 began.

CHAPTER SIX

The Lineups

THE GALLO CREW

Three of the most famous characters in Mafia lore are brothers Lawrence, Joseph, and Albert Gallo. Lawrence, the eldest, born on November 3, 1927, was best known as Larry. The second Gallo boy was Joseph, who initially was called "Joey the Blond" because of the color of his hair. Later on, his moniker became "Crazy Joey," but this was only used behind his back and in the press. Albert Jr. was the youngest boy, and his early nickname was "Kid Blast," which he earned because of his fondness for sex with the ladies. As Albert aged, his nickname became "Blast." Law enforcement and other mobsters referred to them as "The Gallos."

At first glance, Larry Gallo did not give the impression that he fit the mold of the stereotypical gangster. At five foot seven and one hundred and fifty pounds, Larry was not a physically imposing man. However, no one fooled with him. Being the eldest, Larry adopted a protective attitude towards his younger brothers. In the early 1950s, Larry took a one-year prison sentence for possessing a crate of stolen suits that the police thought Joey Gallo had heisted.

Although not formally educated, Larry was reasonably well-read and had a love for music. During one raid, law enforcement officers observed Larry's extensive opera record collection. They even listened to some of the selections as they talked to the hoods. Larry also played the fiddle well, which suggests that he did have enough discipline when he found something he enjoyed.

Joey was the most famous of the three Gallo brothers. He was born in 1929 and grew to a height of five feet six inches and weighed in at one hundred and fifty pounds as an adult. As he aged, his blond hair receded, and his temper seemed to get worse. Hyperactive since childhood, Joey would lash out unexpectedly with his fists, feet, and even his teeth. Add to this package of dynamite a reputation of being a Mafia gunman, and you had someone that everyone, including the toughest of hoods, tried to avoid provoking.

Like his brother Larry, Joey Gallo earned a reputation for being intelligent. He had never done well academically and dropped out before graduating from high school. But, towards the end of his life, Joey came into contact with an eclectic group of actors and writers who moved in the circle of famed actor Jerry Orbach. It was from some of the observations of this group that the public learned that Joey had at least a passing knowledge of the writings of a few significant philosophers.

Those more experienced with criminal life will quickly recognize a characteristic of one type of long-term prisoner. Some cons spend hours poring over books from the bible to law journals. They may quote extensive passages from the book(s) of their particular interests. Of course, having little to do to occupy time will bring out this trait in at least a few bad guys. The point being is that the intellect of Joey Gallo was only remarkable in that he had any at all.

Albert "Blast" Gallo was the youngest of the three Gallo brothers and was/is probably the smartest, both intellectually and politically. Born on June 6, 1930, Albert was swept up into the underworld by merely following the example of his two older brothers. He never had a reputation for violence, although that is a relative term when you are talking about Mafia guys. Few doubted that Albert would turn to violence if necessary.

At five feet seven inches tall, Albert was similar to his brother in height, but he had a larger frame. He, too, was prone to balding and eventually attacked the problem by getting a hair transplant in the early 70s. Albert could dress up and take on the appearance of a businessman rather than that of a poor street hood. This Gallo probably had a more comprehensive view of the world than just La Cosa Nostra due to his constant reading of newspapers.

The two older Gallo boys grew up as street criminals doing hijackings, burglaries, and the like. Eventually, they came into the orbit of more powerful hoods like Frank "Frankie Shots" Abbatemarco. They started collecting gambling debts for the veteran mobster. Gradually they carved out a little kingdom in the Red Hood section of Brooklyn, which was part of the Joseph Profaci territory.

By the mid-fifties, the Gallos had a vending machine business in operation. Like most Mafia enterprises, there was an attempt to create a monopoly in their area, and thus they became active in Local 266 of the Juke Box Union. The government alleged, and they were correct, that Local 266 was a paper entity to allow the creation of a mob monopoly on Long Island. Competitors were squeezed out or made to join the union, and bar owners were forced to use "approved" machines. If threats didn't work, the Gallos weren't hesitant to use violence.

They became so infamous that they received an invitation to appear before the Select Committee on Improper Activities in the Labor or Management Field. Better known as the Rackets Committee, it began on January 30, 1957, and issued a final report on March 31, 1960. The Gallos were just two of some 1,526 witnesses to appear before its members.

Larry and Joey traveled to Washington to testify before the Committee. For Joey, the engagement was another opportunity to be on stage, playing the role of a gangster. By most accounts, he acted like a juvenile in the private session with Committee counsel Robert Kennedy before the public part of their testimony. When appearing before the full Committee in 1958, Joey Gallo looked menacing despite his small stature. His slicked-back hair, dark suit, and sunglasses make him look like a movie gangster. Both he and Larry kept taking the Fifth Amendment, which, when combined with other testimony and the questions, made the Gallos look even more threatening. From this point on, Joey Gallo was a recognizable name when talking about east coast gangsters.

By the time 1960 rolled around, the Gallos had a crew of approximately twenty regular Associates. These guys ranged in age from the early twenties to a few in the late fifties. None of them were great money-makers. They banged out money any way they could, gambling, fraud, extortion, burglary, hijacking, union racketeering, fencing stolen goods, and on and on. Money was always a sore point with the Gallos and their gang. Eventually, they would take an enormous gamble to try to improve this situation.

JUNIOR'S BOYS

Unlike Joey Gallo, Carmine "Junior" Persico was a Mafia hood of real substance. He was cunning, ruthless, politically astute, fearless, and intelligent. Persico learned when to use violence as an instrument of power rather than a reaction to frustration. Persico would climb to the heights of La Cosa Nostra while Gallo remained on the lower rungs all his life.

Persico was born in New York on August 8, 1933, and began a criminal career early in his teens. Carmine was a small man, five feet six inches in height, and weighing around 130 pounds in the mid-sixties. He was not going to terrify anyone with his size. But once he had gained a reputation as a killer connected with the Mafia, few would dare to get lippy with Persico.

Persico climbed the Mafia ladder by starting on the street doing burglaries, enforcement work, and truck hijacking. An arrest on the latter racket would plaque Persico for the next twenty-plus years.

Persico's success was due to the fact he controlled a large crew of loyal friends and relatives. They could be counted on to undertake any assignment, even killing. Included among these men was Dominic "Donnie Shack" Montemarano.

Montemarano was fearless, but some of his actions made outsiders question his intelligence. For example, on January 8, 1962, "Donnie Shack" and another Persico hood decided to snatch a rival Gallo gangster off the street in front of the Gallo headquarters. The trouble was that detectives who were parked inconspicuously in the early morning darkness were closely watching the Gallos. As Montemarano and the other Persico man were trying to muscle the Gallo hood into their car, the two detectives approached on foot. "Donnie Shack" jumped into his car and hot-footed it out of the neighborhood with the detectives in pursuit. The other two hoods took off on foot.

After a chase, Montemarano was finally pulled over. His pursuers were the police instead of the Gallos much to Donnie Shack's relief. Strangely he was trying to pull off the kidnapping using Carmine Persico's car! So much for the Mafia legends of well-planned hits using crash cars and the like! Donnie Shacks didn't talk, so we have no idea whether this was the spur of the moment action or a planned event that went south. Montemarano would be involved in many similar operations right into the next century.

Another Persico loyalist was Hugh "Apples" McIntosh. Before his senior years, McIntosh was a large, powerful-looking man who could intimidate others by his mere presence. McIntosh could never become a formal member of La Cosa Nostra because he was not of Italian heritage. But he was as close to power as many made men due to his friendship with Carmine Persico.

Salvatore "Sally D" D'Ambrosio and his twin brother Alphonse "Funzied" D'Ambrosio were two other Persico men who were not afraid of the rough stuff. Salvatore had a wife and four kids but also a mistress who had two children fathered by "Sally D." If that wasn't enough, Salvatore also had a girlfriend. Surprisingly, Salvatore had time to gamble and strong-arm guys who were behind in their loanshark payments. Chapter Seven will cover three famous murder attempts involving Salvatore.

One of the most loyal of the Persico men was young Gennaro "Gerry Lang" Langella. He was twenty-four in 1960 and was not yet a formal member of La Cosa Nostra. However, Langella was already an experienced street hood that could be counted on to collect loans, hijack trucks, and do anything else to make a buck. If Persico ordered a Gallo murder, Langella would be first in the hit vehicle.

Joseph "Joe Yak" Yacovelli was a much smaller man than Gennaro Langella but just as deadly. A quiet hood who shunned the limelight Yacovelli was known by the public until 1963 when the New York Police Department publicly-listed Yacovelli as a member of the Colombo Family. They knew him as a loanshark, extortionist, and someone involved with stolen goods. Circumstances would place Yacovelli in a pivotal role a decade later.

ANOTHER JOE

Another key player in the Gallo brother's revolt was Joseph Anthony Colombo, who was no stranger to violence. Joe Colombo, born on June 16, 1923, was the first child of young hoodlum Anthony Colombo and his twenty-year-old wife, Catherina. From the birth records, it appears that Colombo was born at the home of his parents, but it is unclear whether this was a question of timing, an economic issue, or a family tradition.

Colombo managed to make it through public school in Brooklyn but found high school, not to his liking. With a recorded IQ of 94, Colombo failed 15 courses before leaving school on December 1, 1939. While this type of academic performance is not a-typical of Mafiosi, in fairness, Colombo did have a legitimate excuse for part of the period.

On February 6, 1938, Colombo's father, Anthony "Nino" Colombo, was found murdered in the rear seat of his automobile along with his girlfriend. It was a startling turn of events for young Joseph. His family had deadly enemies, but there was the added distress of having his mother humiliated in front of the entire neighborhood. Additionally, there was the economic devastation caused by the loss of the family's earner. It's not surprising that Joseph decided to leave school behind.

The Coast Guard called Colombo to active service in October of 1943. He had joined the Coast Guard Reserve shortly after the Japanese attack on Pearl Harbor on December 7, 1942. Despite his patriotism, Colombo's stay in the armed forces was not without its problems. His record indicates that he was officially AWOL (away without leave) three times and received a sentence of 12 months after his third offense.

During this same period, Colombo was suffering from mental problems, which the Coast Guard called "psychoneurosis, mixed type." He spent 19 days in hospital in the fall of 1944 and a further five days in February of 1945.

After this second incident, the Coast Guard honorably discharged Colombo on March 24, 1945.

During his sojourn in the Coast Guard, Colombo found time to marry Lucia Faiello in a ceremony at Our Lady of Peace church in Brooklyn on May 28, 1944. Their first child, Anthony, was born on February 25, 1944, and he was to be followed by four other children over the next two decades.

Colombo bounced around in his quest for legitimate employment. His record lists occupations such as machinist, mechanic, and longshoreman. Finally, he began work at Pride Meat Company, a Brooklyn enterprise, in the late 1950s.

It was at this latter concern that our first hint of Colombo's connections to the powerful Carlo Gambino begins to appear. Pride Meat was a part of the expanding legitimate business interests of Paul Castellano, a brother-in-law of Gambino, and a Capo in Gambino's Mafia Family.

During this same period, we also see a developing interest in Colombo by the NYPD and the FBI. In 1958 the police arrested Colombo two times for vagrancy. Probably this was just the police harassing a known hood. A judge dismissed both charges. The FBI was interested enough in Colombo to interview him on July 1, 1958, and January 12, 1959. While they didn't gain any useful information, their attention to Colombo indicates that they thought he was well connected, which he was.

The surveillance of Colombo by law enforcement revealed his association with Sebastian Aloi, a long-time Profaci member known to control various gambling enterprises. Aloi was a close friend of Carlo Gambino, Boss of his own Family. Colombo had yet another connection to the powerful Gambino besides his supposed employment with the Castellanos and Pride Meats.

According to FBI informant Greg Scarpo, Colombo was also involved in gambling, running crap games out of locations that were changed periodically in the hopes of avoiding raids. This tactic did not always work. When Colombo moved into a new social club on 13th Avenue in Brooklyn, the police quickly raided. Someone must have forgotten to make a payoff to the cops.

Colombo, by 1961, was a recognized Mafia member involved in gambling. No one in law enforcement was predicting that he was a future Boss. Furthermore, informant reports never mention Colombo was leadership material. He looked like a middle-level management type guy who would hover at this stage for the rest of his criminal career.

THE MEDDLERS

In New York City, five distinct Mafia Families continually stumble over each other in their constant quests to make money. The Bosses have a never-ending interest in having "friends" in charge of the other Families. Such was the case as Joseph Profaci entered the 1960s.

Profaci and Joseph Bonanno had been allies since the 1930s. They supported each other in the decisions made by the Commission and made sure to keep this alliance by not intruding on the interests of each other.

In hindsight, it is now possible to see just how vital the alliance with Profaci was to Bonanno. From his writings, Bonanno spoke of a conservative block on the Commission of which he and Profaci were crucial components. According to Bonanno, another conservative member, Buffalo's Stefano Magaddino, had begun distancing himself from the alliance and in particular, Bonanno. For some reason, perhaps vanity, Bonanno couldn't bring himself to court Magaddino and cater to his need to be recognized. Instead, Bonanno plotted his course, confident in his abilities to forge other alliances to protect his broad interests.

But Bonanno's position was slipping away as the 60s began. Not only had he alienated Magaddino, but his arrogant behavior had won him no friends amongst the newer New York Bosses. Perhaps, because of his long tenure on the Commission, Bonanno thought that he was not only more experienced but smarter than these new members. Whatever the case, the power that belonged to Bonanno was in decline. Profaci's influence fell as a result.

Profaci's power had also been affected by the loss of ally Albert Anastasia who had been the head of the Gambino Family until his murder in October of 1957. Carlo Gambino, who had few connections to Profaci and who began building his alliances, which excluded Profaci and Bonanno, replaced Anastasia.

A similar situation existed in the Genovese Family. Frank Costello, a man more inclined to negotiations and compromise than direct action, had led it for decades. Although not always in agreement with Profaci, Costello was not someone that Profaci would have to fear. But, in May of 1957, Costello, weakened by legal problems, was overthrown by his Underboss, Vito Genovese, a man who was not reluctant to use violence to get his way. The authorities sent Genovese to prison in 1960, but his appointed Acting Boss was still listening to his views, and supporting Profaci was not on the agenda.

The fifth New York Mafia Family, the Luccheses, was never in the Profaci camp. In 1953 Thomas Lucchese had taken over leadership of this group after the death of its long-time Boss Gaetano Gagliano. Lucchese was considered a staunch ally of Carlo Gambino due to shared interests and the marriage of a Gambino's son to a Lucchese daughter. As such, Lucchese was not going to be opposed if someone more favorable to him, and Gambino won Profaci's throne.

Besides the New York Bosses and Magaddino, Profaci had to be concerned about the alignment of the Chicago Outfit. At the time, Sam Giancanna was its formal leader. His Consigliere, Anthony Accardo, was the real power in Chicago, Giancanna was out front and attended Commission meetings.

The Chicago Outfit did not like Joe Bonanno. We know this from the transcripts from hidden FBI bugs in various Outfit gathering spots. Profaci would not be able to count on the support of Outfit leaders due to his closeness to Bonanno.

Joseph Profaci was in a precarious position as 1961 approached. The government was hounding him on numerous fronts, and his health was fading. Also, some of his Soldiers were hoping for a change in leadership. With his Commission support falling away, Profaci was vulnerable. In La Cosa Nostra, that means the sharks will be circling looking to attack.

CHAPTER SEVEN

Colombo Emerges

PROFACI UNDER SIEGE

Joseph Profaci was in a lot of difficulty in 1961. He was aging, and his doctors hospitalized the Boss in October of 1958, with severe headaches that incapacitated him for more extended periods as time went by. Some outsiders speculated that these medical incidents were just another example of the time-honored practice of Mafia leaders coming down with medical problems when trying to fend off the government. Unfortunately for Profaci, the health problems were real and sapping his energy.

Profaci received some good news on January 12, 1960. An appeals court overturned his denaturalization order. But, the very next day, Profaci was sentenced to five years in jail for conspiracy to obstruct justice. His answers before a special Grand Jury in the Southern District of New York about the 1957 Apalachin affair were considered not believable. Profaci would remain free while his and other similar cases wound their way through the appeals process.

On March 22, 1960, Profaci had to face the indignity of a marshal's sale of a number of his properties to meet taxes owing to the federal government. This event even hit the papers with a New York Tribune story on the auction. This event had to be a humiliating experience for the man who tried to present himself as a respectable businessman.

Profaci's embarrassment continued. On April 8, Myron Beldock, the United States Attorney for the Eastern District of New York, requested an investigation into Profaci, his wife, and two of their companies. He was inquiring to see if they could pay the more than one million dollars in taxes that were still owing after the marshal's sale. The thought was that Profaci had assets that he was hiding from the government.

All these problems suddenly became minor when, in late February 1961, the Gallo crew kidnapped four of his senior men. The consensus is that Underboss Joseph Magliocco, Capo Frank Profaci, Capo Salvatore Musacchia, and Soldier John Scimone were those taken by the Gallos. Informant reports to the FBI suggested that low profile Cap Joseph Colombo was among those kidnapped.

According to an internal NYPD report, the Gallos kidnapped six men, not four. The victims were: Magliocco, Frank Profaci, Musacchia, Colombo, Harry Fontana, and Charles LoCicero. The number and the names of the victims remain cloudy to this day. The real question was what was going to happen next.

According to Inspector Raymond Martin of the NYPD, Profaci sent negotiators to meet with the Gallos in an attempt to save the lives of his men. One of the mediators was Charles LoCicero, Profaci's Consigliere, who owned a furniture company as his legitimate front. (Obviously, this negotiation role precludes LoCicero from being one of the kidnap victims). While it is not clear as to what the main points of the negotiations were, there must have been a compromise for the captured men were released unharmed.

For a time, everything appeared to return to normal within the Family. Decades later, as made men began becoming government witnesses the public started to get a better understanding of what transpires in the circumstances like this. From what happened a few months later, we can conclude that the Profaci loyalists began planning to attack the Gallo crew. Most likely, there were many missed opportunities before their treachery became known.

Besides back luck, it is also probable that Profaci's continuing health problems played a role in the delay of revenge. On March 2, 1961, a confidential informant told the FBI that Joseph Magliocco said that Profaci had suffered a stroke. This report is backed up by the fact that Profaci was in a Miami hospital during this period.

Another hint that there was a lull in activities in the Family exists. Joseph Colombo felt circumstances were right for him to go through with his marriage to Lucy Faiello on May 3, 1961, at Brooklyn's Our Lady of Peace church. It would seem improbable that Colombo would tie himself down in a known location if the Gallo forces were planning an attack.

WAR

By late August 1961, the gloves came off officially. Joe Gioelli, a violent Gallo gunman, stupidly went off with members of the Carmine Persico crew and was never seen again. Unfortunately for Larry Gallo, this betrayal was unknown to him till it was too late.

Larry Gallo agreed to meet Profaci supporter John Simone at the Sahara Lounge to talk things over. He went despite the warnings from his brother and other crewmembers. Larry felt safe, and he was an experienced La Cosa Nostra member who was very familiar with treason in the killing of rivals.

The ensuing events are well known to mob watchers and those who have seen the Godfather II movie. While in the Sahara, a man came up from behind Gallo and looped a garrote around his neck and began pulling it tight. Later street talk, picked up by the NYPD, claimed that the attackers didn't try to kill Larry right away. They attempted to persuade him to call his brothers to the Sahara. This tale seems unlikely, but in any case, Gallo was near death when good fortune shone on him.

A patrolling police officer, Sergeant Edward Meagher, happened to notice that the door of the Brooklyn tavern was ajar before opening hours and decided to investigate. He saw Gallo's body on the floor just as three men burst past him. Running away, they were accosted by Patrolman Melvin Blei, who had responded to the yells of his Sergeant. One of the three men fired a shot that ripped into Blei's face staggering the officer. The hoods jumped into a parked white Cadillac and tore off. Responding squad cars found the Caddy four blocks away. A battered and bruised John Scimone was lying in the road. Perhaps he had fallen out of the vehicle.

Meanwhile, Larry Gallo slowly regained consciousness but refused to name his attackers. But the Sergeant felt confident that two of the men were Carmine "The Snake" Persico and Salvatore "Sally D" D'Ambrosio.

There was sporadic violence as the two sides attempted to kill each other. The Gallos holed up in their President Street headquarters, which made monitoring by the NYPD and the FBI easy and put the Gallos into the media spotlight. On the other hand, the Profaci loyalists were able to freewheel throughout the city, periodically moving in to fire shots at the Gallo crew.

Among the highlights of this period was the brazen attempt by a Persico wild man, Donny "Donny Shacks" Montemarano, to kidnap a Gallo member from in front of their President Street stronghold. The surveillance cops chased Montemarano, who went on a wild ride through the area before he finally gave up. Montemarano thought the pursuit was by Gallo members and thus his reluctance to pull over.

More serious were the late December convictions of Joey Gallo for extortion and the arrest of Carmine Persico for the attempted murder of Larry Gallo. These were two of the most dangerous opponents, and the legal problems undoubtedly curbed their ability to create havoc.

Carlo Gambino and Tommy Lucchese, two New York Mafia Bosses, were supporting the Gallo revolt. The Gallos had also met numerous times with Anthony "Tony Bender" Strollo, a powerful Genovese Capo. Before the kidnappings, no one knew the significance of the sit-downs.

Joseph Bonanno, then an active New York Boss, revealed more of the intrigue of the Gallo war in his book, *Joseph Bonanno: A Man of Honor* (1982). He related how Joe Profaci appeared before a Commission meeting called by Carlo Gambino in early 1962. At that gathering, Gambino suggested that it would be best for all if Profaci stepped aside to end the conflict. Gambino's strong ally and fellow Boss Tommy Lucchese supported the idea. Mob historians had long speculated about the Gambino/Lucchese support of the Gallos. Bonanno's revelations gave strong support to the theory and provided a better understanding of the Gallo's supposedly irrational act.

Joseph Bonanno supported the continuing reign of Profaci. This position had little to do with his concern for Profaci. Bonanno's desire to have allies in the leadership positions in New York was the motivating factor.

Ultimately the Commission took a neutral position, which meant, at least officially, it was up to Profaci to settle the internal issue himself. It all was academic; however, Profaci had terminal cancer and passed away on June 6, 1962.

BETRAYAL

Profaci's Underboss, Joseph Magliocco, quickly moved to have himself formally selected as the new Boss. Accordingly, he must have called together all the Capos and held an open vote with a show of hands and verbal approval. It seemed, for a short time, that the Profaci dynasty would continue under his long-time friend and relative.

Magliocco was determined to end the Gallo uprising once and for all. As part of this plan, an FBI report said that Magliocco wanted a levy of $100 from each gambling operation as a fund to fight the Gallos.

It is also essential to understand that the majority of the 120 Family members sat out the conflict. They kept their heads down and would respond to orders but didn't actively look for trouble. Those who wanted neither Magliocco nor the Gallos in charge of the Family probably encouraged this lack of action.

Unfortunately for Magliocco, by the late summer of 1963, the forces opposing his leadership had formulated a strategy to unseat the new Boss. The general consensus among historians is that both Bonanno and Magliocco then plotted to kill their enemies Gambino and Lucchese. Capo Joe Colombo betrayed their plan to Gambino.

An FBI report from September 3, 1963, contains the information that Magliocco had told his Capos he was stepping down on orders from the Commission. The Commission had formally disapproved of Magliocco's election from 1962 and ordered him to call a new one. They also fined Magliocco around $40,000 after he confessed to the assassination plan. According to Magaddino, Magliocco claimed that Bonanno had put him up to the plot. A bug in Magaddino's revealed this detail.

Notorious liar and historical revisionist, Bill Bonanno wrote that it was only after the Commission dethroned Magliocco that he plotted to kill Gambino and Lucchese. Like his father, Bill claimed the Bonanno Family had nothing to do with this assassination plan. No one took either of the Bonannos seriously.

While the high-level political maneuvering was taking place, the shootings continued off and on all through 1963. Most of the dead had connections to the Gallo brothers. But in the era, before hordes of Soldiers became turncoats and filled in the details of mob hits, the media and law enforcement were only guessing as to the real reasons behind each killing. The underdog Gallo crew became folk heroes of sorts battling the powerful mob Boss. Only in America.

The spectacle of Joseph Valachi's testimony, in September of 1963 diverted the attention of all the combatants. He was the first La Cosa Nostra member to testify about his life in the secret society publicly. In an appearance before a Senate Committee, the veteran mobster laid out the structure of La Cosa Nostra. Valachi named Joseph Profaci as the former Boss of one of New York's five Mafia Families. Also, a chart of the Giuseppe (Joseph) Magliocco Family was presented on October 8, listing many of the major players in the ongoing conflict. Ironically Magliocco had been dethroned by this point. Notably absent from the Magliocco list was Carmine Persico. Faulty intelligence placed him in the Genovese Family.

Magliocco passed away after suffering a massive heart attack on December 28, 1963.

COLOMBO RISES

Someone had to take over control of the Family. To do so required approval from the Commission. The Gallos may have dreamed of taking the throne, but they didn't have a chance.

Quickly eliminated from contention was Underboss Salvatore Mussachio. He was too close to the old administration. Larry Gallo's name came up, but this was due more to name recognition rather than real power.

Anthony "Tony Bender" Strollo, the powerful Genovese Capo who had been supporting the Gallos, had fallen out of favor with his bitter imprisoned Boss Vito Genovese. On April 8, 1962, Strollo left home and disappeared. With his demise went the Gallo's hope of support from the Genovese interim leaders.

Another factor that ruled out the Gallos that their deadly street war with the Persico faction. There was little chance that the Commission would approve a Gallo regime if it were only going to lead to future hostilities.

Finally, there was the question of Joey Gallo. On December 21, 1961, a judge sentenced Gallo to a minimum of approximately seven years in prison, taking his hot head off the streets. His brother Larry was well respected and experienced. But his control of an eventually released Joey was in question. The Gallos were perfect for fermenting dissent to undermine Profaci and then Magliocco but as rulers--Fuhgeddaboutit!

A serious contender was John "Sonny" Franzese, a powerful Capo who kept out of the active fighting as far as it's known. He as well connected and certainly had a reputation of a man willing to kill if necessary. Franzese attended the wake of Joseph Profaci, and the FBI recorded his presence. His attendance suggests that he was not an open Gallo supporter. Franzese may have been a Profaci loyalist, but it's more likely he was one of the fence-sitters. In other circumstances, Franzese may well have been a serious contender, but the fix was already in, and Franzese was not the choice.

WHAT CARLO WANTS CARLO GETS

Quietly moving among the heavy hitters was Joseph Colombo, a man few outsiders expected to be in the running for the leadership of the Family. Colombo was better connected than any of the other contenders. Previously I discussed his extensive links to Carlo Gambino. FBI files, in October of 1963, contained a least one opinion that Colombo was now a "power" in the Magliocco Family and was "extremely active" in "Family" affairs.

Colombo's Family mentor was Sebastiano "Buster" Aloi, who just happened to be a long-time friend of Gambino Boss Carlo Gambino. While it's pure speculation, it is not too hard to imagine Aloi suggesting Colombo as a viable candidate to his powerful friend.

New York Police reports on Colombo cite information from informers in 1963 that linked Colombo with the operation of Coffee Royal on New Utrecht Avenue in Brooklyn. This club was the home to a floating crap game that Colombo ran in partnership with others. Real estate records indicated that the owner of the building at the time was one Peter Castellano, brother of the previously mentioned Paul Castellano. Colombo was well known to the Gambino/Castellano entourage.

Colombo's ace, in his climb to the top, was undoubtedly his betrayal of the Bonanno/Magliocco murder plot. Without this action, Gambino may very well have been taken out in a spectacular hit.

With Colombo, not only would Gambino be getting a person with whom he was acquainted but a man who seemed well in control of his emotions. Furthermore, Colombo was a neophyte in the political intrigue of the Commission and could be expected to follow Gambino's lead in these matters. Throw in Colombo's presumed appreciation of Gambino's support and the elevation of Colombo seemed a perfect fit for the wily Gambino.

By the summer of 1964, the FBI was receiving reports from a variety of sources, that Colombo had become the Boss of what used to be the Profaci/Magliocco Family. The consensus was that Colombo was the de facto leader for a period, then was formally recognized at a meeting in which the other New York Bosses were present. It is unclear whether Joseph Bonanno was there, but it would seem unlikely.

What also was taking place was a series of meetings, many held at Renato's Restaurant in Brooklyn (86th and Bay 8th), between Colombo and the Capos from the Magliocco regime. He intended to show a willingness to listen. This action would be in stark contrast to the more remote leadership style of Profaci and Magliocco. Their attitudes contributed to the alienation among some of the members leading to open revolt by some. Colombo was trying to avoid a repeat of those troubled times.

As part of his administrative duties, Colombo had to appoint an Underboss, Consigliere, retain some of the existing Capos, and appoint others. These moves were political. He had to return favors, acknowledge loyalty, and recognize power. It did not mean that Colombo could necessarily select everyone he wanted, for that would mean he would have to ignore those who were dangerous when angered. It was a high wire act with his life at stake in a real sense, especially considering the recent history of the Family.

Veteran Capo Simone Andolino was bumped up to Underboss. He was an excellent choice for Andolino wasn't a significant player in the previous revolts and thus would not be objected to by the other factions. Besides, Andolino was old and had no ambitions that would threaten Colombo in the future. He died on September 7, 1969, while visiting Italy and was replaced by Capo Charles Mineo.

A man with vast La Cosa Nostra experience, Benedetto D'Alessandro was Colombo's first Capo. He lasted till 1969 when Joseph "Joe Yak" Yacovelli, an ally of Carmine Persico, replaced him.

Among the veteran Capos that were initially retained to lend some continuity to the Family were, Sebastiano "Buster" Aloi, Henry Fontana, John Misuraca, and John "Bath Beach" Oddo. Also holding their positions were younger Capos John "Sonny" Franzese and Nicholas "Jiggs" Forlano. While the exact dates of their promotions are unclear, Carmine "Junior" Persico, John Bolino, John Muce, Rocco Miraglia, Nicky Bianca, and others were moved up to Capo during the Colombo's reign.

One of Colombo's significant accomplishments was the wooing and winning of Larry Gallo, the leader of the dissident crew that began the revolt. Gallo had had enough of the violence that had resulted in the murders of nine men and the wounding of eleven others. The deaths of Profaci and Magliocco eliminated the targets of Larry's anger. It was time to get back to making money.

Another factor that eased the peace process was the fact that hotheaded Joey Gallo was behind bars and unable to ferment further problems. Besides, Colombo seemed amenable to giving the Gallo crew more leeway to make money than Profaci had been. Finally, it must have been clear to Larry Gallo that Colombo had the backing of the Commission, and it would be useless to continue fighting.

By the end of 1964, Joseph Colombo was sitting atop a powerful La Cosa Nostra Family, and his future in this life seemed limitless. As the youngest Boss, it was not unforeseeable that Colombo would eventually be the dominant player in the Commission as the older Bosses died off. It was heady stuff.

CHAPTER EIGHT

On Top of the Mountain

GETTING STARTED

Once it became clear that Joseph Colombo was the new Boss of the Colombo Family, he became a prime target for the NYPD, the FBI, and a host of other federal, state, and local law enforcement officials. At various times there was a least one agency following Colombo around to see whom he was meeting and at what locations.

Colombo became very concerned about the continued surveillance. One informant told the FBI that Colombo had ordered his men to not come around to his front work place, Cantalupo Reality, unless specially requested to do so.

It was not uncommon for Colombo, once he had spotted his shadows, to go over and exchange pleasantries with the FBI agents. Among the common themes was Colombo's claim to hate narcotics and anyone who dealt with them. Another pet peeve was Colombo's belief that the government was harassing Italian-Americans.

On other occasions, the FBI agents would go to Colombo to ask him questions on specific matters. Such meetings would sometimes expand into areas in which both parties would dance around the topic of Colombo's activities with La Cosa Nostra.

Despite Colombo's tendency to banter with the agents, he forbade his men from doing the same. Colombo felt that only he had the skill to joust with the agents without revealing any Mafia secrets.

In the fall of 1967, agents were questioning Colombo about a particular person, but he would not reveal whether he knew the man or not. Colombo went on to complain about the bad publicity he was getting and that it was ruining his real estate income. He further stated that he trusted the FBI but did not have the same feelings about other law enforcement people. Those positive feelings about the FBI would soon change.

One of the reasons for the good guys' interest in Colombo was the ongoing turmoil in the Bonanno Family. Commission members Carlo Gambino and Tommy Lucchese believed Bonanno was plotting their deaths. At the same time, the authorities were hunting Bonanno because he had avoided appearing before a grand jury.

Bonanno ultimately reappeared in New York and began a futile attempt to regain control of his Family. Sporadic violence broke out that only increased media and law enforcement attention. At this stage of his leadership career, Colombo was a firm supporter of Carlo Gambino, who was opposed to Bonanno and his return to power.

In the spring of 1966, informants told the FBI that there were rumblings of a shooting war erupting between the Bonannos and the Colombos. The incarceration of Colombo, Larry Gallo, and others for contempt added to the uncertainty on the streets.

The Bonanno problem required frequent discussions among the leaders of La Cosa Nostra. Incredible as it may sound today, on September 22, 1966, a group of Mafia leaders sat down in La Stella restaurant in Queen's and began to have lunch. The NYPD arrested all thirteen men for "consorting" with known criminals and hustled them away to jail.

Included in this gathering were: Carlo Gambino, Boss of his own Family; Colombo; Carlos Marcello, Boss of the New Orleans Family; Santos Trafficante, Boss of the Tampa Family; Tommy Eboli, front Boss of the Genovese Family; and Anthony Corallo, acting Boss of the Lucchese Family. Later, intelligence suggested that the hoods were sitting down to eat after attending a Commission meeting. All the men had the "consorting" charges dropped a few days later. However, they became the focus of considerable media interest and had received subpoenas to appear before a Queen's County grand jury.

EGO PROBLEMS

In 1964 Colombo had become the new Boss of one of New York's five Mafia Families and as such, achieved high power and financial gain. Under him were an estimated 120 men sworn to follow his orders. With his position came a seat on the Commission, La Cosa Nostra's board of governors. Counted among his allies was Carlo Gambino, who had emerged as the most powerful Boss in the eastern half of the United States. Colombo was now a significant player, but he would pay the price for this stature.

Back in 1966, Joseph Colombo had applied for a real estate broker's license. This formality would give him much more flexibility in financial matters associated with the buying and selling of properties. Whether there was an ulterior motive to this attempt is not known. What is clear is that the licensing required Colombo to disclose his income and assets to New York's Secretary of State's office. Among the details was the fact that Colombo claimed to own 55% of Prospero's funeral home in Brooklyn.

State hearings on Colombo's application did not commence till November of 1966. By that time, the fiasco at La Stella had taken place, adding even more negative publicity to Colombo's resume. In January of 1967, his attempt at a broker's license was denied partly because of Colombo's association with criminals, as demonstrated by the La Stella meeting. Informants told the FBI that Colombo was "incensed" at this setback. He blamed the FBI and the NYPD for the rejection of his application.

Colombo had better luck with other legal matters. In July of 1967, he had a contempt citation dismissed. Colombo had refused to testify before a King's County grand jury. The judge ruled that Colombo had offered to testify previously. On December 5, in King's County, Colombo's legal problems with the La Stella affair came to an end when his contempt citation was thrown out.

On September 1, 1967, Colombo received a blast of national publicity when he, along with the other La Cosa Nostra Bosses, was featured in a Life Magazine story on the Mafia. Colombo's picture was at the top of a map of the United States, which showed the locations of the various Mafia Families and depicted their rackets in cartoon form. All the mob Bosses, including Colombo, had to know that the FBI had fed this information to the magazine.

FBI Agents twice observed Colombo meeting with Philadelphia Boss Angelo Bruno in New York's House of Chan restaurant, in June 1968. Carlo Gambino joined Bruno and Colombo at the restaurant along with Colombo Soldier John Scimone on July 11, 1968. At this point, the NYPD arrested the four men and charged them with loitering. That action was just a method of police harassment. Wiser superiors dropped the charges the same day. But this incident must have done little to improve Colombo's growing perception that law enforcement was persecuting him.

The following event appeared to confirm this to Colombo. The State Liquor Authority, on March 24, 1968, held an inconclusive hearing concerning a liquor license for the Via Appia Ristorante in Brooklyn. Anthony Colombo, the eldest son of the mob Boss, owned the joint. The Authority's delay in making a decision was a financial blow to the restaurant. This decision frustrated the senior Colombo. He expressed his feeling to FBI Agents in January of 1969. As far as he was concerned, the authorities were continuing to harass him through his son.

It was not all bad news. By late 1968 it appeared as if the long-running Bonanno problem was coming to an end. Bonanno finally came to his senses after suffering another heart attack and gave up his vain attempt to regain power in New York.

After a brief lull, Colombo felt the pressure increasing again. This time, in late 1969, two Colombo men were missing and presumed killed. Salvatore "Sally D" D'Ambrosio was a veteran Colombo Soldier who was rumored to have been chaffing at Colombo's failure to promote him. The street talk had the Persico crew carrying out the actual hit of D'Ambrosio and his buddy Fred "No Nose" DeLucia.

The FBI looked into the disappearances and decided to try to exploit talk of unrest within the Colombo Family by suggesting to friends and relatives of the missing men that Colombo had a hand in their disappearance. As part of this tactic, they visited a social club on 18th Avenue in Brooklyn that was run by Associate Caesar Vitale. Since there was no evidence of a federal violation, the FBI handed the investigation to the NYPD. Someone (probably the FBI) tipped the press to the activities at the social club, and it became big news.

The media produced stories connecting Colombo to the club, although he claimed to those close to him that he had never set foot in the place. Worse yet was the formation, in January of 1970, of a grand jury to look into the disappearance of the two Colombo men. Among those subpoenaed to appear was Joseph Colombo Jr. With this action, law enforcement officials were rubbing a raw nerve in Colombo Sr. and they knew it.

A STAR IS BORN

Often, during his bantering with FBI agents, Colombo would protest what he saw as unfair treatment of Italian-Americans both by law enforcement and the media. He claimed that Italian-Americans were loyal to the United States and would fight to protect their country, even against Italy. Of course, this had been proven long ago when many Italian-Americans served honorably in all theatres of World War Two, including action against Italy.

During one of his rants, in 1966, Colombo revealed that he was a member of AID, which stood for Americans of Italian Descent. This organization's mission was to protect the interests of Italian-Americans. Colombo said all his Family would pay the $10 membership fee and take part in its activities.

Not surprisingly, the agents then began to pump their sources for information on the AID organization and a connection to Colombo. The feedback, which was not necessarily correct, was that a number of the New York Bosses were secretly behind AID, including Colombo. These men would strive to keep their participation secret so as not to taint the organization with links to reputed criminals.

ITALIAN-AMERICAN CIVIL RIGHTS LEAGUE

Law enforcement's pressure tactics against Colombo finally pushed the Mafia Boss over the edge on April 30, 1970. On that day, police arrested his son Joseph Jr. for melting down coins whose silver content was worth more than their face value. Colombo Sr. was incensed, feeling that the FBI was harassing his son to get at him. In a spontaneous move, Colombo and a group of his men began picketing the New York office (201 East 69th) of the FBI. The agents were holding Joe Jr. at that location.

As the FBI men led Colombo Jr., out of the federal building, about thirty angry pickets accosted them. Anthony Colombo, the eldest son of the mob Boss, challenged the agents to fight, and Mrs. Colombo berated them verbally. It was the beginning of a wild ride that few would have ever predicted.

Colombo decided to continue picketing and ordered his Soldiers to make appearances, of which he would keep track. Much grumbling ensued behind his back, but none of the men dared speak openly. Soon volunteers were going about some Brooklyn neighborhoods urging citizens to join in the demonstrations and donate money. Gradually the number of picketers rose.

Within a week of the first protest, Colombo formed the Italian-American Civil Rights League and opened offices at the Park Sheraton Hotel. He announced that there would be a giant rally at Columbus Circle on June 29. Colombo named this date the Italian- American Unity Day. Local politicians and celebrities were lined up to speak at the rally, and the support began to mushroom.

Surprisingly Colombo gained the support of Carlo Gambino, who usually preferred a much lower-key tactic. With this backing, the International Longshoremen fell into line and stated that their members would have the day off to celebrate Unity Day. Following suit, merchants, especially those in Italian areas, served notice that they would be closing on June 29.

No doubt, fear played a role in the compliance of some for Colombo had received much publicity about his alleged role in La Cosa Nostra. But the real reason for the closings and the large turnout for the rally had an explanation. Colombo had struck a chord in a large segment of the Italian-American population in New York.

Unity Day was an event, which would allow Italian-Americans to gather together to celebrate their common heritage and achievements. Demonstrations by American blacks and students had shown the way to power during the same era, and now it was the time for Italian-Americans. It was an excellent idea, but a fatally flawed one. Its leading proponent was a parasitic Mafia Boss, who accidentally created a movement while trying to intimidate the FBI.

The FBI closely monitored the picketing of their headquarters and were able to identify many known La Cosa Nostra members in attendance at various times. Regulars included Colombo's sidekick Capo Rocco Miraglia, Soldier John Cutrone, Soldier Joe Brancato, and Capo Greg Scarpa. Unknown to Colombo was the fact that Scarpa was a secret FBI informer who filled the agency in on the latest movements and plans of the League and of the Mafia Family itself.

One informer told the FBI that even Carlo Gambino demonstrated his support for the League by attending a small rally on Brooklyn's Court Street. This event had been organized to protest the arrest of some connected people. The informant explained that these smaller protests were to encourage neighborhood people to attend the more significant rally at the end of June.

Gambino was also present at another rally in Brooklyn's Carroll Park on May 30, 1970. The crowd was addressed by Gambino Capo Anthony Scotto, who was also a power in the Longshoreman's Union whose offices were nearby. Gambino did not leave his car, so his support would seem to have been less than enthusiastic. However, his poor health may have been the real reason.

Gambino's Underboss, Aniello Dellacroce, was reported walking the picket line in front of the FBI offices on at least one occasion. Another informant passed on the news that Angelo Bruno, the Philadelphia Boss, would demonstrate on behalf of the League on May 15, 1970.

Father Louis Gigante, the brother of future Genovese Boss Vince "Chin" Gigante, was a significant supporter and was observed speaking to the protestors on June 1. Father Gigante was running for congress at the time, so his participation was understandable from both a political and family point of view.

Colombo's pickets suffered a minor setback on June 15. New York Supreme Court Justice George Starke ordered picketing to end at 9 pm. Also, no "amplified or magnified" devices could be used. Previously the demonstrators had been using bullhorns to increase the disturbance they were creating. Not surprisingly, the neighboring businesses were finding this bothersome.

In the weeks before the Unity Day rally, Colombo told his organizers that he expected that he and nine other leaders of the movement would be arrested the night before the rally. He saw this tactic as an effort to disrupt the gathering. Whether Colombo believed this or was using a ploy to inspire his followers is not clear. In any event, the arrests did not take place.

ITALIAN-AMERICAN CIVIL RIGHTS LEAGUE RALLY

July 29, 1970, was the apex of Joseph Colombo's power, both as a Mafia don and a pseudo civil rights leader. An exuberant crowd, estimated to be in the thirty-five to seventy thousand range, packed Columbus Circle. They were there to hear speeches from a guest list that ranged from Colombo to the deputy mayor Richard Aurelio. Singer Jimmy Roselli entertained the crowd along with the Bob Chese orchestra. Notably absent was Mayor John Lindsay, who was waiting to see which way the wind blew on this controversial movement.

Around 2:40 pm, approximately 2,000 marched to the Federal Building to express the anger in front of the FBI offices. Along the way, protesters pushed police barricades aside, and some vandalism took place. Once at their destination, part of the crowd battled with police officers as they tried to storm the building. Finally, Anthony Colombo arrived and persuaded those assembled to disperse. Despite this relatively minor matter, it had been an incredibly successful day for Colombo. Many people were sitting up and taking notice.

THE AFTERMATH

Colombo's euphoria came crashing down the day after the rally. Police arrested him in Mineola, NY, for refusing to answer questions from a Nassau grand jury. The authorities leveled similar charges against twenty-three other men. The New York Times reported these details. Informants later said that this blow to his pride so angered Colombo that he planned to picket the newspaper.

On November 27, 1970, Colombo's organization packed Madison Garden's Felt Forum. The show featured Frank Sinatra, Sammy Davis Jr., and Trini Lopez. The Italian-American Civil Rights League supposedly banked $600,000 from this gala event.

Capo Vinny Aloi was one of the first to feel the results of the ongoing federal push against the Mafia. In November, the feds indicted him in a stock fraud case that was the result of the turning of conman Michael Hellerman. However, this was a minor inconvenience to Colombo for Aloi wasn't going anywhere soon, and even if he did, his brother Benny could quickly fill in.

On December 16, 1970, the FBI hit the jackpot when they arrested Capo Rocco Miraglia for allegedly committing perjury in the coin case that snared Joe Colombo Jr. As he emerged from his vehicle, Miraglia was carrying a briefcase that the FBI seized. That brought an outburst from Joseph Colombo, who was with Miraglia. Despite Colombo's protests that the briefcase was his, the FBI retained it and Miraglia.

Eventually, the briefcase was returned to Colombo but not until the FBI photocopied its contents. Among the papers was a list of nicknames with amounts beside each. It remained unclear whether those values reflected an amount raised for Colombo's League or payments to those listed. Perhaps the money was for another purpose. To clear up these and other questions, Colombo was ordered to appear before a grand jury on February 3, 1971.

As 1970 came to a close, Colombo could look back on the year with a great deal of satisfaction. He had become, almost overnight, a national figure who was being listened to by politicians, entertainers, and moguls of industry. There were faint rumblings amongst his fellow Mafia leaders, but his apparent newfound power stilled their protests. They fought off their instincts to stay in the shadows to see how the Colombo gamble paid off.

For many, it appeared as if Colombo had performed one of the great tricks of all time. He had persuaded tens of thousands of Italian-Americans that he was the man to voice their legitimate grievances and express their ethnic pride. At the same time, Colombo ran a criminal empire, which had no respect for anything but money. The mob Boss understood that law enforcement knew he was a crook. But Colombo must have dared dream that he could become so powerful that he would be untouchable.

When a judge threw out the Joe Jr. coin case, Colombo faced the New Year with optimism. But 1971 would be a horrible year indeed for the new media star.

CHAPTER NINE

Welcome Home Joey

As the first months of 1971 unfolded, tensions were rising in segments of the New York Mafia. Back on December 14, 1971, the FBI had confiscated Colombo's briefcase, along with some suspicious papers it contained. To create pressure on him, Colombo was called before a Federal grand jury in the Southern District of New York and asked to explain the contents of the papers or risk contempt charges.

Colombo reluctantly identified the people who were listed only by their first name or a nickname. He also said that the numbers beside each name represented the dollar value of tickets that person had sold to the Italian-American Civil Rights League's fundraising concert. Madison Square Garden's Felt Forum hosted the event on November 27, 1970.

These revelations allowed the government to call those named before the grand jury and subject them to questions. For many of these figures, including Carlo Gambino and Genovese Family Front Boss Tommy Eboli, their appearances were not only embarrassing but also potentially legally dangerous.

A favorite government tactic was to try to catch Mafiosi in lies during their grand jury testimony. Then the authorities could charge the witnesses with perjury. Another ploy was to grant immunity to some hoods, which meant that they could no longer refuse to testify, based on their Fifth Amendment rights against self-incrimination. If the gangster still refused to testify, he could be charged with contempt of court and jailed. If he did speak and did so falsely, the government could fall back on the perjury charges.

The net outcome was that hoods wanted to avoid being subpoenaed to testify about anything. Colombo's mistake with the briefcase and its contents didn't make happy campers out of his "friends."

Into this tension-filled milieu strode cocky Joey Gallo, determined to re-establish his reputation and pocketbook after his lengthy prison stay. Thanks to Peter "Pete the Greek" Diapoulos, a long-time Gallo Associate, we have an insider's view of the mindset and actions of the hotheaded Gallo during this period.

Gallo began complaining before the prison door shut behind him on March 10, 1971. He was infuriated with his crew's weak financial position and lack of status. Before Gallo had arrived back in Brooklyn, he had determined to move on Boss Joe Colombo. Diapoulos knew there was going to be trouble.

On May 11, a judge gave Colombo a short sentence for perjury on his real estate license application. The mob Boss spoke to the waiting media when he exited the courthouse. Colombo protested that he had checked the wrong box on the application form. He told the press that he wanted to remain on bail so he could direct the building of a hospital, a home for narcotics addicts, and residence for seniors. He explained that the date for the planned Italian-American Civil Rights League's dinner would have to be changed. Colombo was scheduled to begin his prison sentence on May 23, which was before the original date.

About a week after returning to Brooklyn's President Street, Joey Gallo played host to two emissaries from Joe Colombo. Sitting down with Capos Rocco Miraglia and Nick Bianco, Gallo was in a feisty mood. Bianco had been a Gallo back in the early sixties but had eventually migrated into the Colombo camp where he had been promoted and prospered financially. His success must have rankled Gallo, who was not only a mere Soldier but also poor to boot.

According to Diapoulos, Gallo vigorously told the Colombo men that he wanted past promises of financial and power gains met. Furthermore, he stated that neither he nor his men recognized Colombo as their leader. With that, Gallo dismissed the two and began making war preparations.

One can only imagine the reaction of Colombo upon hearing the reports of the Gallo meeting. He was already under considerable pressure from the activities of law enforcement agents and the resulting endless legal problems. Throw in the growing schism with his former mentor, Carlo Gambino, and you had a man under siege.

Some of that bottled up anger came out on March 22, 1971. Colombo was the star attraction at a $125 a plate dinner put on by his Italian-American Civil Rights League in Huntington Station, Long Island. Colombo received the League's Founder Award and was named the Tri-Boro Post's Man of the Year before an enthusiastic crowd of supporters. In his acceptance speech, Colombo tried to send a message to his tormentors, including the FBI and probably Joey Gallo as well. Colombo said, "The League is under God's protection. Anybody who goes against it will feel its sting." It was clear that Colombo was feeling powerful and combative.

If Peter Diapoulos' account of the months between March 1971 and the end of June of the same year is correct, the Gallo crew was continually trying to kill Colombo. Diapoulos described an unsuccessful attempt outside Prospero's Funeral Home on Brooklyn's 86th Street and another in front of Colombo's home on 83rd Street. In neither case did the Gallos fire any shots nor were they seen. By June, informants were telling the FBI that Joey Gallo had definitely rejected the leadership of Colombo, and he and his men were acting independently.

Colombo was aware that Gallo and his men were going their own way. But he didn't take steps to discipline the wayward men. There was more than enough on Colombo's plate to occupy his thoughts as the second annual Unity Day rally approached.

In late March, the feds arrested Italian-American Civil Rights League President Natale Marcone and three others after a violent picketing incident outside the offices of the Staten Island Advance. That paper had angered Colombo and his friend by continuing to print news about the Mafia. The picketing was an attempt to disrupt the delivery of the journal. They hoped to hit the Advance in the pocketbook.

About a week after the Staten Island incident, police arrested Colombo and twenty-one others on gambling conspiracy charges. While not devastating, the pinch forced Colombo to spend more money on lawyers, and he had to post $25,000 bail to avoid staying in jail.

Colombo's problems moved much closer to home on May 14, 1971. While standing outside Cantalupo Reality, where he supposedly worked as a real estate salesperson, Colombo became involved in a street fight. Some of his men and a passing group of strangers came to blows.

While the brawl is unimportant in itself, the fact that Colombo joined in at all seems to indicate a lack of control or thinking on his part. Especially when he now was a public figure under constant scrutiny by both the media and law enforcement.

Carlo Gambino's growing disenchantment with Colombo's public activities became evident. According to turncoat Joseph Cantalupo, Gambino had suggested to Colombo that he recede into the shadows and let others front the Civil Rights League. Colombo rejected any thought of withdrawal, claiming that he was going to continue his activities no matter what anyone thought.

It's impossible to know what was running through Colombo's head after receiving Gambino's advice. It must have shaken the young mob Boss to at least some degree for Gambino was a dominant figure in 1971 despite his declining health. Then Gambino forbade the longshoremen from taking the day off to celebrate Unity Day. The message had to be clear even to a man with a head swollen by his perceived own importance. Nevertheless, Colombo continued to move forward.

In March, Al Ruddy, producer of *The Godfather* movie, announced that the words "Mafia" and "Cosa Nostra" would not be used in the production of the film that became a classic. The decision was weak-kneed, but practical might have been a better description. The year before both the United States Justice Department and New York State Governor Nelson Rockefeller caved under perceived political pressure and banned the use of the offending terms. Ruddy, filming the picture in the heart of Brooklyn, was looking to make money, not trouble.

On June 14, New York Magazine published a story about Colombo's May 14 street fight, but while the gist of the story is correct, the date of the battle is off by about a week. Someone leaked the story to the writer, Nicholas Pileggi, most likely in an attempt to embarrass Colombo.

An announcement that Colombo's League was going to dedicate its Camp Unity for underprivileged children early in July offset the negative publicity somewhat. However, whispers continued that Colombo and his Associates were skimming the funds raised.

As preparations for the second Unity Day proceeded, Gallo's men were moving about the Red Hook section of Brooklyn, tearing down the League's signs. The problem with stories like this is that no one can put a figure to the tales. There may have only been a handful of such incidents. However, what is more telling is that the Gallo supporters felt strong enough to take action like this. The well-known fact that Carlo Gambino was not supporting the second annual Unity Day would have encouraged the Gallos in their anti-rally activities.

JOE GOES DOWN

June 28, 1971, was bright and sunny in New York City. It looked like a perfect day for Joe Colombo to bask in the glory of the second annual Unity Day rally. An hour before noon, the crowd had started to build, and Colombo must have hoped for numbers near fifty thousand or more.

The headcount was going to be necessary for a large crowd would indicate to Colombo and others that the support of Carlo Gambino was not vital.

Gambino, disapproving of Colombo's continued public participation in the League, had tried to undermine its success by forbidding the longshoremen from taking the day off. That decision would have sent a signal to others that it might be best to sit out the 1971 rally. A low turnout would have been an unambiguous indication of Gambino's power and would have probably forced Colombo back under Gambino's wing.

Among the thousands getting ready to attend the June 28th rally was Georgia born Jerome Johnson. After high school, Johnson bounced around and finally ended up in New York City, where he existed on the fringes of society. Most accounts of his New York life describe Johnson as a dreamer and a minor con artist. No one thought Johnson was going places, and this may have been part of his motivation for the actions he was planning to take.

Among Johnson's possessions, that day was a film camera and a pistol capable of firing 7.65 mm bullets. The camera was an essential part of his planned masquerade as a news cameraman. Johnson must have thought that the camera and the press pass he had also obtained would allow him to get close to his intended target. He was right.

It was no surprise that Carlo Gambino had no intention of attending Colombo's sleight of hand show. Gambino hadn't gone to the first one even though he had given it his support. Now that he was opposed to the idea, there certainly wasn't any chance Carlo would be anywhere near Columbus Circle.

Joseph Colombo was dressed casually for the Unity Day rally. It was supposed to be a festive, rather than a formal affair, so his golf shirt and slacks were more than appropriate. As he mingled amongst the growing crowd, Colombo acknowledged shouted greetings, and posed for pictures.

Among those gathering near Colombo was Jerome Johnson. Photographs taken by others confirm eyewitness testimony that Johnson was "filming" Colombo with a camera that he had rented earlier. No one was paying particular attention to Johnson for all eyes were on Colombo. While he did have bodyguards, they were untrained street hoods. While they may have been effective in pounding out gamblers behind in their loanshark payments, they were useless in terms of protecting their leader from an assassin.

Also present at Columbus Square were a host of uniformed police officers and undoubtedly a number in plain clothes. Like Colombo's bodyguards, these men were untrained in protection duties. Their responsibility was crowd control. No one was forming a protective cordon around Colombo.

As the mob Boss moved through the crowd towards the stage, Johnson was standing a few feet away on Colombo's left. Suddenly Johnson dropped his camera, pulled a gun, and began firing. Colombo slumped to the ground bleeding heavily from wounds to his head, neck, and face. Within seconds

Johnson had also been hit by three slugs, one tearing through his heart, and he died face down on the pavement as police officers restrained him.

The Colombo assassination attempt took place before the age of handheld camcorders, and no one had captured the shooting in pictures and film. A later police reconstruction did shed some light on the events. As mentioned earlier, there was photographic and eye witness testimony to the fact that Johnson was acting as if he was filming Colombo. Furthermore, several Colombo men were pictured having pistols in their hands immediately after the two shootings. Later a film showed one of the men running from the scene while the others remained in place.

Doctors at Roosevelt hospital determined that the damage to Colombo's brain was so significant that his days as a functioning human being were over. On August 28, Colombo was moved to his eldest son's Brooklyn home and still later to his own Brooklyn residence (1161 83rd). In 1973 his wife and sons had Colombo transported to their estate in Blooming Grove, where he lingered in a coma for another five years. Colombo finally died in St. Luke's Hospital on May 23, 1978.

ANOTHER JOE GOES DOWN

Immediately after ambulance attendants hauled the body of Johnson and the wounded Colombo away from Columbus Circle, the speculation began as to exactly what had happened and why.

One idea was that Johnson was associated with a black revolutionary group. During this era, several such entities sprang up then quickly faded away as the police and their tendency to violence decimated their ranks. No one could link Johnson to any of these groups ending race as an issue in the Colombo killing.

Time was also spent investigating the role of Carlo Gambino in the shooting. Gambino had distanced himself from Colombo and his civil rights activities. But the authorities could not link the Gambino organization and Johnson. The use of an eccentric person like Johnson would be totally out of character for the veteran mobster. The fact that the shooter would have little chance of escape suggested a Mafia plot was unlikely.

A fundamental building block in most conspiracy theories in the Colombo shooting was the fact that the shooter, Johnson, was himself killed, presumably to prevent him from revealing the plot. At first it this looked feasible in that the person who shot Johnson was not known and thus could have been part of the plan.

However, within days, law enforcement was picking up street talk that a "Chubby" had been the gunman. With the aid of pictures and film taken before and after the Colombo shooting, the NYPD was able, on July 21, 1971, to identify "Chubby" as Philip Rossillo, a Colombo Associate. Further investigation showed that Rossillo was a Colombo loyalist and continued to be trusted by and associated with Colombo's sons. That connection continued during the following decades. Also, Family leaders inducted Rossillo into the organization ending any speculation he was part of a plot.

The last plausible conspiracy theory is that Joey Gallo, the main Colombo antagonist, was the brain behind the shooting. The thinking was that Gallo had become friendly with some black convicts while he was in prison and had recruited one of their associates to kill Colombo.

Some have made several rational arguments as to why Gallo would use a black to carry out the hit. Others suggest that Gambino was supporting the Gallo plan to get rid of Colombo but have the blame fall on Gallo. But the bottom line is this: there is no credible evidence to link Johnson to Gallo. Without this, all conspiracy theories die on the vine, no matter how reasonable and logical they seem to be. The known facts support the hypothesis that Johnson was a nut acting alone like so many other assassins of famous people in the United States.

Joey Gallo was a problem, however. Some Colombo loyalists continued to believe he was behind their Boss' shooting and desired revenge. But they were now effectively powerless as control shifted to another faction of the Family. These new powerbrokers saw Gallo as a wildcard who was sure to continue causing problems for an administration that would be led by caretaker leaders for some time. For this reason, Consigliere Joe Yacovelli sought the Commission's approval for a hit on Gallo. The fact that they could "legitimize" the murder as revenge for the Colombo shooting allowed everyone involved to appear noble rather than self-serving. Gallo's elimination was approved, and it was only a matter of time before Gallo was taken out.

On April 7, 1972, Gallo's wild ride came to a crashing end on the street outside Umberto's Clam House in New York's Little Italy. Purely by chance, a Colombo Associate named Joseph Luparelli saw Gallo and others enter Umbertos on the corner of Hester and Mulberry. Luparelli rushed to the King Wah restaurant a few blocks away on Mulberry and told Carmine "Sony Pinto" DiBiase about what he had seen. The crew phoned Colombo Consigliere Joseph "Joe Yak" Yacovelli, who told them to go ahead and hit Gallo.

The hoods rounded up pistols, and then the five men headed for Umbertos. DiBiase, Frank, and Benny Locicero were in DiBiase's car while Luparelli and Philip Gambino followed in Luparelli's vehicle. DiBiase and his two passengers pulled up opposite Umbertos' side door on Mulberry and raced in.

Immediately upon entering, the three saw Gallo, who was sitting between his sister Carmella and bodyguard Peter Diapoulos. Also seated at the table but with their backs against the wall were Gallo's wife and stepdaughter, and Diapoulos' date Edith Russo. The three hoods opened up on Gallo, creating an uproar in the restaurant.

Everyone dove for cover as the bullets from three guns flew. Diapoulos took a shot to the hip and went down. Gallo was hit two times in the back and once in the left elbow as he fled out the front entrance. Crazy Joey fell in the middle of Hester Street and died. The three shooters ran to their car and exchange shots with Diapoulos as they sped away. Luparelli and Phillip Gambino watched it all unfold from Luparelli's auto parked at the intersection.

Eventually, both Luparelli and Diapoulos rolled over and described the events of that night. Their stories confirmed the spontaneity of the attack, as did the statements of Gallo's wife and sister. The shooting diagram produced by the NYPD, along with ballistic evidence, totally supported the accounts of four direct participants in the shooting.

Gallo's death was an event of very low significance in terms of the Colombo Family and La Cosa Nostra. Gallo had no power and even less financial resources. He depended on his motley crew to keep him in spending money by running minor gambling events, hijackings, and the like. There was no union local under his thumb that would provide high paying jobs and skimming opportunities. No one saw Gallo as a man who would be in power someday. Even if he had survived the shooting at Umbertos, Gallo would have continued being a fringe player.

Note:
See Appendix C for a detailed analysis of the Gallo hit.

CHAPTER TEN

Making Money

GAMBLING

Like most mob Families, gambling was the lifeblood of the Colombos. Wagering comes in many forms, such as numbers, card games, and sports betting. Various members and Associates of the Colombo Family engaged in all of these and more. The following brief look at sports betting should give the reader a sense of this form of Colombo Family income.

Michael Bolino, the son of a one-time Colombo Capo, was involved in a variety of scams, including sports betting. One method used by Bolino to gain business was to take on Associates who would push bets in some geographical regions or segments of society in which they had connections. For example, Colombo Associate Joseph Cantalupo hung out in a Chinese Restaurant and soon had many of its workers as gambling customers.

Cantalupo would keep a small percentage of the wagers for himself, then turn in the betting slips and the rest of the money to the bookmaker. There was always a great temptation for Cantalupo to gamble himself. That, of course, meant that inevitably, he would be a loser.

Others in similar positions would sometimes not turn in a betting slip and the money associated with it. They would be hoping that that particular bet would be a loser. That would mean the person who bet would not be expecting any money, and the bookmaker would not even know a wager existed. It was an exciting way for the Associate to "skim" money from the bookmaker. Of course, it was also an excellent way to end up dead in the trunk of his car if the bookmaker found out about the scam.

Most bookmakers also took sports bets over the phone. The betting money did not physically change hands. What kept the system running was the clear understanding that the bookmaker or his backer would come after a deadbeat gambler who didn't pay for his losses.

One of the weak points of sports gambling is that the operation has to have a base where the betting slips are received, the wagers balanced, and the money counted. This static location makes the process susceptible to police raids. The betting slips and the money are crucial evidence in any ensuing court case.

While the legal penalties for a first offense might be light, the disruption caused by the loss of the betting records, not to speak of the confiscated money, can be significant. When Joseph Cantalupo became an FBI informant, he would rent apartments to various Colombo bookmaking operations and then immediately tell the agents their locations.

For decades the Mafia and other gamblers avoided being severely damaged by police raids by paying off co-operative cops and local politicians. While this type of corruption was still present in 1973, in New York, it was in decline. The regular movement of the gambling headquarters and stringing phone lines to an apartment other than the one registered for the phone were other tactics employed the mobsters.

For a hood, participation in a sport's betting operation while lucrative is a lot of work and full of headaches. A Mafioso, being inherently lazy and unwilling to work, loved the money involved but not the effort. Consequently, many of them found a better idea. They would go to established bookmakers, threaten them, and demand a specific amount each week. Of course, the bookmaker would have to make the payoff whether he made or lost money. Besides, he couldn't run to the police for protection. It was the perfect situation for the Mafia.

It is impossible to accurately estimate how much money the Colombos were making from gambling of all types. The take must have been considerable, considering how many members were involved in the racket.

In the long run, regular gamblers will lose money, thereby draining their bankrolls. Standing by with cash is your friendly Mafia hood. His terms are steep, and they average about 150 percent a year. But a compulsive gambler is not thinking long-term, and he wants to be able to bet again - today - he'll worry about tomorrow, tomorrow.

LOANSHARKING

The loanshark loves having a lot of money on the street in the hands of regular customers who make their payments on time. The reality is that many of the fees have to be chased down, and the debtor threatened. A menacing hood whose mere looks sends pangs of fear coursing through a debtor is the ideal. A debtor who is so beat up he can't beg, borrow, or steal his required payments is useless. Unfortunately for the loanshark, many collectors have brains of concrete. These Neanderthals periodically hurt or scare the victim so severely that they run to the cops.

Joseph Cantalupo, the Colombo Associate, revealed a twist to the typical insolvent loanshark customer's problems when he related his difficulties with Alphonse Persico. In his book, *Body Mike* (1990), Cantalupo explains how he arranged a loan for another person through Persico. When the businessman didn't need the money, Cantalupo kept it rather than returning the cash. Cantalupo made regular payments on the loan but never told Persico that he, rather than the businessman, was the real borrower.

Eventually, Persico discovered Cantalupo's subterfuge and called him to a meeting. There, the hood viciously beat Cantalupo demanding the return of his money. Now the street people knew he was in Persico's bad books and thus no longer protected. Inevitably Cantalupo had to go into hiding in the Witness Protection Program.

CIGARETTE SMUGGLING

Another lucrative racket in the early seventies was the smuggling of cigarettes. The hoods would purchase cigarettes in North Carolina, which had much lower state taxes on smokes than did New York. They would move the cartons into New York and sell them at corner stores, truck stops, factories, and other locations for about a dollar cheaper than legal cigarettes.

The financial backer of the cigarette racket did not participate in the transportation or sale of illegal merchandise. In this manner, he avoided any chance of being caught. If the authorities arrested a participant, he rarely rolled over due to the lightness of the penalties.

DRUG DEALING

Another lucrative but dangerous Mafia racket was drug dealing. Theoretically, the Bosses forbade this activity. Nevertheless, Colombo members periodically took their chances with fate. Gambino Associate Joseph "Joe Dogs" Iannuzzi told of an incident in which he arranged to purchase 580 pounds of marijuana for Colombo Soldier Dom Cataldo. According to Iannuzzi, Cataldo made $45,000 for merely acting as a middleman in the dope deal. It is impossible to estimate how much money the Colombos gained from dealing with drugs, but for some, it was lucrative.

STOCK MARKET

While not a major income producer for the Family, stock market manipulation was part of the Colombo repertoire. On November 18, 1970, an indictment named Capo Vinny Aloi and several Mafia hoods and Associates based on information from conman Michael Hellerman.

Hellerman and another man, representing the hidden interests of Vinny Aloi and some major Lucchese Family hoods, bought approximately 150,000 shares in a Miami based financial company called Imperial Investments at prices not much above zero. In a series of moves, the shares were traded back and forth between the participants creating the illusion of high demand for them. The stock price was artificially inflated and sold to gullible investors. Then insiders unloaded their shares at around $24, reaping about a $2 million profit. Shortly after that, the stocks held by the public were worthless.

OTHER RACKETS

Besides stock manipulation, a wide gamut of illegal activities ranging from labor racketeering, extortion, burglaries, hijackings, stolen cars, credit card fraud, and on and on provided income for the mobsters. Basically, like most hoods, a Colombo Soldier would do almost anything if it meant he made some money with the least amount of work possible.

An FBI report from October of 1973 included these brief, real-life sketches of the activities of several Colombo Soldiers as related by an FBI informant.

Soldier 1

"A shylock (loanshark) and has a hidden interest in a travel agency."

Soldier 2

"...active as a backer of pornographic movies."

Soldier 3

"working in construction and is a union shop steward."

Soldier 4

"has nothing going for him."

Soldier 5
"in real estate enterprises plus shylocking (loansharking)"
Soldier 6
"Strictly a bandit."

Like any other mob Family, the Colombos' primary purpose in life was making money. Having stable leadership was essential to this goal. Unfortunately for the Soldiers, stability was an elusive property.

UNSTABLE LEADERSHIP

When Joe Colombo was gunned down in late June of 1971, turmoil resulted. First of all, there was the question of the extent of Colombo's injuries and whether he would be able to return to power.

The doctors who operated upon Colombo must have been reasonably sure that he would never again be able to function as a complete human being. One of the three slugs Jerome Johnson had fired into Colombo tore into his brain, causing irreparable damage. But the extent of Colombo's wounds was not immediately apparent to everyone outside his Family, thus creating a period of uncertainty.

While everyone waited for the Colombo situation to clarify itself, the Family required leadership, even if it was to be temporary. According to an FBI informant, a group of Colombo Capos held a meeting shortly after Colombo was shot and asked Underboss Charles Mineo to "assume interim leadership" of the Family. For the Colombo loyalists Mineo would have been the right choice for he had never openly exhibited the ambition to be Boss and thus would be unlikely to try to seize permanent power. Even for those Capos who coveted the top slot for themselves, Mineo was acceptable as Acting Boss for the same reasons. But Mineo wasn't having any part of these attempts. Mineo refused the offer citing his age and poor health. Left unspoken was the possibility that Mineo was too smart to step into the limelight and thus become a target for the FBI or an ambitious Capo.

The media centered on Joseph "Joe Yac" Yacovelli as the heir apparent to the incapacitated Colombo. For example, the New York Times of September 1, 1971, carried a front-page story that claimed Yacovelli was running things in Colombo's absence. The story, written by Nicholas Gage, also mentioned that Yacovelli might have been acting on behalf of Capo Carmine Persico, who was appealing a hijacking conviction.

Gage's story was very accurate. The Carmine Persico faction was the most powerful in the Family. If Persico didn't have legal problems, he would have been the natural choice to replace Colombo. But the chances of Persico winning his appeal were slight. At the same time, everyone had to take into account the wishes of the powerful Carlo Gambino. The compromise was placing compliant Capo Vincent Aloi in the Acting Boss position, backed up by Persico loyalist Consigliere Joseph Yacovelli.

This latest Colombo Family administration setup made Aloi and Yacovelli prime targets of law enforcement. Aloi had been indicted for a stock fraud back in November of 1970. Another indictment, on November 13, 1972, charged that Aloi and Carmine Persico had participated in a conspiracy to help a Colombo Associate avoid murder charges from the killing of two people at a New Year's Eve party in 1970. Finally, a January 1973 indictment meant that Aloi was facing perjury charges for denying that he attended Colombo Family meetings at a Nyack apartment back in 1972.

Yacovelli soon was facing his legal roadblocks. In August of 1971, the feds hauled the Consigliere before a Brooklyn Federal Grand Jury after he tried desperately to avoid a subpoena. In November of 1972, the Aloi indictment included Yacovelli charging him with conspiracy to obstruct justice. A month later, legal papers named Yacovelli as one of the conspirators in the Joey Gallo murder.

All these legal charges signaled the end of Aloi and Yacovelli as Colombo leaders. In late December of 1972, aging Capo Tom DiBella became the new choice of Carmine Persico to head the organization. On April 9, 1973, informer Greg Scarpa confirmed DiBella's selection. Anthony Abbatemarco, a veteran of the Gallo wars, became the Underboss with Alphonse Persico as Consigliere. Everyone understood that Carmine Persico was the real power despite the Bureau of Prisons sending him to Atlanta Penitentiary in January of 1972.

The New York office of the FBI sent a report to its Washington headquarters on October 10, 1973, that outlined the structure of the Colombo Family, as it was then known. According to several informers and intelligence gathering, the FBI felt that DiBella, Underboss Abbatemarco, and Consigliere Alphonse Persico led a Family that was broken down into six crews. Dominick "Mimi" Scialo and Joseph Brancato were new Capos while Aniello Giannattasio was bumped up to Acting Capo.

MORE PROBLEMS

The wounding of Joe Colombo and the killing of Joseph Gallo a year later ended two of the major problems facing the Colombo Family as it entered the 1970s. Colombo could not have continued his civil rights charade indefinitely, and it was just a matter of time before someone killed Gallo after his release from prison. It was just a question of how Colombo would fall and who would murder Gallo. By 1973 both those questions had been answered.

As for the Italian-American Civil Rights League, its future appeared shaky in the immediate aftermath of the Colombo shooting. Former Underboss Sal Mussachio, Carlo Gambino, leader of the Gambino Family and informer Greg Scarpa, all told the FBI they had no interest in the league before or after the Colombo shooting.

By November of 1971, FBI informants were commenting that league activities had fallen off, and it looked like the entity was going to die a slow death. A few months later, the FBI heard that a scam was unfolding that involved the league. An insider at the Kings County Lafayette Trust had convinced league officers to move the league's accounts to that business. In turn, the banker would arrange phony loans for various Colombo hoods.

Eventually, on February 17, 1972, the FBI arrested eight individuals connected to the Colombos and charged them with fraudulent bank loan applications. Among those charged were: Rocco Miraglia, a close Associate of Colombo; Salvatore Profaci, son of the former Boss; and Philip Rossillo, the alleged shooter of Jerome Johnson. Three months later, a Federal Grand Jury indicted the Italian-American Civil Rights League and two of its officers, Natale Marcone and Caesar Vitale, with fraud in their loan applications from the same trust company. The indictment also revealed that the league was at least $100,000 in debt.

During this same period, Anthony Colombo made headlines with his statement that there was a possibility that Joseph Colombo might be able to attend the 1972 Columbus Day rally. In a further attempt to bolster the sagging league fortunes, Anthony claimed that league membership had grown to nearly 100,000. While the backers of the league had another successful rally at Madison Square Gardens, the Italian-American Civil Rights League was fading into obscurity as 1973 ended.

THE DISPERSING GALLOS

The murder of Joey Gallo signaled the beginning of the end for the infamous crew named after the three Gallo brothers. While all the events did not happen by 1973, this is the appropriate place to discuss their fate.

For a short period, Albert Gallo tried to hold his crew together under the Colombo umbrella. Still, with his archenemy, Carmine Persico, in charge, it was only a matter of time before someone killed the youngest Gallo. With that thought in mind, Albert called upon his friendship with Capo Vincent

"Chin" Gigante of the Genovese Family and transferred there. Also moving with Gallo was veteran mobster Frank "Punchy" Illiano.

Peter Diapoulos, Joey Gallo's bodyguard, became disenchanted with the criminal milieu, turned his life around, and reportedly has been a productive citizen ever since. Along the way, he co-authored his life story, *The Sixth Family* (1976), which was very successful.

For a long time Gallo hood, Gaetano Basciano, the future was not as bright. He bounced in and out of the Gallo crew after Joey Gallo's murder but finally fell totally out of favor. After an unsuccessful attempt on his life, someone eventually killed Basciano on June 16, 1976.

Note:
Gallo Associate Frank DiMatteo wrote that street talk indicated that the Gallos gave Bobby Boriello and Preston Geritano the hit order on Basciano. Both were Gallo Associates at the time.

On October 5, 1977, John "Mooney" Cutrone was gunned down in Danny's Luncheonette in Brooklyn. Along with Larry and Joey Gallo, Cutrone was the only other Gallo crew member who inducted into La Cosa Nostra. In an odd twist, the two different vehicles involved in the Cutrone and Basciano hits were both registered to the same fictitious name.

Note:
Gallo Associate Frank DiMatteo wrote that his father, Ricky DiMatteo and Tony Bernardo committed the killing. Both were Gallo Associates.

The Commission approved the murders of Cutrone and Basciano, who had continued their internal feud with members of the Gallo crew after being ordered not to.

Bobby Boriello moved into the Gambino camp and eventually became a close confidant of both John Gotti and his son. Over the years, he was heavily involved in loansharking and other rackets as his stature improved. On April 13, 1991, a Lucchese Family crew, on orders from Underboss Anthony "Gaspipe" Casso, killed Boriello. Casso believed Boriello was part of a murder attempt against him.

Roy DeMeo went on to infamy for his part in a murderous group of car thieves whose exploits were immortalized in the book *Murder Machine* (1992) by Jerry Capeci and Gene Mustain. In 1983, Gambino Boss Paul Castellano, worried that DeMeo might talk after being indicted, ordered his murder.

Anthony "Tony" Bernardo did significant prison time. The authorities jailed him on March 30, 1976, and the Bureau of Prisons finally released

Bernardo on March 22, 1983. Bernardo had been a partner of Peter "Pete the Greek" Diapoulos in several schemes before the murder of Joey Gallo. When the court sent Diapoulos to prison on a weapons charge related to the Gallo shooting, Bernardo was supposed to give Diapoulos' cut of various rackets to his wife. According to Diapoulos, Bernardo gambled the money away, which added to Diapoulos' growing disgust with his criminal life. Bernardo died of natural causes years later.

An examination of the Gallo crew reveals them to be ideal subjects for writer Jimmy Breslin's *The Gang That Couldn't Shoot Straight* and the movie of the same name. Carlo Gambino and his allies used the Gallos in a successful attempt to create unrest in the Profaci regime. Much to their disappointment, the Gallos didn't benefit from their activities. Gambino quickly deserted them for Joe Colombo, whom he thought would be easier to control.

With the death of Larry Gallo in 1968, the crew no longer even had one made man in their group for John "Mooney" Cutrone had broken off on his own, and Nicky Bianco hooked up with the Colombos. As mere Associates, without any strong backing, the Gallos existed on the fringes of the mob, scraping out a living. Joey Gallo tried to change their fortunes in 1971, but things only got worse, and inevitably, Gallo wound up dead.

In reality, the Gallos were only important in the early 1960s when they were used by Carlo Gambino to achieve his ends. Media attention made them seem larger than life when, in fact, they were minor Mafia figures who had no real power. On the other hand, Carmine Persico and his crew were the real thing, and as 1973 drew to a close, the Persico era was about to begin.

CHAPTER ELEVEN

The Other Families

THE BONANNOS

Joseph Bonanno had led the Family that bears his name from 1931 till 1964. At that point, the Commission deposed Bonanno for refusing to appear before them to answer charges that he had plotted to murder rival Bosses Carlo Gambino and Thomas Lucchese.

For approximately four years, Bonanno and a few loyalists tried to retain control of the Family but finally gave up the losing battle. Bonanno retired permanently to Arizona and never again was a factor in La Cosa Nostra's affairs.

Gaspar DiGregorio briefly held power from 1964 till 1966 when he resigned due to ill health and declining confidence in his leadership abilities. Capo Paul Sciacca took over and spearheaded the fight against Bonanno loyalists. However, by 1970, Sciacca was fighting both health and legal problems, and the apparent end of his reign caused others to try to position themselves as next in line for the throne.

On September 18, 1969, Underboss Frank Mari and Consigliere Mike Adamo disappeared. Sciacca and his loyalists did not like the rising ambitions of the two hoods.

When Paul Sciacca stepped down in 1970, veteran Capo Natale Evola was elected to replace him. Evola had been a close friend of Joseph Bonanno and had even served in his wedding party back in the early 1930s. Regular Mafia rackets occupied Evola's time, but he also became involved in narcotics.

Before Evola could unify the Family, he died of natural causes in late August of 1973. A gathering of Family Capos, in November of the same year, elected Philip Rastelli Boss. Unfortunately for Rastelli, his rise roughly coincided with the release from prison of veteran Bonanno mobster Carmine Galante.

Galante was a man Carmine Persico could understand. Both had grown up on the streets and made their bones as young men. No one had handed them everything on a silver platter. Surrounded by a core of loyalists, the two had used intelligence, cunning, and ferociousness to rise to the top of their respective Families.

Back on July 10, 1962, Galante had received his most serious prison term when a judge sentenced the mobster to thirty years for a massive heroin conspiracy. An appeals court reduced his sentence to twenty years, of which Galante did twelve. The prison authorities released Galante from Atlanta penitentiary on January 24, 1974, just in time to see Boss Phil Rastelli become bogged down with his legal problems.

On July 10, 1975, Rastelli began a prison term for loansharking. He would remain behind bars till June 15, 1977. Galante almost immediately began acting as if he was Boss. Galante's reputation for violence, his long service, his street experience, and the length of his stay in prison without turning on anyone, were crucial factors in many members accepting his role. The earlier murder of James Fernandez, Rastelli's stepson, on March 7, 1974, has long been cited as another factor that caused Rastelli to keep quiet. By mid-1975, Galante was Boss as far as the FBI, and many mobsters were concerned.

Under Galante, the Bonanno Family slowly became less involved with the majority of Commission business. There were three main reasons for this development: Galante had seen his Boss, Joe Bonanno, deposed by a Gambino led Commission. He did not want a repeat of that mess. Second, Galante's primary connections were in the heroin business, and he quickly returned to this lucrative racket, which did not require any interfacing with the other Families. Finally, the Commission members, fearing Galante and being greedy, did not include the Bonanno Family in their major construction industry shakedowns. The net result was that the Bonanno Family had few ties to the four other New York Families.

Despite his growing bankroll due to the heroin trade, Galante was not in a position to solidify his control over his Family. On October 11, 1977, Galante was arrested on a parole violation and was in prison till March 1, 1979.

During this period, the dissidents within the Bonanno Family had plenty of time to plot his demise.

At some point before July 1979, the New York members of the Commission met and voted to sanction the killing of Galante. According to testimony by Fred DeChristopher, a relative, Persico claimed to have voted against the murder. On July 12, 1979, three men charged into Joe and Mary's restaurant in Brooklyn and blew Galante away along with two other men. One of the shooters then immediately drove to the Ravenite Social Club in Brooklyn, where he and higher-ranking Bonannos met with Gambino Underboss Aniello Dellacroce. Years later, a jury accepted that this action was proof that the Commission had sanctioned Galante's murder. The killer was reporting success to the Commission representative.

Philip Rastelli once again became the accepted Boss but was handicapped by his endless prison sentences. Consequently, his Capos began to grow independent. A group was soon conspiring to replace Rastelli. Those Capos loyal to their Boss sought and finally received permission from the Commission to murder the leading dissidents. On May 5, 1981, three rebel Capos were lured to a Brooklyn social club and gunned down in a violent ambush, thus putting an end to any thoughts of a revolt.

The killings did not end, however. For example, Dominick "Sonny Black" Napolitano, a leading Rastelli loyalist, was killed because he had unknowingly permitted an FBI agent to infiltrate the Family. From the carnage, Capo Joey Massino emerged as the new Acting Boss and then Boss when Rastelli finally died on June 24, 1991.

Although he was in prison from 1987 till November of 1992, Massino was able to control the Family through Acting Bosses, such as his brother-in-law Salvatore Vitale. However, Massino was not a big supporter of Carmine Persico, and this fact would play a role in Persico's battles to retain his throne.

THE GAMBINOS

In the early to mid-1950s, the Gambino Family's leadership was unsettled. Boss Vincent Mangano disappeared in 1951, and then new Boss Albert Anastasia was gunned down in 1957. Finally, stability came when Carlo Gambino took over the throne.

To gain nationwide approval from the 26 some Mafia Bosses, Gambino attended the ill-fated 1957 Apalachin National Meeting. Much to his regret, NY State Troopers detained and identified the new Boss. This notoriety brought the Immigration people down on Gambino's head.

Gambino's troubles with the INS were extensive; I will use a point-form summary below. The reader may choose to skip the long list. It shows Gambino's use of his poor health to avoid INS hearings.

November 25/57
The INS issued an arrest warrant for Gambino. They claim he illegally entered the US at Norfolk, Virginia, on December 23, 1928.

December 3/57
Doctors admitted Gambino into a hospital.

December 9/57
Gambino had heart surgery.

January 10/58
The hospital released Gambino.

August 6/58
Gambino and his lawyers traveled to an INS office. There they accepted a deportation warrant. The INS authorities released Gambino on a $10,000 bond. September 3, 1958, was set for a hearing.

September 3/58
Authorities postponed the meeting to September 28.

September 28/58
A doctor certified that Gambino was too ill to appear before the INS. They set October 2, 1958, as the new date.

September 29/58
Doctors admitted Gambino to a hospital.

October 2/58
The INS postponed Gambino's scheduled appearance.

November 3/58
At an INS hearing, Gambino complained of heart problems. Authorities had him rushed to a hospital. They postponed the discussion until November 19, 1958.

January 19, 1960
Gambino had heart surgery.

Florida
Gambino spent most winters in various locations in Florida.

March 1962
An illegal bug in the Gambino's Florida apartment (Golden Gate Motel) caught a series of interesting comments. An FBI summary of the tapes revealed that Gambino, bet on horses, regularly insulted his wife, and cursed. They added that Mrs. Gambino made racist comments.

November 5/62
The INS postponed Gambino's appearance. (Probably due to his health issues.) The new date set was November 13, 1962.

November 13/62
Gambino's lawyer told the INS that he was too sick to appear. The new date set was Nov 19/62.

November 23/62
A neutral doctor ruled that Gambino was well enough to appear before the INS.

January 14/63
The INS postponed Gambino's appearance. The new date set was January 17, 1963.

January 17/63
The INS postponed Gambino's appearance. The new date set was February 26. 1963.

February 27/63
Gambino's son-in-law, Dr. Thomas Sinatra, phoned the INS revealing that Gambino was too ill to attend the hearing. The new date was March 4, 1963.

March 4, 1963
At the INS hearing, Gambino requested a doctor. They rushed him to a hospital where they admitted him.

July 26, 1963
The INS decided to postpone Gambino's deportation due to ill health.

September 3/63
A hospital admitted Gambino. While there, he had a heart attack.

October 25/63
The hospital released Gambino.

March 2/64
A doctor at US Public Health concluded that it would be too dangerous to submit Gambino to an INS hearing.

March 29/65
An INS doctor examined Gambino in a hospital.

April 2/65
The hospital discharged Gambino.

Meanwhile, a notorious bank robber, John "Red" Kelly had told the FBI that Carlo Gambino was involved in a conspiracy to rob an armored car. The claim was total nonsense, but Kelly was trying to escape severe charges of his own. The justice system pounced all over Gambino leading to great aggravation for the mob Boss, lawyer costs, and precious time.

Based on the Kelly allegations, the District Attorney obtained several search warrants for various Gambino locations. At one, the good guys opened a safe, which contained a stolen jewelry piece. They charged Gambino with possession of this article on March 23, 1970.

In February of 1967, an informant told the FBI of a Gambino leadership meeting hosted by Capo Paul Castellano. Big Paul announced that he was now the Acting Boss for Gambino was too ill to carry on day to day duties. Other appointments revealed by Castellano were the earlier promotions of Joe N. Gallo to Acting Consigliere, and Aniello Dellacroce to Underboss.

In hindsight, this informant news clarified the participation of Gallo and Dellacroce at the infamous September 22, 1966, La Stella meeting discussed earlier. Gambino was too ill to attend, so new Underboss Aniello Dellacroce and Acting Consigliere Joe N. Gallo represented the Gambino Family. A grand jury later indicted the two men on matters centered on the La Stella event. They were now firmly in the headlights of the feds.

Then a Grand Jury indicted Gambino on the armored car conspiracy, and the authorities arrested him on May 23, 1970. Fortunately for the mob Boss, a judge severed him from the trial of the alleged robbers due to his poor health.

Note:
After Gambino died, the government dismissed the armored car charges against him. They were a joke.

During this same period, more negative publicity came down on Gambino's head. The FBI named him a Boss of the Cosa Nostra Family. News outlets such as the New York Post and Newsday carried articles repeating the claims. Gambino probably was furious with the stories.

Not to be forgotten, the INS revealed its power once again. On January 7, 1970, an Appeals Court upheld the legality of Gambino's deportation. Then the Supreme Court backed this ruling in June. Gambino was in serious trouble.

On November 2, 1971, the INS served Gambino notice that they would deport him on November 5. The very next day, doctors reported that Gambino had another heart attack. Nevertheless, a Federal Judge ruled that the INS could move him out of the country on November 5 as scheduled. But on that date, two doctors from US Public Health ruled that Gambino was too ill to move. At that point, the INS relented once more. It has been a close call for the aging and sick mob Boss.

KIDNAPPING

If the fear of deportation didn't create enough stress, a group of mutts sent Gambino's blood pressure soaring. They kidnapped Gambino's nephew, Manny, on March 18, 1972. Surprisingly Carlo allowed the FBI to become involved. The Gambinos paid a $40,000 ransom, but Manny was not released.

Eventually, the authorities interviewed suspect Harold Sentner and convinced him to roll over on the other three kidnap conspirators. With his information, the police found Manny's body in a shallow grave on June 26, 1973. Senter and John Kilcullen received fifteen-year sentences for this crime. A judge handed out lesser terms to the two other participants. It is important to note that James McBratney played no role in the Manny Gambino affair despite countless stories that he was. John Gotti was involved in the death of McBratney, which later made McBratney famous.

During this ordeal, Gambino suffered further heart problems. The doctors admitted him to the hospital on September 30, 1972, and kept the aged Boss until October 22. The next spring, the INS was after him yet again. From April 1973 till June 5, 1974, the INS required Gambino to report to their office every second week. This order must have been extremely frustrating for Carlo.

The beginning of Gambino's long physical decline began on May 31, 1975. He was in and out of the hospital numerous times. Finally, on October 15, 1976, the veteran mobster passed away.

Aniello Dellacroce, Gambino's Underboss, did not attend the funeral. On June 2, 1972, he began a one year sentence for criminal contempt before a Grand Jury. Upon his release, Dellacroce faced tax evasion charges involving his alleged ownership of some stock. The jury found him guilty early in January of 1973, and the judge sentenced Dellacroce to five years and a fifteen thousand dollar fine on March 12, 1973. The prison authorities still had the veteran mobster as a guest by the time a priest conducted Gambino requiem mass.

Once the prison gates opened for Dellacroce, he blessed Paul Castellano's rise from Acting Boss to Boss. In response, Castellano asked Aniello to continue as his Underboss. The new administration was complete with Joe N. Gallo remaining the Consigliere. To outsiders, the Gambino Family looked strong and unified in 1976. They did not appear to pose any problems to Carmine Profaci's plans for his Colombo Family.

THE GENOVESE

On May 5, 1957, a Vito Genovese flunky attempted to kill Boss Frank Costello. Vincent Gigante only managed to wound Costello, but that was enough to convince the aging leader to resign. The other Capos accepted Genovese as their new Boss, and it seemed like the future would be rosy. Oops!

The first thing that went south for Genovese was when New York State Troopers identified him as being present at the Mafia gathering near Apalachin in 1957. Then there were a host of hearings and investigations that gave Vito little peace. But that was not the worst of his problems.

On July 8, 1958, the authorities arrested Genovese (and others) on a heroin conspiracy. In April of the following year, a jury convicted Vito, and a few weeks later, a judge sentenced him to 15 years and a $20,000 fine. His appeals failed, and the Bureau of Prisons send Genovese off to Atlanta Penitentiary to do his time. Despite these severe setbacks, the Genovese Family continued to recognize Vito as their Boss. The courts would allow further appeals, and not many wanted to act as if Vito was never coming home.

Veteran Genovese aide, Anthony "Tony Bender" Strollo was not too careful. Someone passed the word to Genovese that Bender had been dealing in heroin and was continuing to do so. Also, he was meeting with the Gallo crew as they planned an uprising against Joe Profaci. On April 8, 1962, Bender left his home for a meeting, and no one ever saw him again. The message was unmistakable; Vito was still in charge.

Veteran mobster Gerardo "Jerry" Catena became the Acting Boss. Genovese appointed hot-headed Tommy Eboli as Underboss. Genovese completed the administration by placing aging Mike Miranda in the Consigliere seat. Some illegal FBI bugs revealed that there was not always harmony in the front office, but this trio managed to hold things together for a few years.

On April 8, 1965, the FBI taped Underboss Tommy Eboli mentioning that Catena wanted to step down as Acting Boss. As a replacement, Eboli suggested veteran Capo Phil Lombardo. According to Eboli, Lombardo wished to be very cautious. For him, a consultation with Catena was in order. Lombardo knew full well what had happened to the ambitious Tony Bender.

It wasn't until March 28, 1967, that an informant confirmed Philip Lombardo's official status as Acting Boss. From his jail cell, an ailing Genovese anointed Lombardo as the Family's new leader. When Genovese died on February 14, 1969, Lombardo became the official Boss.

Lombardo liked the confusion created when law enforcement was not sure who the real leader of the Family was. Accordingly, Lombardo ordered his Underboss, Tommy Eboli, to continue acting as the Boss while he remained in the shadows. For simplicity, I'll use the term "Front Boss" for this position.

Like any Mafia Boss Lombardo had to watch his back continually. There were always ambitious underlings waiting in the wings, hoping to move up the ladder. Underboss/Front Boss Tommy Eboli may have had these thoughts. Whatever the reason, some hoods filled Eboli full of slugs as he exited the residence of a mistress on July 16, 1972. His replacement, Eli Zeccardi, also didn't fare very well. Zeccardi disappeared in 1974, a mere two years after being promoted. Lombardo was not fooling around.

Next up as Front Boss was veteran Capo Frank "Funzi" Tieri. He was a strange choice in that he was in poor health and had little energy. Perhaps Lombardo picked Tieri for these very reasons and his lack of ambition. By January of 1975, an informant was telling the FBI that Tieri had stepped down, but the situation remained unclear.

Tieri continued as the face of the Genovese Family until the late 1970s. At that point, he was too ill to continue. Lombardo appointed Anthony "Fat Tony" Salerno as the replacement. Unfortunately for the very sick Tieri, although out of power, the feds did not know this. They made him the focal point of a RICO case.

In the summer of 1980, the FBI arrested Tieri on RICO charges. On November 21, a jury convicted the sick, older man much to the delight of the authorities who proclaimed he was the first sitting Boss found guilty under RICO. A judge sentenced Tieri to ten years, but he would never serve a day for on March 29, 1981, Frank Tieri went to meet his maker. A judge vacated Tieri's conviction since his appeals never took place.

For a short period Anthony "Fat Tony" Salerno was moved up to Underboss and Front Boss. But, in 1981, Salerno suffered a stroke and was hospitalized. At the same time, Boss Phil Lombardo was lying in a hospital bed in feeble health. At that point, Vincent Gigante, Sammy Santora, and Bobby Manna visited the two men and announced that they were the new administration of the Family. Salerno and Lombardo were now mere Soldiers.

After a period recuperating at his farm, Salerno received permission from the new Boss Gigante to return to New York. Gigante also decided to let Salerno continue as the Front Boss in the hopes of shielding himself from the law. One result of this decision was that Salerno ended up in the Commission trial labeled as Boss of the Genovese Family. His sentence of 100 years must have been galling to Salerno as Gigante had dodged that bullet.

THE LUCCHESES

Thomas "Tommy Brown" Lucchese became that Family's Boss with the 1951 death of Tommy Gagliano. Lucchese was very well connected politically, and this fact caused him a lot of grief. In 1952 the new mob Boss made numerous appearances before the New York State Crime Commission, where the members questioned him on his many connections. Lucchese admitted knowing many mayors, judges, and political heavyweights. He also acknowledged being friends with several notorious gangsters, including Boss Jack Dragna of Los Angeles and Frank Costello. As far as Lucchese was concerned, all these contacts were innocent.

As with many other major suspected hoods, the INS launched a lengthy attempt to have Lucchese deported in the 1950s. By the end of the decade, the US Supreme Court ruled that Lucchese could safely remain in America.

For some reason, Lucchese never went to the infamous Apalachin National Convention of LCN on November 14, 1957. The New York State Troopers may have missed him as they identified the many hoods in attendance. However, there doesn't seem to be any evidence of his presence there.

In the early 1960s, Lucchese was involved in an attempt to replace Colombo Boss Joe Profaci with someone who would be allied with himself and Carlo Gambino. Eventually, Capo Joe Colombo took the throne of his Family and presented a solid block on the Commission.

Unfortunately for Lucchese, he would not see Colombo rise to the heights of fame. The mid-1960s saw the feds inundate Lucchese with subpoenas to appear before various hearings. As usual, he said little. Sickness overcame the Boss during testimony on July 22, 1965. He began a long, slow slide to death due to cancer. On July 13, 1967, Lucchese breathed his last.

Note:
There have been two versions of the spelling of Tommy Lucchese's name, Lucchese and Luchese. However, on his tax forms, the Boss spelled it Luckese, the same text that appears on his gravestone.

Carmine "Mr. Gribbs" Tramunti became the next Lucchese Family leader. Favorite Anthony "Tony Ducks" Corallo was jammed up with legal problems involving the bribing of a New York City official, which put the veteran Capo out of the running.

Tramunti spent the seventies appearing before various grand juries and other investigations. The authorities charged him with contempt several times, but his most pressing problem was a drug conviction on March 13, 1974. He received a fifteen-year sentence and died behind bars on October 15, 1978. A series of Acting Bosses stood in for the incarcerated Tramunti.

After Tramunti's death, the Lucchese Capos elected Anthony "Tony Ducks" Corallo as their new Boss. It was a time of great success as the Family had their hands in very lucrative garbage, construction, and concrete rackets. Unfortunately for Corallo, the feds were finally getting organized for a severe onslaught against LCN. Corallo didn't know it, but his time was nearly up.

CHAPTER TWELVE

The Past Haunts Junior

Carmine "Junior" Persico seemed to find trouble throughout his entire life. On February 25, 1951, Persico was with a group of youths when longshoreman Steve Bove was gunned down. Police pursued Persico and arrested him for murder. Fortunately for him, his older brother, Alphonse, turned himself into police. Alphonse began serving a twenty-year sentence on September 20, 1951. Unsubstantiated rumors claimed that Alphonse was taking the rap for his younger brother.

Eight years later, police accused Carmine and some of his buddies of hijacking an Akers Motor Lines truck full of linen. Also charged were: Hugh McIntosh, Sal Albanese, Joe Magnasco, and George La Fonte. Little did they know that this mundane July 28, 1959 hijacking would start a legal battle that lasted more than a decade. A point form recital of the various stages of this epic follows. Keep in mind that all kinds of other actions took place during these dates due to Persico being free on bond most of the time.

May 13, 1961
Carmine Persico et al. won a mistrial.

June 9, 1961
The court convicted Carmine Persico et al. of a violation of the theft from interstate shipment statute. The judge released them on bond while awaiting sentence.

October 4, 1961
A gunman killed hijack defendant Joe Magnasco. The murder had nothing to do with the hijack case.

Fall 1961
A judge sentenced Persico to fifteen years but released him on bond. A crew of Gallo men verbally assaulted Persico as he left the courthouse. (Albanese, McIntosh, and Spero received ten years. George La Fonte got three years.)

July 1962
An Appeals Court reversed Persico convictions and those of his Associates.

May 20, 1963
A judge declared another mistrial in the Persico case.

June 19, 1964
A jury finally convicted Persico and his Associates. A judge sentenced Carmine to 14 years and nine months. The judge released him on a $35,000 bond. (Spero--ten years, McIntosh nine years and nine months, Albanese-six years, La Fante--two years six months.)

July 29, 1965
An Appeals Court overturned the convictions of Persico and his Associates.

April 23, 1968
Famous turncoat Joe Valachi testified in the fifth Persico hijacking trial.

May 9, 1968
A jury convicted Persico and his Associates.

June 6, 1969
A judge sentenced Persico to 14 years but also released him on a $15,000 bond.

April 16, 1970
An Appeal Court upheld Persico's hijack conviction.

January 13, 1972
An Appeal Court refused to grant Persico a new trial.

January 27, 1972
Persico began his hijacking sentence.

PERSICO VS. THE GALLOS

As mentioned earlier, the Gallo crew, along with other young Profaci members and Associates, were not happy with their lack of success under Profaci. Egged on by Carlo Gambino and Tommy Lucchese, these dissidents began to act independently. The kidnapping of several Profaci big wigs was the highlight of this era's revolt.

According to the later testimony of Joseph Valachi, Carmine Persico and his crew were initially lined up with the Gallos. However, Profaci lured them back into his fold by offering increased riches. From that point on, the Persico crew led the attack on the Gallos.

August of 1961 would see a lot of Persico aggression. On August 16, feared Gallo enforcer Joseph "Joe Jelly" Gioelli disappeared. Street talk indicated the Persicos had lured him onto a boat and finished him off.

A few days later, Larry Gallo stupidly accepted an invitation to conduct peace talks with the Persicos. At this point, Larry was not aware that Gioelli was sleeping with the fishes. He should have been more careful.

Larry went to the closed Sahara Lounge for what he believed would be friendly talks. Suddenly a garrote was around his neck, squeezing the life out of him. By pure chance, an NYPD Sergeant entered the bar, wondering why there was activity inside. Three hoods burst through the door, with one of them shooting a second police officer in the face once they reached the street. The entrance of the Sergeant had saved Larry's life.

One of the cops identified Carmine Persico and Sally D'Ambrosio as two of the hoods in the bar. Surprisingly Larry Gallo signed a statement that acknowledged that the police had told him the names of the two attackers.

It appears that Gallo was sending a message to his rivals that he knew full well who they were.

Four days later, Persico was on the move once again. On August 24, 1961, he and Dom Montemarano did a drive-by shooting in Gallo territory. They only managed to wound Larry "Big Lollipop" Carna in the foot before racing off.

A Grand Jury indicted Carmine Persico and John Scimone for the attack on Larry Gallo. But, on October 5, 1961, a judge released the two hoods on bonds. The mayhem would continue.

1962 was a year of turmoil and intrigue as Profaci's physical deterioration increased. The old mobster finally passed away on June 6, 1962.

MAGLIOCCO VS. THE GALLOS

Endless meetings ensued as Underboss Joseph Magliocco tried to round up support for his elevation to Boss. One of his initial decisions was to assess each member $100 a month to fund the war against the Gallos.

According to Peter "Pete the Greek" Diapoulos, a Gallo loyalist, Larry Gallo carried out a bombing attack on Carmine Persico in January of 1963. He hired a young man to rig and place the bomb under Persico's Cadillac. When Carmine sat down, he pushed the starter button, and the Caddy jumped off the ground. The doors swung open, glass burst, and the explosion sent metal pieces flying. Diapoulos commented, "But Junior, the sonofabitch, wasn't dead. The explosion had gone down not up, and Junior had only gotten a concussion."

Persico did not fare so well in court the following month. A judge sentenced him to a year in jail for an assault on a Gallo Associate. Carmine and Jiggs Forlano had accosted Sidney Slater in the Copacabana Nightclub in an attempt to discover the location of Joey Gallo. The two hoods believed the authorities had released Gallo from prison. That was true, but he was back in the slammer at the time of the assault on Slater. As usual, the judge released Persico on bond.

On May 19, 1963, the Gallos made another attempt on Carmine. Shooters hid in a panel truck outside Persico's girlfriend's home. When Persico climbed behind the wheel of his vehicle, the panel truck's back doors opened, and a hail of gunfire hit Persico. One round struck his mouth, another a shoulder, and the third smashed into his hand. But, once again, although very seriously wounded, Persico survived.

As outlined in a previous list, the courts occupied much of Carmine's time during this period. But there was some good news. Alphonse "Allie Boy" Persico, Carmine's brother, won an appeal of his murder conviction from back in the early 1950s. The net result was that a judge resentenced Allie Boy, and the prison authorities released the elder Persico on November 14, 1967.

The release of Alphonse was timely in that Carmine was off to prison on January 27, 1972. The elder Persico made numerous trips to Atlanta Prison to confer with his brother. They weren't planning a Christmas gathering.

With the incapacitation of Joe Colombo and the killing of Joey Gallo in 1972, the Persico faction was firmly in charge of the Colombo Family. But the de facto Boss, Carmine, was behind bars, and he needed leadership on the street.

Persico first appointed aging Capo Tom DiBella as his stand-in. To this day, it is not clear whether DiBella was the formal Boss or just Acting Boss from 1974 until 1980. This detail would become important many years later. For a short period, Capo John Brancato replaced DiBella while the latter did a brief stint in prison.

CHAPTER THIRTEEN

The Scopo Era

What follows is a summary of the high rise construction process in Manhattan. A general understanding of this type of contract is needed later when I outline a major Colombo Family racket.

After much study, a wealthy developer decides that if he built a 20 story building on a particular Manhattan lot, his company could make a fortune renting out space. An architecture firm draws up plans for the structure then the city has to approve a host of permits for the enterprise. At this point, the developer puts the building construction up for bids.

A prospective general contractor will look at the different phases of the construction and query sub-contractors on how much they would charge for completing their part of the structure. For example, he might contact four excavation companies for a price for digging the foundation and hauling away the dirt. Usually, the developer will pick the lowest bid on each segment of the development.

Once the general contractor has firm bids from each subcontractor, he will submit an overall proposal to the developer. At the same time, other general contractors are going through the same process in the hopes of winning the contract to construct the building.

The very rough outline of the construction business I've provided above looks like a straight forward process on the surface. It's not. Even without the interference of the Mafia, development has a million complications, which we won't discuss here. Throw in the greedy hoods, and the potential for financial ruin hangs over the head of every prominent Manhattan developer.

Imagine for a moment that you are a general contractor and have won the bid to construct a $50,000,000 office tower. Without a doubt, the developer will have set a completion date. If you don't meet that benchmark, severe financial penalties come into play. Any delay will be devastating. The mobsters are well aware of this weakness.

The Colombo Family ran Local 6A of the Cement and Concrete Workers Union as well as the larger District Council. This control meant that even if concrete arrived on a job site, the workers would not pour the material unless Local 6A officials had received a kickback. Such a delay would hold up the entire construction process costing tens of thousands of dollars for each short stoppage of work. Knowing this potential disaster, both the general contractor and the subcontractor would have made arrangements to pay the bribes.

The subcontractor would build the cost of his bribes into his bid. The general contractor would do the same. The developer would fully understand that these criminal operations were the price of doing business. Thus he would raise the dollar amount for rental space passing the bribe costs on to his new tenants.

The criminal operations in constructing a Manhattan building was far more complicated than my simple example demonstrates. A subcontractor doing the drywall would have made payments to a union so he could use non-union labor, which would be much cheaper. The same scams took place with the painters, electricians, window installers, and on and on. It was a boondoggle.

At first, these rackets were happening sporadically with wild fluctuations in the price of bribes and who would win specific contracts. The leaders of four of the five NYC Mafia Families decided to bring order to the process and thus more guaranteed riches in their pockets.

They created a monopoly on providing concrete to Manhattan construction sites. The Colombo Family would "own" all concrete contracts under $2 million. For deals between $2 and $5 million, only six approved companies were able to make bids. The hoods devised a system called the "Concrete Club" so that each of the six companies would get their fair share of contracts. They all understood that a 2% kickback would be required. If the concrete work were estimated to be worth $2 million that would mean the company would pay $40,000. Four NYC Mafia Families would split the kickbacks. The Bonanno Family had been suspended from the Commission and did not get a piece of this action.

A semblance of legitimate bidding would be maintained. All six concrete companies would submit bids. Beforehand, the mob would have chosen one company for the contract. They would provide a price, and the five other companies would make sure their rates were higher.

While that system seems simple, there were endless conflicts. The mobsters and other involved never kept the details on paper. Consequently, people would have different memories or understandings of what had taken place in a complicated business. There were times that the disputes would require the Commission to settle things.

Ralph Scopo, a Colombo Family Soldier, was head of Local 6A and the District Council of the Cement and Concrete Union. The Bosses designated Scopo as their point man for the "Concrete Club." He made a lot of money in these operations but was fully aware that his life always hung in the balance.

A legal bug in the Casa Storta restaurant caught Colombo Family heavyweights Gerry Langella and Donnie Montemarano talking about the construction scams. What puzzled the FBI was the presence of lowly Soldier Ralph Scopo at their table. They began looking into Scopo's activities. The use of bugs was critical in their investigation.

On March 19, 1984, Scopo revealed the main details of the concrete scam to a contractor who was sitting in Scopo's vehicle. This incident was the first time the FBI heard a clear outline of the racket.

An April 5, 1984 transcript of a conversation Scopo had in his vehicle demonstrated his vulnerability. The mobster told contractor James Costigan that the Gambino Family had killed one of their tough Soldiers just in case he might talk to the feds in the future. Scopo was sure that Roy DeMeo would never have informed. Scopo went on to explain that he'd be one of the first arrested in if the concrete scheme blew up. Left unsaid but clearly understood was the possibility the Boss would have him killed to isolate themselves from the crimes.

On February 26, 1985, Scopo's world exploded. The feds announced their massive Commission indictment, and Scopo was one of the main defendants. He had little choice but to resign from his positions in Local 6A and the District Council. However, he left his two sons in charge of the store.

Judge Richard Owen sentenced Scopo to 100 years on January 13, 1987. A jury had convicted him and others in the famous Commission trial. All his appeals would fail, and the old mobster died in prison in March of 1993.

SCOPO FAMILY

When Scopo resigned from his union positions, his blood family remained in charge. Ralph Jr and Joe, Scopo's sons, became the Colombos new control agents. But their reign did not last long.

In March of 1987, the parent Laborer's Union (LIUNA) ousted the two Scopos and put a trustee in charge after the feds filed RICO charges. That wasn't the worst news for the Scopos. Around 1991, the Colombo Family split in two. One faction supported the jailed Carmine Persico while the other rallied behind Acting Boss Vic Orena. Gambino Boss John Gotti endorsed the latter. A sporadic but deadly shooting war broke out. It lasted into 1993

The police arrested Ralph Scopo Jr. for possession of a handgun early in 1992. Scopo and others were out "hunting" for Persico loyalists at the time. The case dragged on into 1993 with a variety of appeals, but the good guys finally won.

1993 would be a terrible time for the Scopos. Ralph Senior died behind bars in March. Then the feds decimated the Orena faction convicting most of their leaders. Orena Underboss Joseph Scopo was still on the streets, but a Persico hit team wiped him out on October 20. The rebellion against Persico was over, but the feds fight to clean up Local 6A continued.

Despite being permanently barred from the union, Ralph Scopo Jr. was in control of Local 6A. Boss Carmine Persico appointed Capo Dino Calabro to oversee the operation. He was Scopo's boss. Unfortunately for Scopo, a jury convicted him of extortion involving the local in 2006. The judge took pity on the very ill mobster. He ordered a $40,000 fine and a sentence of time served as Scopo awaited trial. Scopo went free.

The feds later jammed up Calabro, and he rolled over. He explained how he had control of the local and that he approved the elevation of Ralph Scopo III to be in charge. It appeared that the feds would never get the Scopos totally out of the union.

The International Labor Union's internal investigation team finally became involved again. Starting in 2008, they looked into the operation of Local 6A and concluded that the Colombo crime Family still had control. On December 21, 2010, LIUNA filed a formal complaint. It included an allegation that Ralph Scopo III had cashed out fake vacation time to the tune of $10,000. Also, LIUNA accused the Local of shaking down a cement contractor. Everyone knew that Ralph Scopo Jr. was still in charge despite being banned way back in 1987.

On March 11, 2011, LIUNA put Local 6A under trusteeship and ousted the entire executive board, including Ralph Scopo III. Among the charges was that Scopo III ran a "coffee boy" extortion scam. At each job site involving Local 6A, the contractor had to provide for a "coffee boy" operation run by the local. That meant the union held a monopoly on providing coffee and other foods to the workers. Way back in the 1980's Ralph Scopo Jr. forced each "coffee boy" to kick in $250 a week for the right to hold that position. If

Local 6A had four work sites that would mean a tax-free $1000 a week would be going to the Colombo Family.

Scopo III appealed his ouster to no avail. Meanwhile, his father, Ralph Scopo Jr., had been rounded up with a host of other Colombos in 2011. The feds charged him with running the "coffee boy" extortion scam. Over the next two years, most of the Colombos made plea deals but not Ralph Jr. He used his legitimate feeble health to delay the trial. Finally, it was all academic as the grim reaper took him on October 8, 2013. The Scopo's control of Local 6A of the Cement and Concrete Workers Union was finally over. It had been quite a ride.

CHAPTER FOURTEEN

Persico Problems

FATTY RUSSO

The 1970s saw Carmine Persico involved in endless misadventures. The first incident did not initially include Persico. On New Year's Eve 1970, the home of Joseph "Fatty" Russo was the location of a party. Russo had hired a young black man and his wife to serve the guests. At some point, the waiter started dancing with one of the white visitors, which infuriated the inebriated Russo. An argument ensued and quickly became violent.

Russo went and retrieved a pistol and emptied its bullets into the waiter in front of the guests. Everyone was screaming and yelling, but that didn't stop Fatty. He went and reloaded his gun, then came back and killed the black man's wife. Some male relatives took the bodies and dumped them along a road where a passerby discovered them the next day.

In a panic, Russo loaded all thirty guests on a plane and took them to Florida. At this point, Fatty consulted with a friend, Carmine "Sonny Pinto" DiBiase, the man who would later kill Joey Gallo. Sonny Pinto arranged a meeting with Consigliere Joseph "Joe Yak" Yacovelli to discuss the problem. In the summer of 1971, Yacovelli consulted Carmine Persico as to how to handle the mess. The meeting took place in the apartment of future turncoat

Joseph "Joe Fish" Luparelli. It was the latter who provided all the details of the events to the police.

A few months later, the police captured Fatty Russo when he returned to the New York area to complete the sale of his home. To everyone's surprise, the first murder case ended up in a mistrial on December 8, 1971, when Judge George Postel declared the jury was exhausted. Russo was back in court in June of 1972, and yet another mistrial was declared. Finally, an Appeals Court ruled that there should never have been a second trial and dismissed all charges against Joseph Russo for the murders.

JAIL HOUSE ROCK

Carmine Persico knew how to stir up trouble whether he was in prison or out on the street. In November/December of 1971, Persico was facing trial for extortion conspiracy involving loansharking. Judge Postel had warned the press not to prejudice the prosecution by mentioning details of Persico's criminal life. When the newspapers came out the following day, the judge and Persico's attorney were incensed. Some papers had mentioned Persico's connection to organized crime Boss Joe Colombo. The judge then barred the press from the rest of the trial. This action caused an uproar.

Persico got lucky. Judge Postel dropped 27 of the 37 charges Carmine was facing. The jury found the mobster not guilty on two conspiracy charges then did not address the remaining eight counts as per the judge's instructions. Persico went free on December 8, 1971.

The next month the sting had run out on Persico's attempt to avoid prison time for his 1959 hijacking. On January 27, 1972, the mobster was sent off to Atlanta to do his fourteen-year sentence. As always, trouble followed.

In the fall of 1972, Persico had his first parole hearing. On October 11, the parole board turned him down and ordered a further review in April of 1975. Considering his background, Persico didn't have a chance of gaining freedom at his first parole date possibility. However, Carmine had other brands in the fire.

In November of 1972, the prison system moved Persico to New York. He was about to face a conspiracy to hide a fugitive in the Joseph "Fatty" Russo matter. The transfer suited Persico ideally. It was much easier to run the crime Family from New York than Atlanta. It wasn't long before he was receiving daily visits from his brother Alphonse and assorted other mobsters. Also, Persico had the use of private phones that were off-limits to other inmates. It didn't take a rocket scientist to figure bribe money was changing hands.

Persico pushed the envelope too far. In February of 1973, the authorities transferred Carmine to the hell hole of Marion, Illinois. At that maximum security institution, the mob leader spent every day in solitary confinement with only a brief exercise period. He was not a happy camper. But in March, his lawyer obtained an order to bring Persico back to New York City for consultation on his upcoming trial for harboring a fugitive.

A one week stay in the Big Apple turned into three. At that point, Judge John Bartels ordered Persico back to Marion, stating that the trial wouldn't get underway for quite some time. Persico was not happy.

In September, the well-traveled mobster was back in a New York courtroom. He and Fatty Russo faced a jury on obstruction of justice charges related to Persico helping Russo hide from the authorities. Judge Bartels urged the press not to mention the criminal record of any defendant. Oops.

The next day the New York Daily News printed that Persico's present address was a federal prison. The New York Times story included the facts that Persico was doing a 14-year sentence and that his nickname was "Snake." Persico's lawyer demanded a mistrial. Judge John Bartels granted the request and dismissed the jury.

At the end of September 1973, Judge Bartels began a non-jury trial for the two defendants. After four days, he dismissed the indictment. Russo walked free, but Persico went back to prison to do his hijack sentence.

Persico appointed Tom DiBella as Boss during this period, although everyone knew Carmine was the real power. To ensure his men were following his edicts, Persico appointed his older brother, Alphonse, as Family Consigliere. Veteran Capo Anthony Abbatemarco was the Underboss.

Meanwhile, Persico decided to go to the courts to improve his chances of gaining freedom. The authorities had labeled him a dangerous offender due to his past criminal record. This moniker significantly reduced Carmine's chances of winning early parole. Persico wanted to see the justification for this label and demanded his files.

The proceedings were very complicated, so I am summarizing them significantly to avoid confusion. The US Court in the Eastern District of Illinois partially denied Persico's requests. One positive for the mobster was that if he requested an explanation for the dangerous offender label, the parole board would have to meet that demand.

The parole board held Carmine's scheduled hearing in April of 1975. Much to Persico's fury, his next conference would not be until April of 1978. Meanwhile, some of the troops were getting restless back home in New York.

In 1977 Underboss Anthony Abbatemarco and Soldier Sal Albanese started chafing under Al Persico's heavy hand. Amazingly they went to the Commission to make a complaint. To no one's surprise, the Commission ruled that Al Persico could do anything he wanted. Abbatemarco and Albanese were in big trouble. Persico minions killed Albanese while Abbatemarco went into hiding and was never again involved in mob affairs.

BRIBERY

Sensing a possible more significant revolt Carmine was extremely anxious to get back to New York. Underling Victor Puglisi approached a supposedly corrupt IRS agent named Richard Annicharico to facilitate such a move. The IRS agent suckered the Colombos, for he was working undercover and taping nearly all the interactions with the hoods.

For a bribe of $3500, Annicharico arranged to have Carmine moved back to New York for a few days in August of 1973. According to later information, Persico was not aware his men were attempting this bribe. Nevertheless, by all accounts, he was extremely pleased to be back in the Big Apple and wanted a repeat.

On December 19, 1977, the prison authorities authorized a second move from Marion to New York for Persico. This time Puglisi gave Annicharico $3400 and kept $1600 for himself. Persico wanted to stay in New York while he worked to have his hijack sentence reduced. The hoods offered Annicharico $250,000 if he could make both dreams come true.

Nothing came of these fake efforts, but the parole system did release Persico in 1978. During that period of freedom, Carmine arranged a meeting with up and coming Soldier Michael Franzese. Persico informed the young hood that he had ordered the death of one of Franzese's Associates. This man was part of a kidnap ring two decades before. They targeted made members of La Cosa Nostra, which was a capital offense. Not long afterward, some young prospects carried out the killing of Tommy Gambino. (No relation to Carlo Gambino)

Later in 1978, Persico violated his parole. The good guys sent him to a harsh prison in Ashland, Kentucky, on November 7, 1978. His brother Alphonse called him regularly, which allowed Carmine to retain control of the Family. Fortunately for Persico, the parole authorities released him from his hijack sentence on December 7, 1979.

Note:
The Commission sanctioned a hit on Bonanno Family power Carmine Galante in July of 1979. Persico told a relative that he had voted against the death sentence. If true, this meant that Persico was able to cast his vote despite being locked up.

On November 7, 1980, Persico's involvement with bribing the IRS officer Richard Annicharico came back to haunt him. The feds indicted Persico and three other mobsters in the affair. The judge released the mob Boss on a $250,000 bond. At about the same time, a high-level informant told the FBI that Persico was now the official Colombo Family Boss rather than the power behind figurehead leader Tom DiBella.

Persico's lawyer obtained a delay in the bribery trial in January of 1981. Instead of a start in February, the judge set May 11 as the new date. For the casual reader, the change might seem insignificant, but these types of maneuverings prolonged Persico's time on the street and thus aided his control of the Family.

While on parole from his hijack conviction, Persico was not supposed to associate with any bad guys. The FBI knew this was not possible if Persico was going to continue as Boss. Thanks to an informant, they learned of a meeting Persico had planned with other powers in the Family on May 6, 1981. Eight days later, Persico turned himself in, and the authorities immediately locked him up on a parole violation.

Note:
On June 29, 1981, Colombo hoods killed Capo John "Johnny Irish" Madera in Miami. Informants attributed Madera's death to the fact the good guys followed him to the May 6, 1981 meeting with Persico. The mob Boss blamed Madera for his latest problem.

In early August of 1981, Persico moved to have the bribery indictment dismissed. He lost and on August 11, 1981, decided to plead guilty to conspiracy to bribe an IRS official. The authorities kept him locked up at the Municipal Correction Center in New York City. Persico wanted to remain there and was willing to do whatever to do so. This plan led to even more trouble for the mob leader.

During Persico's latest legal problems, a Gambino Associate had become an informant for the FBI. The story of Joseph "Joe Dogs" Cantaluppo is a long and complicated tale. I will concentrate on those parts that directly affect Persico.

In October of 1981, Cantaluppo had arranged for a Colombo hood to do time at a "country club" prison. The authorities arranged this to enhance Joe Dog's stature with the bad guys. The Colombo mobster was so impressed that he asked Cantaluppo to arrange for Persico to stay in New York. With the FBI's consent, Cantaluppo promised to try and arrange this for a payment of $20,000.

A judge sentenced Persico to five years for his bribery guilty plea. This legal event took place on November 9, 1981. However, for some reason that is still not clear, Persico's minions did not come up with the $20,000 until April 17, 1982. Prison authorities shipped Carmine to the federal prison in Danbury, Connecticut. The Mob Boss was fairly content there.

Meanwhile, some of Persico's men on the streets were having varying degrees of success and or failure. The next chapter will cover some of their adventures.

CHAPTER FIFTEEN

Alphonse Persico

Alphonse Persico was Carmine's older brother. In the family, there was also a younger brother named Theodore and a sister named Delores. Alphonse was the first one to end up behind bars.

In July of 1949, police arrested Al Persico and his buddy Steve Bove. The two hoods had beaten up a cop in some dispute. The DA later reduced the charges, and the judge gave the two suspended sentences. Things would not go so well a few years later.

Seventeen-year-old Carmine Persico was standing outside his family home in Brooklyn on January 12, 1951, when someone wounded him by gunfire. The police picked up Bove, although it is not clear whether Carmine ratted him out. In any case, no criminal penalty ensued, but the Persico brothers were incensed.

On February 23, 1951, Bove, Al Persico, and three others were driving in a vehicle through the streets of Brooklyn. Suddenly Persico pulled out a gun and fired several shots into Bove. The hoods then threw the body into the street. At that point, they drove to the nearby Gowanus canal and disposed of the weapon. It didn't take the cops long to link the Persico brothers to the hit.

The police arrested Carmine Persico on March 2, 1951, when he turned himself in. At first, he faced a murder rap, but the District Attorney soon dropped that charge. The court held Carmine as a material witness with a bail amount of $50,000. Meanwhile, the good guys were looking for Alphonse, whom they believed was the shooter.

A few months later, Alphonse's lawyer arranged for his client to surrender. On May 16, 1951, Alphonse denied committing the murder and was locked up. During his first-degree murder trial, Alphonse gave up the fight and pled guilty to second-degree murder. The judge gave Persico 20 years to life on September 20, 1951, and he was sent off to Sing Sing prison. (In Ossining, New York)

It wasn't until 1967 that Alphonse had a change in fortune. On October 24, 1967, a judge resentenced him to 10 to 13 years which meant he would soon be released. That dream came true on November 14, 1967, when Alphonse went free. He was quickly back into the criminal life with his brothers and friends.

Carmine and Alphonse had chips on their shoulders when it came to cops. Carmine demonstrated this attitude on September 12, 1969. A beat cop was writing Alphonse a ticket for some minor offense when his younger brother started verbally berating the officer. The net result was that Carmine had yet another arrest on his lengthy record.

When a lone nut gunman shot and permanently incapacitated Boss Joe Colombo in 1971, the Persico brothers' power increased dramatically. Within a few months, Carmine was the de facto Boss with Alphonse as his right-hand man.

Alphonse's influence increased significantly on January 27, 1972. That date is when Carmine finally began serving his hijacking sentence. The Bureau of Prisons locked him up in Atlanta. It wasn't long before Alphonse had created a beaten path to the visitor's room there.

A grand jury briefly interrupted Alphonse's life on April 4, 1972. It indicted him for providing false information on a loan application. Fortunately for Persico, the judge released him on $5000 bail. This problem would come back to bite Alphonse at a later date.

In March and April of 1972, Alphonse made numerous visits to see Carmine in Atlanta. When a drunken crew of mobsters killed Joey Gallo on April 7, 1972, it would have been reasonable to conclude the Persico's were planning Gallo's death. That was true, but the Gallo shooting came about by fluke without direct Persico involvement or approval. Nevertheless, Alphonse was quickly on the plane to Atlanta, a few days after the Gallo hit, to see what Carmine's strategy would now be.

The feds had been searching for Alphonse to serve him with a federal warrant on the false loan application charges. They had the benefit of having a high echelon informant in the Family. That person told the feds that Alphonse and some other members were going to be present at Carmine Persico's Blue Mountain Farm in Ulster County. On April 24, 1972, the feds and State Troopers stopped two vehicles leaving the location. The lawmen arrested five people.

Alphonse Persico and Jerry Langella were in the first vehicle, which also contained a cache of illegal fireworks. Charles Panarella, John Pate, and Panarella's girlfriend occupied the second car. In it, the feds discovered two pistols, which allowed them to charge the two hoods with the illegal possession of guns. The feds transported Persico to New York City, where a judge formally charged him for the false loan affair. The court freed Persico after he posted a $5000 bond. The next day he hopped a plane for Atlanta.

These events permitted a judge to issue a search warrant for the farm. The feds moved in the day after the arrests. The search turned up seven rifles, six shotguns, one revolver, plus ammunition. During the stop the previous day, illegal fireworks were discovered in the Langella car. Over the decades, this cache increased and changed magically. In 2005 noted author Selwyn Raab wrote that there were 50 rifles and 40 bombs. The illegal fireworks had turned into lethal "bombs," and the "gun" count had shot up from 13 to 50.

Note:
On May 3, 1972, Jerry Langella pled guilty to possessing illegal fireworks, illegal possession of a rifle, and driving with a suspended license. The judge fined him $750. These three counts originated from the arrests at Carmine Persico's farm.

On April 26, the good guys accosted Alphonse yet again as he was leaving the Atlanta pen. This time they served him with a subpoena to appear before a Fulton County (Georgia) grand jury investigating drug dealing. No legal ramifications resulted from this event.

NEAPOLITAN NOODLE MASSACRE

One of the worst events in New York Mafia history took place on August 11, 1972. Someone in the Colombo Family tipped the Gallos that Alphonse Persico and other heavyweights in his crew would be dining at the Neapolitan Noodle Restaurant. They decided that this would be the location for their revenge for the Joey Gallo murder. It was a fiasco.

A lone hitman gunned down four innocent males, two of them died. He had mistaken them for four Persico men who had just moved from the shooting location at the bar. According to later information from Gallo member Peter "Pete the Greek" Diapoulos, the hitman had been brought in from Las Vegas. From his observations that day in a Gallo hangout, Diapoulos fingered Al Gallo, Frank "Punchy" Illiano, Louis Hubela, Sammy "Sammy the Syrian" Zahralbam, and Bobby "Darrow" Bongiovi, as being in on the planning of the hit.

This outrage caused an uproar in the media. Mayor Lindsey told the police, "to do everything in their power to make it virtually impossible for mobsters to do business in this town." The NYPD responded by rousting hoods and bringing them before various grand juries. In the end, there was a temporary disruption of mob activities, but the justice system never convicted anyone for the Neapolitan Noodle shootings.

Meanwhile, the incident at Carmen Persico's farm came back into Alphonse's life. He had to appear in court to face charges about the cache of guns on the farm on August 15, 1972. The judge released the mobster on a $100,000 bond, the same amount imposed on Jerry Langella a few days earlier for similar charges.

There was some positive news for Alphonse in mid to late 1972. His brother Carmine made some formal changes in the administration of the Family. Tom DiBella became the official Boss, although everyone knew Carmine was the real power. Persico promoted Tony Abbatemarco to Underboss, and Alphonse became Consigliere. Again, everyone understood that if Carmine were locked up, Alphonse would be wielding his power.

Perhaps in an attempt to gather some positive publicity, Alphonse turned a good deed for a local church. Early in 1973, two drug addicts stole some jewelry from the Regina Pacis Roman Catholic Church. An informant told the FBI that Persico might have some knowledge of the whereabouts of the jewels. Alphonse reportedly agreed to help the FBI recover the valuables, and he did. On January 21, 1973, veteran hood Charles Panarella placed the gems in a box at Grand Central Station where the feds recovered them. There is no evidence that this gesture gained Persico any slack from the good guys.

Alphonse faced a series of legal battles in 1974. Like many other hoods, the police hauled Persico before a grand jury. He refused to testify, at which point the judge gave him a grant of immunity. The authorities could not use his testimony against him in the future. But Persico still refused to testify. At that point, the judge placed him in civil contempt and imposed a two-month sentence.

Thinking Persico might have changed his mind, the authorities brought him in front of the grand jury in February. However, he once again refused to testify and received another sentence. He lost appeals of both these convictions and served 60 days in the slammer.

In 1977 Alphonse Persico had long been well established in his Diplomate Social Club in Brooklyn. According to future turncoat Joseph Cantaluppo, the joint was always filled with hoods of varying importance. On April 22, 1977, Cantaluppo, a degenerate gambler, was ordered to the joint to meet with Alphonse.

Within a short period after entering the club, Persico severely beat Cantaluppo in front of all the other hoods. The mob leader had recently learned that Cantaluppo had lied to him about a loan. Persico believed a purse maker was the recipient of the money, but he wasn't. This information was an embarrassment for Persico, so he made Cantaluppo pay physically. It was yet another loss of control for the volatile Persico.

In November of 1979, police arrested Alphonse and another man on a six-count loansharking indictment connected to the Cantaluppo affair. The following May, the two hoods were convicted of the offenses. But when Persico was to appear for sentencing in June 1980, he failed to show and went on the run.

Fortunately for the Colombo Family, the Bureau of Prisons released Carmine Persico on parole in December of 1979. Once his brother Alphonse got into the wind, Carmine appointed long-time loyalist Jerry Langella as Acting Consigliere. From this point forward, Alphonse's power shrank.

For the next seven years, Alphonse Persico remained hidden, and he quietly lived in four different towns in Connecticut. In the late fall of 1986, the US Marshalls were concentrating their search in that State.

Using driver's license records and other means, the Marshalls discovered a home where Persico had lived just months before plus the name of the woman who had been living with him. A phone book revealed her new address, and when the Marshalls arrived at the location in West Hartford, they found the fugitive.

Persico's lawyer claimed the mobster had suffered a heart attack and wore a pacemaker. Also, Alphonse was battling cirrhosis of the liver due to his years of heavy drinking. He was not a healthy man when hauled in front of a judge on December 18, 1987. The judge lowered the boom on Alphonse for his extortion conviction. On the three counts, Persico received a penalty of a total of 25 years plus a $30,000 fine. Not long afterward, Persico was in residence in the federal prison at Lompoc, California.

The Second Circuit Court of Appeals rejected Persico's plea to change his sentencing on August 4, 1988. The old gangster passed away from cancer in the Springfield, Missouri prison on September 12, 1989. It had been quite a ride, but mostly he wasted his life.

Note:
In a tragic aside to the tale of Alphonse Persico's years in hiding involves one of his former girlfriends. Mobsters, including Carmine Sessa, feared that Mary Bari might reveal Persico's hiding place to the feds. They lured her to a closed nightclub, and Greg Scarpa killed her with three shots. It is not clear whether Alphonse knew of the plans to kill his former lover.

CHAPTER SIXTEEN

Underboss

ANTHONY "ABBY" ABBATEMARCO

Underboss
1972-1977

Abbatemarco grew up in a Mafia environment. His father, Frank "Frankie Shots" Abbatemarco ran a significant gambling operation in Brooklyn under Boss Joseph Profaci. Unfortunately for Abby, his father angered his mob superiors in 1959, leading to his murder. At the time, speculation was that Frankie Shots was regularly late in making tribute payment to Profaci. The best evidence, although very slim, is that Profaci ordered the Gallo gang to carry out the hit.

Whoever killed Frank Abbatemarco made sure the target was dead. Nine shots from two different .38 revolvers hit the victim. Five of them were from Abbatemarco's gun, which the police found at the scene. If the killer was a member of the Gallo crew that meant Frankie Shots' son was an Associate of his father's murderers. That must have been awkward for Abby continued to run in the Gallo milieu.

Bad luck continued to follow the young Abbatemarco. On August 20, 1961, the Persico crew tried to kill Larry Gallo in the Sahara Lounge. Gallo escaped death by fluke. A policeman walked into the tavern just as hoods were attempting to finish strangling Gallo. The gangsters fled with one of them, shooting a second police officer in the face in the escape. Unfortunately for Tony Abbatemarco, the wounded cop mistakenly identified him as his assailant.

On August 23, 1961, a King's County Grand Jury indicted Abbatemarco and one of the Gallo attackers. Initially, a judge denied bail for both men, but the court released the two later after Larry Gallo refused to testify. To waiting reporters, Abbatemarco said, "I'm innocent, I'm being framed. The Gallos are my best friends." Later the charges were dropped by the District Attorney as more information on the attempted hit became available.

Abbatemarco had his fifteen minutes of fame on February 1, 1962. On that day, the New York Daily News carried a story and pictures of some of the Gallo crew. The day before, seven Gallos, including Abbatemarco, had rescued six small children from an apartment fire near their President Street HQ. This deed captured the imagination of many Americans, turning the violent Gallos into folk heroes.

By the fall of 1962, things had changed. Boss Joe Profaci had died, and Underboss Joe Magliocco was attempting to establish himself as the new leader. Part of his strategy was to finish off the Gallo rebellion. Abbatemarco finally decided that his future no longer was with "his best friends." He left the Gallo compound, and the Magliocco forces welcomed him back into the fold.

Magliocco's dream of becoming the new Boss died in late 1963. The Commission discovered that Magliocco and Joe Bonanno had been plotting against them. They dethroned Magliocco, and he died in disgrace in December. Capo Joe Colombo became the new Commission, approved Boss in early 1964.

At first, Colombo assigned Abbatemarco to a crew belonging to Underboss Charles Mineo. But Mineo was seriously ill, so Colombo promoted Carmine Persico to Capo over that group of men. This information came to the FBI courtesy of an informant in January of 1965. By this time, Abbatemarco was well on his way to establishing a lucrative gambling business in the Bedford-Stuyvesant section of Brooklyn.

In 1971, a deranged gunman turned Boss Joe Colombo into a total invalid by firing shots into his head at a Colombo civil rights rally. After some initial confusion, Carmine Persico began to assert his control. This increase in power meant that his crew member, Anthony Abbatemarco, would also move up in influence.

Persico went off to prison in 1972 but appointed veteran Capo Tom DiBella to be his stand-in. Abbatemarco became the Underboss with Carmine's brother Albert serving as Consigliere. This promotion put Abbatemarco entirely in the FBI's sights.

Unbeknownst to Abbatemarco, the federal agents planted a bug in his 1971 Chevy. They recorded conversations from March till September 1974. Sal Albanese was a regular passenger with Charles "Moose" Panarella occasionally riding along. Among other things, Abbatemarco boasted about the success of his policy racket in Bedford-Stuyvesant.

But he made a big mistake when he bad-mouthed powerful Boss Carlo Gambino. Those remarks would come back and bite him.

The good guys kept the pressure on Abbatemarco in the fall of 1974. In September, the feds served him with a grand jury subpoena requiring an appearance on October 7. A week before the show, Abbatemarco was admitted to Brooklyn Veteran's Hospital complaining of stomach pains. But the feds went to his sickbed and put another summons in his hands. The Underboss responded by hiring a psychologist. His report was fascinating.

According to Dr. Bruce Finch, Abbatemarco was psychologically unfit due to brain damage. His judgment, thinking, and memory was severely impaired. It was the doctor's opinion that his patient was not fit to appear before the grand jury as a witness. Other evidence from Abbatemarco's lawyers included the fact that Anthony had received a medical discharge from the US Marines in 1945. They claimed that the Underboss was a boozer who had been drinking a quart of vodka for the last 25 years. Wow!

In 1976 Abbatemarco appeared to have recovered from his medical problems. He continued to act as Underboss, plus he hosted a massive reception after his daughter's wedding. Famous future turncoat Jimmy "The Weasel" Fratianno was in New York at the time, and Abby invited him to the celebration. According to Fratianno, hundreds of made men were in attendance, plus the Bosses of four of the five New York Families. It is interesting to note that the Weasel reported that Abbatemarco was loaded.

Perhaps it was his alleged alcoholism that caused Abbatemarco to make a potentially lethal political move in 1977. According to informants, Abbatemarco and his right-hand man, Sal Albanese, were unhappy with how Boss Tom DiBella was running the Family. The two felt that DiBella was favoring Consigliere Alphonse Persico to their detriment. Of course, DiBella was just a Carmine Persico puppet, so his supporting of Alphonse should not have been a surprise. Nevertheless, the two malcontents took their complaints to the Commission. It was a mistake.

The Commission backed the Persicos, which meant Abbatemarco and Albanese were now in jeopardy. The Persico faction invited Albanese to a reconciliation meeting from which he never returned. Abbatemarco got the message and fled never to be a factor in Colombo Family affairs again.

Despite rumors that the Persicos had killed their Underboss Abbatemarco managed to survive many years before dying of natural causes on July 7, 2005. Whether he gave information to the FBI during this period remains an interesting question.

CHAPTER SEVENTEEN

Informers

Informers have been the lifeblood of the FBI's investigation and decimation of La Cosa Nostra. They have provided inside information so that the good guys were able to construct organization charts of the Families. The FBI was able to focus their attention on the more powerful mobsters if they knew who they were, thus making the best use of their time and resources.

From informers, the good guys learn the location of meetings, gambling centers, and the like. This knowledge makes surveillance much more productive, plus it tells the agents where to plant their bugs.

Often, an informer will tell the law enforcement officers about a crime that was committed by someone they don't like. For the bad guys, the hope is to rid himself of a rival. For the good guys, the plan is that they may accost the culprit and hopefully use pressure to turn him into another informer.

When a hood is vulnerable because of a pending court case or even after a conviction, the FBI might approach him, suggesting informing might be an escape hatch. Often another informer has told the agents that this potential client might be open to ratting due to large debts or fear of prison.

Some agents have the right combination of knowledge, skill, and personality to develop top informers. Often luck is involved in the process. In the 1960s, all agents were required by Director Hoover to develop informers. The quality and quantity of the mutts they brought in from the cold played a significant role in the evaluation of the agents. At different times in the move on the mob, the pressure to have informants was intense.

If an agent developed a Top Echelon informant, he suddenly gained considerable power and influence within his office. Other agents would consult him to see if his informer could shed some light on their investigation. If arrests resulted from this work, especially if it garnered headlines, the agent's influence grew.

Handling an informer could be exciting, nerve-wracking, financially rewarding (promotions), but also very dangerous. The agent was always walking a tightrope. The informer had to continue his criminal ways to remain active in the crime Family. Boundaries were spelled out by the FBI, but the hood often crossed them. Sometimes the agents did too.

If the transgression were not too severe, the handler would reprimand his charge, sometimes with a wink and a nudge. But if the hood went off the deep end and beat or killed someone, the proper response would be an arrest. That choice would mean the end of a valuable source. Sometimes an agent gave in to ambition and ignored or covered up his source's transgression. There have been instances when even the agent's superiors turned a blind eye to this kind of behavior. Several famous scandals have resulted in greatly diminishing the reputation of the FBI.

From 1959 till mid-1965, the FBI conducted hundreds of illegal bugging and wiretapping of Mafia guys and locations. None of the gathered information could be used in court but was invaluable as the FBI tried to understand the organization of La Cosa Nostra and who the key players were.

Everyone in law enforcement realized the importance of electronic surveillance in investigations. Accordingly, they were extremely pleased when Congress made it legal with the passage of the Omnibus Crime Control and Safe Streets Act of 1968. Title 3 was a particular passage, and the authorities use this label even today when dealing with this method of eavesdropping.

It is safe to say that without legal electronic surveillance, law enforcement would never have decimated La Cosa Nostra as they did. Nearly every big Mafia case included devastating recordings of the hoods talking to each other about various rackets. Two examples would be the famous Commission case in 1986 and the conviction of John Gotti in 1991.

Without informers, these legal electronic surveillances would not have been possible. The law requires probable cause before a judge will sign an authorization for a Title 3. The good guys partially meet this stipulation by using the knowledge gained from an informant. He might have told the FBI that the Boss of his Family regularly meets with his Capos on Thursday night at Restaurant A.

The FBI confirms this information by conducting surveillances of the hoods and the location. The agent throws in other details from previous investigations to bolster the application. Sometimes they use material emanating from other Title 3s operating elsewhere. At this point, the agent has to convince the judge that using electronic surveillance is the only way to find the required information. The judge puts a time limit on each successful application.

Planting the bug(s) and phone taps are the next steps. Over the decades, the FBI has developed specialists to achieve these goals. From their successes, it's clear they are good at their job.

GREG SCARPA

Greg Scarpa was a long-time member of the Colombo Family who died from complications of having AIDs. Scarpa was violent, charming, ruthless, ambitious, treacherous, cunning, fearless, protective, and a killer. As you can imagine, his FBI handlers had their hands full trying to keep him under control. Unfortunately, in the 1980s and 1990s, the imaginary leash broke, resulting in mayhem.

In this book, I will not address the question as to whether an FBI agent helped Scarpa kill some victims. Nor will I delve into the issue of morality in dealing with informers. Those interested in these and other questions might find answers in two books which take opposing views:

We Are Going to Win This Thing by DeVecchio and Brandt and *Deal with the Devil* by Peter Lance.

Scarpa's connections to the F.B.I. and the information he provided is complicated and vast. I will summarize the material to make it easier for the reader to follow this confusing, long-running tale. Thousands of details will be left out, but you may easily access all his FBI files. Here's how:

Type in "FBI Vault" in Google.
"FBI Records" will pop up.
Click on the subheading "Search Vault," which will be on the left.
A "Disclaimer" box will pop up.
Click on "Close."
Type in "Gregory Scarpa" in the search box.
8 Scarpa files will pop up.
They will NOT be in order. Start with file 1.

In 1960 the FBI jammed up Scarpa over truck hijacking and possession of stolen goods. He briefly became an informant before quitting. By 1961 the Gallo rebellion had heated up, and the FBI was desperate for inside information. They began unannounced visits to Scarpa's social club much to his displeasure. Finally, the agents promised to stop dropping in as long as Scarpa took their phone number.

On October 27, 1961, Scarpa called an FBI agent. The two met, and Scarpa quickly began supplying low-level Mafia news and was officially opened as an informant.

Scarpa provided a great deal of misinformation, perhaps not deliberately, but due to the fact, he did not know everything. For example, he messed up the details of the killing of Gallo hood Joe Magnasco. Then Scarpo told the FBI that the Mafia Commission was made up of all the Bosses in La Cosa Nostra when, in fact, it was only seven. Another colossal error occurred when he stated that Boss Joe Profaci made an additional 200 men after the Apalachin fiasco of 1957, making the Family size 400 members. In fact, after Apalachin, all the Families curtailed inducting men until things calmed down. Where Scarpa got the idea of Profaci quickly making 200 members continues to puzzle researchers.

But Scarpa had tons of factual information. He provided the FBI with the history and structure of the Mafia. They were very interested to learn that a peace attempt by Consigliere Charles LoCicero had been turned down by the Gallos. Scarpa described the process of preparing a prospect to be inducted into the Family. It was also interesting to learn that the Bosses removed the requirement to kill someone to be eligible for membership. The recruit had to pledge to be willing to commit murder.

From Scarpa, the FBI learned that Carlo Gambino had financed Joe Colombo's loanshark operation, and the two shared in the profits. Also, the two mob leaders had been working with Bonanno Capo Thomas "Smitty" D'Angelo in 1967 before the Joe Bonanno faction killed him. They wanted D'Angelo to become the new Bonanno Boss so they would have a friend on that throne.

For the rest of the 1960s, with a brief pause, the FBI paid Scarpa as he provided a variety of information on the world of La Cosa Nostra. From him, the FBI knew who was up and who was down in that life. This news helped them focus their surveillance on the more critical members. The informant even provided details on the activities of a future participant in the Joey Gallo murder. The parole office busted Frank LoCicero taking him off the streets for two years. Scarpa was a gold mine for the FBI.

Scarpa stopped providing information around 1975 in what appears to have been a dispute over his compensation. However, in 1980, FBI Agent

Lin DeVecchio was able to convince the mobster to return to the fold. The results would be a combination of great success, murders, deceit, court cases, and endless hatred. I will outline the significant events of this period in a later chapter.

CHAPTER EIGHTEEN

Michael Franzese

Michael Franzese is one of the most interesting La Cosa Nostra members ever. He followed his father's footsteps into the Mafia, had great financial success, then, after a short prison term, left that life and became a public persona. It was a fantastic ride.

Franzese's father was a powerful Colombo Family Capo who was greatly feared. Unfortunately for John "Sonny" Franzese, the good guys were all over him in the 1960s. A jury found him not guilty in a well-publicized murder trial, a home burglary case, and a bookie ring, but he lost in a very controversial bank robbery trial. The judge hit him with a fifty-year sentence, although he only did nine years before being freed in February of 1979. But the parole authorities found him in violation of this parole many times resulting in numerous return visits to prison.

The younger Franzese slowly but surely slid into his father's life. In the spring of 1970, one of his father's friends told Michael that Boss Joe Colombo expected him and his mother to join a picket line. Colombo, incensed at the arrest of one of his sons, decided to picket the New York headquarters of the FBI. Michael was a willing and enthusiastic participant.

One day the hot-headed Franzese ended up in a shoving match with a cop then punched the officer. Off to jail he went, but ultimately a judge only gave him a $250 fine. Joe Colombo showed his appreciation by appointing Michael, a captain in his Italian American Civil Rights League. The critical point was that the young Franzese was now in the milieu of the bad guys.

The following year Franzese was present at Columbus Circle when Joe Colombo was gunned down. Lone nut Jerome Johnson had walked up to Colombo, exchanged a few words, and then shot the Boss in the head when he turned. The short reign of Colombo was over. He went into an irreversible coma and died in May of 1978

Unlike Colombo, Franzese's life was beginning, and business became his focus. He first became involved in a body shop followed by a car leasing operation in Hempstead, Long Island. Next up was a pizza shop named after his father. According to Franzese, he was making $5,000 a month profit. To his credit, he also focused on freeing his father from prison. That endeavor did not go as well as his businesses.

In desperation, Franzese hooked up with the wife of one of the bank robbers supposedly involved with his father. Eleanor Cordero was a tough, street smart woman who played Franzese like a fiddle. He lavished time, money, and attention on Eleanor, who promised she had information which would prove Sonny Franzese innocent.

Using Eleanor's evidence and a variety of other material, Franzese and his mother managed to obtain a judicial hearing about Sonny. The judge destroyed their hopes by dismissing the case quickly. Michael Franzese hated and distrusted the justice system more than ever.

In 1974 the good guys steamrolled Franzese charging him with three different cases involving a variety of charges including conspiracy, grand theft, extortion, and coercion. The details of these cases are not that important. The fact that Franzese was found not guilty on two of them and only fined $250 on the third is of interest. In any case, Franzese was now a big target for law enforcement. Instead of backing away from this life, he jumped in the deep end.

Michael Franzese traveled to Kansas to visit his father in 1975. Sonny explained that he would like to see Michael become a member of the Colombo Family. At yet another critical point in his life, Michael made the wrong choice to please his father. On Halloween 1975, Boss Tom DiBella put Michael and five other recruits through the induction ceremony of the Mafia. He was no longer in control of his life if he had ever been so.

In the mid-1970s, Franzese invested in a Mazda dealership with a financial plan based on bribery. His repair shop continued to flourish, so he had money to put to work. Not surprisingly, Michael put his money on the street in a profitable loanshark racket. Success in this business requires an understanding that the lender would not hesitate to use violence if the payments did not appear on time. With his father's name behind him, Michael usually did not have too much trouble getting his money.

The parole authorities released Boss Carmine Persico from prison in 1978. It wasn't long before he demonstrated his power to Franzese. In the late fall, Persico informed Franzese that one of his men had to die. According to the Boss, the target was a member of a long-ago kidnap gang. Their crime was grabbing Mafia members for ransom. Someone had finally ratted out the Associate, and Persico's men quickly dispatched him. Despite his shock Franzese, once again, decided to continue in that violent life.

He made the same decision early in 1979 after a close Associate. Larry Carrozza allegedly murdered another member of their crew. The fear was that this man, Joseph Laezza, might turn informer. Franzese insists that he did not order this hit but only learned about it after the fact. Nevertheless, his Mafia life proceeded despite the rising body count.

On May 15, 1981, police found the body of Franzese Associate Thomas Genovese in the trunk of a car in the Bay Ridge section of Brooklyn. Franzese wrote that this death was another settling of accounts for past misdeeds. He guessed that Genovese was another long ago kidnapper of Mafia members.

The same year as Genovese's death, Franzese went into the gasoline business. A friend of his father put him in touch with Larry Iorizzo. The latter was running an extremely lucrative gasoline tax scam, but some low-level hoods were pressuring him. Iorizzo wanted protection.

THE GASOLINE TAX FRAUD.

Initially, the hoods worked at the service station level. Legally they were required to pay 27 cents a gallon in taxes. But they never intended to do so. This decision permitted the hoods to set their prices lower than the competition. It didn't take long for there to be a lineup of eager vehicle owners. The trick was to carry on the fraud as long as possible, then disappear with the tax money. Iorizzo's crew had about 300 locations, thus multiplying the profits.

Finally, New York State changed the rules. They now required the gasoline wholesalers to pay the taxes, not the service stations. Iorizzo was happy beyond imagination. He created a blizzard of gas wholesale companies and, on paper, moved the gasoline between them. He placed the final stop at a fake company located in Panama. Meanwhile, the hoods had the gas trucked to hundreds of locations and sold at a discount. Iorizzo and his crew were making millions not paying the taxes, and it took the tax people forever to work their way through the mass of paperwork.

Once Franzese understood the scheme, he was an eager participant. With the blessing of Boss Carmine Persico, the fraud expanded significantly, allowing Michael to provide various types of jobs for his ever-expanding crew. In an interview long after the fact, Franzese claimed he was giving Persico $2 million A WEEK!

More drama followed in 1983. Capo Jimmy Angelino told Franzese that his close friend Larry "Champagne Larry" Carrozza, a married man, was carrying on an affair with Franzese's sister. On May 20, 1983, the police found Carrozza's body in his mother's vehicle. To this day, Franzese vehemently denies demanding the hit. Some disagree.

Sal Miciotta was a veteran Colombo hood who started informing to the feds in 1993. Later the government took him into the Witness Protection Program, and he testified in some cases. This situation turned into a disaster. Miciotta continued his criminal ways, and eventually, the feds booted him from the program, plus he was now worthless as a witness. However, he had already spoken about Michael Franzese.

According to Miciotta, Franzese demanded the head of Carrozza, and presumably, Boss Carmine Persico gave his blessing. Miciotta lured Carrozza to his death by telling him they had to perform a hit. While sitting in the driver's seat, Big Sal turned and fired a one-shot into Carrozza's head, killing him. Whether he told the truth about Franzese demanding Carrozza's death remains questionable. The critical point is that even this hit of someone very close to Franzese still didn't cause him to withdraw from this horrible milieu.

Note:
Miciotta claimed that Chucky Russo picked him up after the hit, and Billy Russo drove a second backup vehicle.

Things continued to go south the following year. The feds convicted Big Larry Iorizzo for his massive gasoline tax fraud. Larry fled to Panama before sentencing, but Panamanian dictator Noriega forced him back to the US in October of 1984. It wasn't long before Iorizzo rolled over and eventually testified against his Associates, including Franzese.

In January of 1985, the feds took Franzese and some Associates to court on loansharking charges. A lengthy four-month trial ensued. But before the verdict, Franzese faced a much deadlier jury. Colombo leaders had heard street rumors that Michael Franzese had not been passing along a fair share of the gasoline fraud taxes. Mob power Andy Russo (Carmine Persico was back in prison) called both Franzeses in for separate sit-downs. Michael, fearing death, did not want to attend, but his father insisted. Against all his self-preservation instincts, Michael showed up.

Franzese emerged in one piece from the sit-down. The leaders decided that he was not cheating them of the profits. Perhaps they concluded Franzese was bringing in so much money some cheating didn't matter. Franzese lived but was shaken to the bone by the experience and the lack of support from his father. Relations between the two would never be the same again.

The loanshark jury gave Michael some good news on April 19, 1985. They found him and his Associates not guilty of all charges. But on December 19, 1985, the past came crashing down on the young Colombo Capo. He was in a world of hurt.

Florida hit Franzese with a 65 count indictment related to his gas tax fraud in that state, and the feds jumped in with their own 28 counts. It appeared that Franzese's Hollywood lifestyle was over forever. Guess again.

Franzese and his lawyers negotiated plea deals in both Florida and the federal charges in New York. The feds dropped 26 counts leaving Franzese to plead to federal racketeering and a tax fraud conspiracy. A judge would sentence him to ten years plus $35,000 in fines, the surrender of nearly $5 million in assets plus the promise to give up 20% of his future earning until he paid $10 million in restitution.

The Florida deal was even better. He pled guilty to all 65 counts and agreed to a nine-year sentence and $3 million in restitution. On the surface, that seems like a severe penalty, but there was a hook. The prison term ran concurrently with the federal time, plus the restitution would come out of the $10 million federal agreement. With good behavior, Franzese would be free in less than four years. It only got better when Franzese appeared before a New York judge.

Franzese formally pled guilty on March 22, 1986. Judge Eugene Nickerson ruled that Franzese could spend three months in a half-way house in Los Angeles while awaiting sentencing. The Franzese team convinced Nickerson that it would be better for all concerned if Franzese were out on the street earning restitution money. It turned out to be a fiasco.

Instead of laying low in Los Angeles, Franzese continued to live a Hollywood lifestyle, including touring around in a white, convertible Caddy. Worse yet, the US Marshalls who were supposed to keep tabs on the young mobster, at his expense, treated the assignment as somewhat of a lark. They might follow Franzese to a location but would not go in to see what he was doing. That honeymoon came to an abrupt end when NBC reporter Brian Ross came to town.

Ross' crew filmed Franzese tooling around in his Caddy. They even shot the US Marshalls, leaving their post outside Franzese's residence to go for coffee. When NBC put the segment on national TV, Judge Nickerson had Franzese hauled back to New York. Then the judge discovered that Franzese's check to pay for the US Marshalls bounced. Franzese got a go directly to jail card.

For the next period, Franzese bounced around from prison to prison, finally ending up at the federal pen on Terminal Island in California.

By this time, Franzese was fully committed to finally withdrawing from Mafia life. He had secretly made that pledge during his plea agreement. The former mob Capo was hoping to be out of prison within a few years. Unfortunately, his past came back to bite him once again, starting at Thanksgiving 1987.

Years before, Franzese had invested in an agency firm owned by Norby Walters and Lloyd Bloom. His infrequent role was to influence artists to sign with Walters. On a few occasions, Franzese used his Mafia reputation to convince several artists not to leave the Walters organization. Later the two agents branched out into the college sports world and began using illegal means to sign up college players. These methods soon created a national scandal. The prosecutors were anxious to convict these two men and gain great publicity. Learning of Franzese's role in their enterprise, the prosecutors were eager to talk to him.

Prosecutors had Franzese flown into Chicago and had preliminary talks with the former mobster. Eventually, the authorities flew Franzese back to Terminal Island, where the prosecutors and Franzese held further discussions. It was at this time that Franzese became an informer as far as Mafia law was concerned.

On August 24, 1988, a grand jury indicted Walters and Bloom on a variety of charges. The prosecutors did not name Franzese, for he had agreed to testify under a grant of immunity. On March 14, 1989, Franzese took the stand in Chicago. What follows are a few relevant quotes about Michael from the report in the Chicago Tribune the next day.

"A former New York crime syndicate figure turned informant testified yesterday..."

"...he used threats, muscle, and money to help...."

"...testifying under a grant of immunity..."

"...he provided $50,000 that allowed Walters to begin his sports-agency business..."

"Yes, I was reputed to be a high ranking member of the Colombo family."

"...and quite often he (Walters) would have problems with club owners...I would sit down and resolve these problems."

"...he was co-operating with the government in the hopes of obtaining a reduced sentence."

The government rewarded Franzese for his testimony by giving him a one-year reduction in his sentence. In May of 1989, the prison gates opened for Franzese on Terminal Island. He was a free man.

A natural follow-up question might be, "Did he make the $10 million restitution? A YouTube piece provided the answer. To an interviewer and an audience, Franzese explained how he traveled to New York once a year to sign papers in connection with the payments. He finally convinced the judge to transfer his case to California. The IRS agent there seemed more interested in closing out the situation rather than having to deal with it regularly. Franzese stated that he made a deal to pay $250,000 over five years. The IRS signed off on the agreement. So much for having to pay $10 million!

For a short period, in the early 1980s, Franzese's Mafia star was in the ascent due to the money he was bringing in to the Family. However, he never had any significant power within the Family. That lay in the hands of Carmine Persico and his close Associates. It follows that Franzese had zero influence in the Commission.

Franzese has probably come to terms with the possibility that someone might kill him. He knows that scenario is unlikely, plus his strong Christian faith tells him there is life after death. By most accounts, Franzese appears relaxed in public, and we assume that is also true in his private life.

The more likely scenario is a lone nut shooting such as has happened to celebrities like John Lennon and other famous figures. But that danger has probably also faded as Franzese's public appearances have become so common that they rarely make national media accounts.

There was no strategic reason for Boss Carmine Persico to order a hit on his former Capo. Franzese was not going to go into court and testify against Persico or any of his men. There was no incentive for him to do so. Perhaps Persico, out of jealousy, wanted to have the now free Franzese killed, but if that thought crossed his mind, Persico must have moved on to other ideas. Franzese does not fear an official Mafia hit.

Franzese hurt several innocent people in his quest to be a prominent Mafia member and Hollywood producer. He abandoned his wife and two children to marry a dancer whom he met on the set of one of his movies. In this age, that type of behavior is not uncommon. But once the law tied Franzese in knots, his alleged plan to provide money for his first family went down the tubes. Franzese wrote that some crooked Associates skimmed the cash, leaving his first wife penniless. She had to go to work to provide for her children and herself. Even their home was not mortgage-free but covered with liens. Whether he eventually righted these financial wrongs and spent time with his children is not known to me.

Franzese became a celebrity and thus was and is far more famous than most La Cosa Nostra powers. His fame came partially from the fact he was living a Hollywood lifestyle, including making movies. Add to this the stories of the vast amounts his crew was generating through the gas tax fraud, and you had the elements to create a star. To this day, he has made a living talking about his former life to naive audiences. In the end, Franzese deserves respect for abandoning the criminal milieu, and for the last twenty years living a respectable life surrounded by his loving family.

CHAPTER NINETEEN

The Colombo Tsunami
1980-1989

THE INVESTIGATION

The FBI and other law enforcement agencies hammered the Colombo crime Family (and others) in the 1980s. Congress laid the foundation for their work in two bills passed in 1968 and 1970.

The 1968 Omnibus Crime Control and Safe Streets Act permitted legal electronic surveillance. Law enforcement had to seek permission from a judge before undertaking the monitoring. These affidavits are called Title 3s after the relevant section of the law dealing with this matter. In the war against La Cosa Nostra, Title 3s would be invaluable.

In 1970 the Organized Crime Control Act became law. It contained the elements of the RICO statutes, which permitted the government to charge leaders of criminal groups for crimes they ordered or helped to carry out. Convictions under this Act resulted in longer prison terms for members of an ongoing criminal organization. Previously it had been challenging to convict Mafia leaders since they rarely personally carried them out. The passage of this Act was a huge step forward in the fight against La Cosa Nostra.

Agents Jim Kossler and Jules Bonavolonta were two key figures in the FBI's war against the Mafia. In 1980 they attended a seminar at Cornell University given by Robert Blakey, who was one of the instrumental people in the drafting of the RICO law in 1970. Blakey educated the two agents on the potential power of this law, and they returned to New York invigorated. Their focus would now be on long term investigations of the hoods with Title 3 applications at the core of their work. This method would prove devastatingly useful.

The good guys put a full-court press on all five La Cosa Nostra Families in New York. This book focuses just on the Colombo Family, but it is essential to keep in mind that these investigations are all interrelated.

In 1980 a low-level mob Associate named Vincent DiPenta asked the FBI for help. He owed a lot of money to mobster Alphonse "Sonny Red" Indelicato of the Bonanno Family. The agents began paying DiPenta a weekly sum, plus they decided to fund a pasta import business for the degenerate gambler. The hope was to lure mobsters into the premises where the FBI could record them.

A judge gave his approval for the Title 3 applications permitting the agents to install cameras and bugs at the Lower Manhattan location. Eventually, to their surprise, a member of the Colombo Family, Frank Falanga, began to make regular appearances. Information gleaned from Falanga's talking helped lead to a bug on Acting Boss Tom DiBella's phone. Informer Greg Scarpa also contributed to the probable cause material needed for Title 3.

The DiBella information moved the FBI to the home of Capo Donny Shanks Montemarano, then to his Maniac Club. From Montemarano's home phone, the feds learn that the Colombos are involved with Genovese Acting Boss Tony Salerno. The feds follow Montemarano and Gerry Langella to the Casa Storta Restaurant in Brooklyn. Surveillance showed them that this was a regular meeting place for the hoods. Accordingly, in December of 1982, the agents sought and received approval to install a bug above Langella's favorite table. Greg Scarpa's information was beneficial here, as well.

From the Casa Storta Title 3, the FBI discovered that Soldier Ralph Scopo played an essential role in the Colombo Family's construction rackets. Consequently, they sought and received permission to bug Scopo's vehicles. On March 19, 1984, Scopo outlined the details of the "Concrete Club," which was a very highly lucrative racket for four of the five New York Mafia Families.

THE CONCRETE CLUB

All concrete jobs in Manhattan, under two million dollars, belonged to the Colombo Family. Scopo would award the jobs in return for a 2% kickback.

If a contractor did not pay, his job site would come to a standstill. Scopo's control of a Laborer's Union local made that possible. It wouldn't take long for the contractor to cave in and pay.

Larger concrete jobs, between $2 and $5 million, were shared by four Mafia Families. The Bonanno's did not participate, for they were no longer members of the Commission. Making sure that each Family got their fair share of the kickbacks required endless discussions. The hoods had to retain all the details in their heads. That process often led to disagreements. The Gambino and Genovese Families shared the kickbacks on all concrete contracts over $5 million.

Only six concrete companies were allowed to bid in Manhattan. They belonged to the "Club," and all their owners fully understood what the mob powers expected of them in the bidding process. If the mob decided it was company A's turn to win a bid, the other five firms would make sure to turn in proposals higher than that of company A.

Anthony Salerno and Paul Castellano controlled S&A Concrete. The primary concrete producer in Manhattan. With the other aspects of the "Club" in place, it was easy for them to sell concrete at inflated prices.

During the 1980s, it was nearly impossible for a prominent developer to work without coming into contact with the mob in some way. They had their hands in concrete, windows, drywall, electrical, plumbing, and on and on. The developer had little choice but to go along and pass the inflated prices on to his tenants.

THE FEDS LOWER THE BOOM

Thanks to an informant, the Gambino squad was able to take pictures of Commission members and Associates, leaving a non-descript home on Staten Island on May 15, 1984. Among the Mafiosi caught on camera were Colombo Acting Boss Gerry Langella and Soldier Ralph Scopo. These photographs would be valuable in later trials.

On October 24, 1984, the feds brought their StarQuest investigation to an end by announcing a massive indictment against the Colombo Family. Named were: Carmine Persico, Domenic Montemarano, Gerry Langella, Alphonse Persico Jr., Anthony Scarpati, Tom DiBella, and six others. There were 51 counts, including extortion, bribery, loansharking, drug dealing, thefts, illegal control of unions, etc. A vast mountain had fallen on these hoods. Carmine Persico and Donny Shacks Montemarano fled.

On January 29, 1985, a federal jury found Gerry Langella guilty of perjury and obstruction of justice. When called before a grand jury about a May 1981 meeting, Langella had lied in an attempt to prevent Carmine Persico for being cited for violating his parole. That tactic didn't work, and now Langella would pay for it. It was the least of his problems.

A relative by marriage ratted out Persico and Montemarano. The FBI scooped them up on February 15, 1985, and took them directly to prison. It would be the last day of freedom for Persico. The relative, Fred DeChristopher, testified against them later and pocketed a $50,000 reward.

The seven-month-long StarQuest trial came to an end on June 13, 1986. The court found the following Colombo hoods guilty of a variety of charges. Going down for the count were: Carmine Persico, Gerry Langella, Al Persico Jr., Dom Catalado, Capo Anthony Scarpati, Capo John DeRoss, Capo Andy Russo, and Associates Hugh McIntosh and Frank Falanga. Judge John Keenan would sentence them on November 17, 1985. Falanga died a day after the verdict. Earlier, the court severed Donny Shacks Montemarano and Ralph Scopo from the trial due to health reasons. Both would be convicted later.

On October 30, 1986, the justice system sentenced a Colombo crew headed by Anthony Colombo, the eldest son of the former Boss. The judge gave Anthony 14 years, and his brothers Joseph and Vincent five years apiece. The rest of the motley crew received a variety of penalties. This good guy victory was a minor accomplishment in that the Colombo boys' team were street thugs and had zero power in the Family.

Persico et al. had very little time to catch their breath after the StarQuest verdicts. The Commission trial began early in September and concluded on November 19. The Commission jury convicted Persico, Langella, and Scopo on all counts. The rest of the defendants also went down. In a curious turn of events, Carmine Persico, with the aid of a court-appointed lawyer, conducted his defense.

Two days previously, Judge Keenan sentenced the Colombo mob for their earlier StarQuest convictions. Carmine Persico received 18 years, Langella got a 65-year hit, while Alphonse Persico Jr. had 12 years to serve. Sometime later, a judge separately sentenced Montemarano and Scopo to 18 and 12 years, respectively.

On January 13, 1987, Judge Richard Owen sentenced Carmine Persico, Gerry Langella, and Ralph Scopo to 100 years each for their Commission case convictions. Most observers believed that Persico's reign at the top of the Colombo Family was over.

Two months later, the feds achieved another victory against the Colombos. This time it was a civil RICO case. A verdict barred Ralph Scopo and a bunch of relatives and Associates from Laborers Local 6A and the District Council of the Cement and Concrete organization. Several months later, the court amended the decision. Now anyone involved with La Cosa Nostra was forbidden from union participation.

Even Ted Persico Jr. had legal problems. A jury found him guilty of dealing cocaine, which resulted in a judge giving him a 20-year sentence on June 29, 1988. Another Mafia son, Greg Scarpa Jr., went down on a variety of charges on February 27, 1989. This conviction ended with another 20- year sentence. His story would get more and more complicated as the years went by, but the bottom line was that the young Scarpo went to prison and has not been out since.

The Colombo Family was reeling. The next chapter will describe how Carmine Persico attempted to hold on to power from his prison cell.

CHAPTER TWENTY

Chaos, Confusion, and Murder

When juries convicted Carmine Persico in both the Colombo Family case and the Commission one, he was never going to be free again. Nevertheless, Persico was determined to hold on to the reigns of the Family. His son Alphonse Junior was the chosen successor, but he had to complete a 12-year sentence from his StarQuest conviction. To hold the position, Carmine Persico appointed a committee of three. After a short period, he adjusted the membership of that committee. The new group still wasn't a success, so Persico decided to appoint an Acting Boss in July of 1987. His choice was Vincent "Jimmy" Angelino, the Consigliere. It didn't work out.

VIC ORENA

Early the next year, informant Greg Scarpa told the FBI that the new Acting Boss was Vic Orena, a loyal Capo. Any confusion about Angelino's status was cleared up on November 28, 1988. A crew led by Carmine Sessa killed the unsuspecting Angelino with Sessa firing the gun. It was an approved hit by both Persico and his Acting Boss Vic Orena.

The genesis of the next hit remains controversial to this day. On November 13, 1989, soldier Jack Leale drove Tommy Ocera to the home of Pat Amato. There, according to hearsay testimony by Harry Bonfiglio, Amato threw Ocera down and held him while Leale strangled the victim with a wire. The hoods placed the body in the trunk of Leale's vehicle, who later met with Bonfiglio and Michael Mattefore.

They transferred the corpse to Mattefore's car, and Leale ordered the two men to bury it. Later, Mattefore, Bonfiglio, Bonfiglio's son, and a fourth man put Ocera's body in a shallow grave on a golf course. The knowledge of this location would prove very valuable to some and disastrous for others. I will discuss this case further in the next chapter.

In the spring of 1990, Persico changed the leadership yet again. He demoted Underboss Billy Cutolo replacing him with Consigliere Benny Aloi. The new Consigliere was Persico loyalist Carmine Sessa. Street talk indicated that Cutolo lost his position due to Persico's fear that he was gaining too much power and influence. About a year later, Ben Aloi had legal problems, so Joey Scopo became the Acting Underboss.

Persico was in a dilemma late in 1990. For Acting Boss Vic Orena to sit on the Commission, official status was required. Probably reluctantly, Persico passed the word that Orena had his blessing, and the Commission should approve him. Reportedly Persico promised not to remove Orena without Commission approval. Persico made this move so that the Commission included the Colombos in their decisions and rackets. It turned out to be a mistake.

In June of 1991, those men loyal to Carmine Persico believed that Orena was attempting to become the full-time Boss. According to Consigliere Carmine Sessa, when he later rolled over, Orena asked him to poll the Capos. In Mafia language, this means Orena was hoping a majority of the Capos would support him replacing Persico as the official Boss. Also, Sessa believed that the Orena side was planning on killing him. Whether that was paranoia or reality remains controversial. But the critical point is that Sessa thought it.

COLOMBO WAR

Sessa set out to kill both Orena and his Underboss Joey Scopo. A typical Mafia hit involved inviting an unsuspecting victim to a meeting then killing him. With tensions high between the Orena and Persico groups, this standard method was not possible. Taking out one man in a "cowboy" hit would be complicated enough, but two was highly improbable. Nevertheless, Sessa proceeded.

On June 20, 1991, Sessa, accompanied by John Pate and Bobby Zambardi, set out to discover Orena's location. Once the Acting Boss was spotted, Sessa would call in a hit team to finish him off. At the same time, another group was looking for Joey Scopo. Unfortunately for Sessa, Orena spotted him and the others and raced away. As for the Scopo situation, he managed to make it safely home before the hit team could strike. Sessa and his men were in huge trouble. Orena now knew the Persico group had targeted him.

By most accounts, Orena quickly consulted leaders of the Gambino, Lucchese, and Genovese Families. Whether he was seeking peace or their support of his move to official Boss is unclear. But his next step seemed to clarify his position. In July, he dismissed five Capos who were Persico supporters, plus he demoted Carmine Sessa and replaced him as Consigliere with Vinny Aloi. To most observers, that move didn't look like a compromise peace initiative.

From his California prison cell, Carmine Persico responded to the Orena move by appointing Joseph "Joe T" Tomasello as the new Acting Boss. In the fall of 1991, most observers were waiting for the shooting war to break out. The interlude wasn't long.

Early in November of 1991, informant Greg Scarpa made a report to his handler FBI Agent Lin DeVecchio. He stated that hostilities would soon break out in violence. Scarpa named Orena Underboss Joey Scopo, and possibly Billy Cutolo as targets for the Persicos. The Orena side would probably hit himself (Scarpa) and Carmine Sessa.

Two agents visited Cutolo on November 13. In the conversation, they warned the mobster that the Persicos had plans to kill him. This action remains controversial. Lin DeVecchio has written that Agent Chris Favro didn't handle the talk well. He would have preferred if Favro had softened the blow by saying it would be logical for the Persicos to target him rather than directly saying it. Whether Cutolo would have reacted violently to either approach is debatable. The bottom line is that he got very hostile.

On November 18, 1991, Scarpa and some Associates left his home on 82nd Street in Brooklyn. His daughter and her young son followed in a second vehicle. Suddenly a van pulled up in the rear while the corner was blocked off by a panel truck. Two hoods fired a storm of shotgun slugs at the Persico car, but the occupants were able to escape by driving around the blocking panel truck. Little Linda Scopo's vehicle was also hit. Within hours Scarpa learned that the shooters were members of the Billy Cutolo crew on the Orena side. How Scarpa learned who his assailants were is interesting. Orena's apologists suggest the source was Lin DeVecchio, Scarpa's FBI handler. DeVecchio has vehemently denied this accusation.

Five days later, the Orena side struck again. They caught Persico loyalist Hank Smurra unawares in his red Caddy at a doughnut shop. Cutolo crew member Vincent "Chickie" DeMartino later admitted to being the shooter who fired the three shots into Smurra's head.

Before the Persico side could retaliate, a New York Post article rocked them to their core. It claimed that Scarpa was an informant. Where this information came from remains murky. Nevertheless, Scarpa was in great danger unless he could prove the report wrong. In that life, the only way to accomplish this would be to kill someone. The thinking would be that the FBI would never allow an informant to commit murder. That theory, and especially when it pertains to Scarpa, causes great debate even in the present.

DEATH COUNT CONTINUES

December 3, 1991
Veteran Genovese soldier Gaetano Amato died in a drive-by shooting. The Scarpa hit crew believed they were firing at prime target Nicky Grancio, but it was his look-a-like nephew. Amato just happened to be there. Larry Mazza did the shooting. Jimmy Del Masto drove the hit car, which also contained Greg Scarpa.

December 5, 1991
Seventy-nine-year-old Persico soldier, Rosario "Black Sam" Nastasi died in his Brooklyn social club after receiving five shots in the head and one in the chest.

December 6, 1991
Scarpa, Larry Mazza, and Jimmy Del Masto happened upon Orena member Vince Fusaro stringing lights at his home. Scarpa killed Fusaro with three shots from his M1 carbine. Mazza testified to this shooting later.

December 8, 1991
Matteo Speranza, an innocent worker, died after being shot six times in a bagel shop connected to the Persico faction. In 1995, the shooter, Christopher Libertore, testified to his actions. He claimed Orena Capo Louis Malpeso ordered a hit on a Persico loyalist because he, Malpeso, felt they were responsible for the wounding of his son that morning. At trial, Malpeso went down on other charges, but the jury hung on the Sparanza murder count.

January 7, 1992

Nicholas "Nicky Black," Grancio an Orena Capo, was killed by the Persico faction. Jimmy Del Masto was driving the hit car with Greg Scarpa in the passenger seat with Larry Mazza in the back. Mazza claimed he killed Grancio with a shotgun blast. Allegations later arose that Scarpa was able to call off the surveillance on Grancio so the hit could proceed. The evidence to support that theory is suspect plus a maneuver like that would involve a significant number of people making it nearly impossible to keep hidden. The reader should make up his or her mind by reading the two books mentioned earlier.

March 25, 1992

The Persico faction killed John Minerva and Michael Imbergamo in a car in Massapequa, Long Island. Later, a jury convicted Joseph "Jo Jo" Russo, Anthony "Chuckie" Russo, and John Monteleone for these murders. After their convictions, many legal maneuvers ensued as evidence of Greg Scarpa's activities emerged. Unfortunately for the three hoods, the Second Court of Appeals ultimately upheld their life sentences in July of 2001. Years later, in May of 2012, then Acting Boss Thomas Gioeli was found not guilty of these (and other) murders in a federal trial.

May 22, 1992

Greg Scarpa, Larry Mazza, and Jimmy Del Masto ambushed Lorenzo Lampasi outside his home. The prevailing wisdom is that this was not a Colombo war-hit but a personal matter for Scarpa. Lampasi suggested that Scarpa might be an informer, thus inflaming Scarpa.

THE QUESTION OF SCARPA

Joseph "Joe Waverley" Cacace was a dangerous Capo in the Orena faction. Greg Scarpa had him on his hit list and nearly succeeded on February 26, 1992. Cacace lived despite serious gunshot wounds to his stomach.

Word soon spread that Scarpa was involved in the hit attempt. Secondly, the FBI developed information that Scarpa was involved in a plot to kill a man in prison. Accordingly, Lin DeVecchio was ordered to drop him as an informant on February 27, 1992. This decision did not go over well with the FBI Agent. Scarpa didn't slow down his aggressive behavior but continued it, as shown by the Lampasi murder described above. However, on April 22, DeVecchio was able to open Scarpa as an informant again. Whether the Agent misled his superiors over Scarpa's illegal activities remains in question.

Due to the pressure from law enforcement, the two rival Colombo groups declared a truce according to information received from Scarpa on July 13, 1992.

Scarpa made the news again on August 29, 1992. He won a $300,000 civil case against Victory Memorial Hospital. During surgery there, the doctor gave Scarpa some blood that was infected by HIV. Ironically that blood had been donated by a Scarpa Associate. Scarpa had developed full-blown AIDS and blamed the hospital.

Two days later, Scarpa turned himself into the police on a weapons charge stemming from a March 31, 1992 incident. The judge released him on $1500 bail. As Scarpa was leaving the court, the feds arrested him on a conspiracy charge. It stemmed from the February 26, 1992 attempt on Cacace. A federal magistrate, unaware of the full extent of Scarpa's violent activities, released the mobster on a $1.2 million bond. Also, Scarpa's home arrest was to be monitored by an ankle bracelet. The killing continued nevertheless.

Scarpa's son Joseph, from his relationship with Linda Shiro, was a mob wannabe. On December 29, 1992, some local street hoods got into a dispute with Joseph, who promptly ran home to his father to complain.

Scarpa was enraged. He and his son and another friend set off to find the culprits. Within minutes a gunfight broke out. Scarpa lost an eye while the young friend was hit and died a few days later. Scarpa's days of freedom were over.

New York State and the feds agreed to make a deal with Scarpa. He would serve a one year sentence in the AIDs wing of Rikers Island for a gun offense. The location was essential to Scarpa, for it permitted his family to visit regularly. The second part of the agreement required Scarpa to plead guilty to federal murder and racketeering charges. For this, he received a life sentence on May 6, 1993. The thinking was that the mobster would be long dead before the federal sentence began.

As Scarpa's state sentence neared its end, he appeared before Judge Weinstein on December 15, 1993. The latter reduced his federal time to ten years so that Scarpa could go to prison with excellent medical care. In return, Scarpa publicly renounced his life in La Cosa Nostra. As usual, Scarpa stunned the experts by living until June 8, 1994. Few mourned the passing of this devious sociopath.

CHAPTER TWENTY-ONE

More trials

There were so many events and trials from 1989 onward that I have decided to list them in point form. In the hopes of making this massive amount of detail easier to follow, I have outlined each case chronologically so the reader can follow what happened over many years.

VIC ORENA

November 13, 1989.
Tommy Ocera was a successful member of the Colombo Family until November 13, 1989. On that date Associate, Gioachino "Jack" Leale drove him to the home of Capo Pat Amato. Later testimony indicated that Amato held Ocera down while Leale strangled him with a wire.

Leale drove to a rendezvous with Associates Harry Bonfiglio and Michael Mattefore. The hoods transferred the body to the trunk of one of their vehicles and then buried it. Two other men helped with this assignment.

October 4, 1991

The feds arrested Michael Mattefore, and he quickly made a deal. The first order of business was to take the agents to the body of Tommy Ocera. Shortly after that, arrest warrants went out for the men involved in the burial. Leale, knowing he was now in big trouble, went on the run. He didn't do an excellent job of hiding.

October 30, 1991

Leale had been hiding out at the Plainview Motel for a few days. When he left the building, two men gunned him down in the parking lot. On March 16, 1996, the prosecution laid murder and weapons charges against Vic Orena Jr. He pled guilty to murder conspiracy in the Leale hit and witness tampering counts. After he completed a four-year loansharking sentence, Orena Jr. had another three years to serve. It was a great deal.

April 1, 1992

The good guys arrested Vic Orena at the residence of a girlfriend. At the location, they seized four loaded shotguns in the home, and six pistols under the back deck. The indictment charged Orena with racketeering, murder, murder conspiracy, and loansharking. Five days later, a judge denied Orena release on bail. His freedom was over.

November 12, 1992

A jury found Michael Sessa, brother of Consigliere Carmine Sessa, guilty of eight counts of racketeering, conspiracy, murder, and loansharking.

The charges included the murder of Anthony Coluccio in 1989. This hit had nothing to do with the war. Prime witnesses in the trial were turncoats Joseph Ambrosino and Carmine Imbriale. In May of 1993, Judge Jack Weinstein gave Sessa a life sentence. As of this writing (2019), Sessa remains in Lewisburg.

November 19, 1992

Opening arguments in the Orena trial began on this date. The main charge was the murder of Tommy Ocera in late 1989. For the government, the probable reason behind the killing was Orena's belief that Ocera was skimming money from a loansharking operation. Secondly, Orena may have feared that when the feds found Ocera's loansharking records, they might implicate Orena.

There was some thought that the hit would win the favor of John Gotti. The claim was that he had a revenge motive for some alleged killing Ocera had committed.

The feds trotted out high profile informers Sammy Gravano and Al D'Arco to prove the Gotti angle. Years later, the integrity of their stories came under high suspicion, but during the trial, their testimony was compelling. Two Orena men who participated in the disposal of Ocera's body also took the stand against their former Boss. The government also used surveillance information and bugged conversations to bolster their case.

December 21, 1992
The jury convicted Vic Orena of all nine counts in the indictment.

January 25, 1993
A jury convicted Capo Pat Amato of the Ocera murder, a weapons possession count plus loansharking charges. Earlier his lawyers were able to prevent Amato from being tried with Orena.

May 26, 1993
A judge sentenced Orena and Amato for their separate convictions. In total, each received life sentences without parole, along with fines in the millions of dollars.

1993
Judge Weinstein rejected the two men's pleas for new trials based on the alleged perjury of witness Sammy Gravano and prosecutorial misconduct in the testimony of witness Montesano.

August 15, 1994
The Second Circuit Court of Appeals confirmed the conviction of Orena and supported Judge Weinstein's rejection of a new trial. They had earlier refused to overturn the conviction of Amato.

March 10, 2007
District Court Judge Jack Weinstein rejected Orena and Amato's plea for new trials or dismissal of the indictment. In a very long and thorough review of the relevant material, Weinstein stated that despite the questionable behavior of FBI Agent Lin DeVecchio,

there was more than enough evidence to convict the two men of the 1989 murder of Thomas Ocera.

Amato died in prison on March 13, 2015. Orena, in ill health, is located at FMC Devons, in Ayer, Massachusetts.

PERSICO HOODS

March 23, 1993
A jury convicted five Persico hoods of six counts related to the war against the Orena faction. Going down were Associates: Frank Pontillo, Alan Brady, Robert Montano, and Michael Dematteo. They also convicted inducted member John Pate. For good measure, the jury hammered Pontillo and Brady for a loansharking conspiracy and Dematteo for a gun charge.

Three turncoat mobsters testified for the prosecution: Joseph Ambrosino, Carmine Imbriale, and Allan Quatrache. The DA also used tapes from Ambrosino's Nissan, along with various other pieces of evidence. FBI Agent George Gabriel put all the material into perspective.

The prosecution put particular attention on the April 1992 attempt on Orena Capo Louis Malpeso and a plot to kill William Cutolo. The witnesses described 17 plans to kill Orena rivals.

At sentencing, the judge gave Pontillo, Brady, and Montano 156 months, three years of supervised release, and fines under $1000. Dematteo received one month longer, probably for his conviction of being a felon in possession of a gun. Judge I. Leo Glasser later sent John Pate to a mental institution for 15 years rather than sentence him. Doctors had convinced him that Pate was mentally ill.

Note:
Before the trial, five co-defendants pled guilty to various charges.
(Robert Donofrio, Joseph LeGrano, Lawrence Micciolo, Joseph Sangiorgio, and Anthony Sayh)

Pontillo, Brady, Montano, Dematteo, appealed their convictions. However, the Second Court of Appeals rejected all their arguments and affirmed the district court decisions.

JO JO AND CHUCKIE RUSSO

April 24, 1994

A jury found Joseph "Jo Jo" Russo, Anthony "Chuckie" Russo, Joseph Monteleone, Ted Persico Sr., and Lawrence Fiorenza guilty of a host of charges related to the Colombo War. The government used turncoat witnesses, Carmine Sessa, Larry Mazza, Joseph Ambrosino, and Sal Miciotta, to outline various crimes. Also, tapes and surveillance details finished the picture for the jury. The judge sentenced the two Russos and Monteleone to life.

Judge Charles Sifton severed Richie Fusco from the case due to ill health. The prosecutors made a deal with Robert Lombardi before the trial. He agreed to plead guilty to one count of racketeering in return for a fifteen-year sentence. He had been facing life. Just before his separate trial in May, the prosecutors agreed to let Fusco plead to one count of racketeering and a fourteen-year term.

After hearing of the misdeeds of Gregory Scarpa and the alleged misconduct of FBI Agent Lin DeVecchio, Judge Charles Sifton altered the convictions of three of the above Colombos. On February 19, 1997, he awarded new trials to the two Russos and Joseph Monteleone. However, he upheld Anthony Russo's loansharking conviction. Ted Persico and Lawrence Fiorenza were out of luck. He also rejected the appeals of Fusco and Zambardi to have their guilty pleas thrown out.

The Russo cousin's euphoria didn't last long. On January 15, 1999, the Second Court of Appeals reversed Judge Sifton's ruling and reinstated the convictions of the two Russo cousins and Monteleone. Although there was concern over the behavior of Scarpa and the FBI, the court felt there was more than enough proof to substantiate their guilt.

Also, in January of 1999, a jury found Joseph Russo's father guilty of trying to contact an alternate juror in the Russo cousin's trial and for hiding a witness who aided in the juror identification. The alternate juror was dismissed, along with the other alternative jurors, before deliberations began.

ALPHONSE PERSICO JR.

August 8, 1994

A jury found Alphonse Persico Jr., not guilty of racketeering conspiracy. The indictment alleged that Persico had ordered six hits during the Colombo war. In a surprise move, the dying Greg Scarpa signed an affidavit stating that Persico had played no role in the conflict. Another boost came from turncoat John Pate who testified that Persico was not involved in the war. Nine other defendants had either pled guilty or went down on various charges, unlike Persico.

WILLIAM CUTOLO

December 20, 1994

The notorious reputation of Greg Scarpa and allegations against his handler FBI Agent Lin DeVecchio seemed to have played a role in a critical Colombo Family case. The defense was successful in casting doubt on the testimony of turncoats Larry Mazza and Sal Miciotta. The jury found Cutolo not guilty of the murder of Vincent "Jimmy" Angelino from 1989. They also rejected conspiracy to murder and gun charges against Cutolo and six Associates. These allegations were from the Colombo war.

ORENA'S SONS

June 30, 1995

Seven members of the former Orena faction hit home runs in their federal trial. Capo Tom Petrizzo, Capo Vic Orena Jr., John Orena, Vincent Cascio, Joseph "Chubby" Audino, Frank Polite, and Paul "Paulie Guns" Bevacqua went free. Testimony about the misdeeds of Greg Scarpa and the alleged misconduct of FBI Agent Lin DeVecchio swayed the jurors. A grand jury had indicted the seven on conspiracy to murder and weapons charges related to the Colombo war.

Note:
In an appeal court ruling before the trial, the prosecution was ordered not to use Paul Bevacqua's nickname "Paulie Guns."

Defendant Rocco Miraglia Jr. pled guilty to conspiracy to murder in a plea deal before trial. The judge sentenced him to two years.

ORENA MEN

> August 21, 1995
> A jury convicted another group of former Orena members on this date.

Joseph Amato, an Acting Capo, Louis "Bobbo" Malpeso, and Associate Robert Gallagher went down on a series of charges related to the Colombo War. The jury was unable to reach a verdict on the murder of innocent Matteo Speranza on December 8, 1991. However, the jury found Amato guilty of being an accessory in that case. The men were convicted of the wounding of another innocent, Dan Norden in a wild shootout on June 4, 1992, where they attempted to kill Tom McLaughlin.

Christopher Liberatore, the man who shot Speranza, was a chief government witness along with his father, Anthony. Tape recordings also played a role.

At a later date, the judge gave out the following sentences: Amato received 211 months, Malpeso 95 years, and Gallagher 39 years. All three lost appeals in the Second Circuit on June 3, 1997. Malpeso died in 2003, Amato was released in 2009, while Gallagher remains in prison till 2029.

THE GREGORY SCARPA JR. SAGA

Note:
Greg Scarpa Jr. was the eldest son of notorious Mafia informer Greg Scarpa. By any measure, a father like that does not predict good things for the son's future. Scarpa Jr.'s life was a mess. Much of it, his fault.

The young Scarpa was a drug dealer who used his father's fierce reputation and the fear of the Mafia to intimidate competing street-level dealers. Inevitably violence would occur, leading to a series of murders. He operated out of his father's Wimpy Boy's Social Club, and with his father's name, all these things made him a big target. Greg Scarpa Jr. was toast long before he knew it.

November 1987
The government indicted Scarpa Jr. and nine Associates on various racketeering charges involving drug dealing and violence. Superseding indictments would soon follow as more information became available. The indictment charged the crew with controlling drug dealing in the Bensonhurst section of Brooklyn as well as running some marijuana sales on Staten Island. The murders of two rival drug dealers were also part of the charges. The government stated that they were a crew earning money to support the Colombo crime Family. In total, there were 11 counts, but not all of them pertained to each defendant.

July 15, 1988
A jury slammed the Greg Scarpa Jr. crew with guilty verdicts on the majority of the 11 counts. Only one of the four charged for the murder of Albert Nocha was found guilty. Another dodged a weapons charge.

At a later hearing, the following sentences were given out by Judge Leo I. Glasser: Kevin Granato 15 years, Catanzano 7 years, Mario Parlagreco 20 years, Billy Meli 15 years, and J Parlagreco received probation. They all had extended probation terms, as well. Their appeals to the Second Circuit failed.

Note:
In 1994 Mario Parlagreco and Billy Meli rolled over in the hopes of reducing their sentences.

August 29, 1988
Authorities were anxious to capture Greg Scarpa Jr., who had been on the run since the fall of 1987. In a controversial move, US Attorney Valerie Caproni asked the US Marshalls Office to get on

the case. She had lost confidence in the FBI and DEA. Afterward, FBI Agent Lin DeVecchio agreed to introduce a lead agent from their fugitive squad to Greg Scarpa Sr. but that led nowhere.

Some believe the featuring of Greg Scarpa Jr. on America's Most Wanted TV program on Fox was the reason for his arrest. In any event, a combined squad of FBI and DEA agents arrested the mobster.

August 31, 1988
Judge Leo I. Glasser refused to grant Scarpa Jr. bail.

December 1988
A jury convicted Scarpa Jr. of all counts from the indictment.

February 23, 1989
District Judge I. Leo Glasser sentenced Scarpa Jr. to 240 months. He said, "You were running a group of very bad guys."

February 23, 1990
Greg Scarpa Jr. lost his appeal in the Second Circuit Court of Appeals.

July 6, 1995
Scarpa Jr. pled not guilty to 13 charges in a racketeering indictment. Also charged were his brother Frank and 11 others.

1996
Scarpa Jr. contacted authorities and offered to spy on convicted World Trade Center bomber Ramzi Yousef. Both men were in New York's Metropolitan Correctional Center. Later, Scarpa's defense lawyers claimed Scarpa did this work till mid-1997

October 23, 1998
A jury convicted Scarpa Jr of loansharking, conspiracy to murder four victims, and tax fraud. They found him not guilty of five deaths.

During the trial, Scarpa Jr. took the stand. He admitted being a member of the Mafia and also outlined the alleged schemes of terrorist Ramzi Yousef. Scarpa Jr.'s central theme was that it was his father and DeVecchio, who were the bad guys. Interestingly neither Linda Schiro (Scarpa Sr.'s mistress) nor Scarpa Jr.'s mother was willing to take the stand to support Junior's contention of the corrupt relationship between his father and Lin DeVecchio.

May 7, 1999
Judge Reena Raggi dismissed Scarpa Jr.'s mitigation claim of fighting terrorists by calling it "part of a scam." She then hit the mobster with a forty-year sentence to be served after he completed 20 years from an earlier conviction. The Bureau of Prisons sent Scarpa to the Supermax prison in Florence, Colorado.

Note:
Scarpa Jr. reportedly turned down a 17-year plea deal before trial. Ouch!

1999
Scarpa Jr. claimed to have once again entered into correspondence with fellow inmate terrorist Ramzi Yousef. Scarpa Jr. stated that Yousef told him in coded terms that there would be an attack on America in September of 2001. The mobster later testified that he tried to contact the FBI to no avail. Then he worked through a Special Investigations Supervisor at the prison. Another prison official said that the FBI would be coming to interview Scarpa Jr. but never did.

March 2003,
Dr. Stephen P Dresch and Angela Clement, a legal researcher, visited Scarfo Jr. They were looking for dirt on Lin DeVecchio, the handler of Greg Scarpa Jr.'s late father. Scarpa Jr. told them lots of stories about the crimes of his father, which were sometimes aided by DeVecchio in Junior's version. He also detailed his contacts with Yousef. Dresch and Clemente accepted these stories. They hoped the government would use Scarpa Jr. during their investigation of DeVecchio.

January 7, 2004
Judge Jack Weinstein was holding hearings to determine whether the government should award Victor Orena and Thomas Amato new trials or dismissal of the indictment. Scarpa Jr. testified by teleconference from his prison.

Scarpa Jr. claimed it was his father and FBI Agent Lin DeVecchio, who had murdered Thomas Ocera in 1989. According to Junior, the two men were also responsible for the Colombo War. He went on to describe a very corrupt relationship between the two men. Scarpa Jr's suspect testimony and other evidence did not persuade Judge Weinstein to grant new trials. This Second Circuit upheld Weinstein's ruling.

September 31, 2004
The Bureau of Prisons transferred Scarpa Jr. to a unit in Florence that also held Oklahoma bomber, Terry Nicholls. It wasn't long before Scarpa Jr. was in communication with the terrorist. As usual, the mobster was looking for an angle to improve his situation.

Early 2005
Scarpa Jr. contacted a prison official and asked to see the FBI on a national security emergency. He didn't believe the prison official took him seriously.

March 1, 2005
Gregory contacted Dr. Steven Dresch and explained his situation. In the fax, Dresch passed the information about possible hidden explosives to Representatives William Delahunt and Dana Rohrabacher. Delahunt passed the information on to the FBI.

March 3, 2005
An FBI Agent administered two polygraph tests to Scarpa Jr. relating to his Nicholl's information. He failed them both. At this point, the FBI dropped the matter.

March 10, 2005
Dresch and Angela Clemente met with Scarpa Jr. at his prison. They had a long discussion about Nicholls evidence. Scarpa Jr. would not give up the location of the explosives unless he had a co-operation agreement with the government.

Dr. Dresch claimed an associate in Homeland Security promised Scarpa Jr. a co-operation agreement. At this point, Scarpa Jr. revealed the location of the explosives. They were in a crawl space under a home Nicholls rented in Herington, Kansas.

Without success, Dresch and Clemente attempted to interest various agencies in Scarpa Jr., revelations. Later the chagrined FBI explained that Scarpa Jr.'s failed lie detector results played an essential role in their non-movement on the case.

March 31, 2005
Acting on a tip, the FBI searched the former Nicholls home and discovered the explosives. They called in the Topeka, Kansas bomb squad, which removed the materials the next day.

The discovery was a massive blow to the prestige of the FBI. They had searched the location many times back in 1995. Representative Rohrabacker called the failure "inexcusable." It is safe to say the public agreed.

Scarpa Jr. did not receive any benefit from the discovery. His reward, although temporary, would come later.

March 30, 2006
A grand jury indicted FBI Agent Lin DeVecchio for four murders committed during the Colombo war. Information uncovered by Dr. Dresch and Angela Clemente played an essential part in the decision to investigate DeVecchio.

December 4, 2006
Scarpa Jr. began his trip from Florence, Colorado, to the Metropolitan Correction Center in Manhattan. He was to testify for the prosecution in the trial of Lin DeVecchio in the spring.

October 10, 2007
The murder trial of retired FBI Agent Lin DeVecchio began with jury selection. DeVecchio waived his right to a jury trial and opted for Judge Gustin Reichback to decide his guilt or innocence.

November 1, 2007
Lead prosecutor Michael Vecchione asked Justice Gustin L. Reichbach for dismissal of the case against DeVecchio. The previous day the credibility of crucial prosecution witness Linda Schiro came into question. Interview tapes from 1999 showed she gave a different story on the tapes and then in her testimony. The

judge set DeVecchio free. Scarpa Jr. never got to testify and was flown back to Colorado early in December.

Note:
For those interested in more detail and different versions of the Scarpa Jr., story (and his father), the following readings will be helpful. I do not necessarily support all the arguments and claims in any book.

Author Sandra Harmon's book *Mafia Son* (2009) details Scarpa Jr.'s life and is very supportive of his version of history.

Lin DeVecchio, with the aid of author Charles Brandt, presented his side of the story in *We're Going to Win This Thing* (2011).

Peter Lance's thoroughly researched book, *Deal with the Devil* (2013), took a very critical look at the actions of the government, the FBI, DeVecchio, and others.

Note 2:
As of this writing (October 2019), the Kansas City field office of the Residential Reentry Management Agency holds the 68-year-old Greg Scarpa Jr. His projected release date is on January 29, 2027.

CHAPTER TWENTY-TWO

The Acting Bosses

In a successful attempt to retain control of the Colombo Family even while imprisoned, Carmine Persico appointed a series of Acting Bosses. Most often, legal problems caused a change in leadership.

Below is a chronological list of the Acting Bosses and then a detailed outline of each one's career. Often the dates have to be approximations since the Colombos didn't mail out updates each time a change took place.

My apologies in advance for there are a ton of Acting Bosses, each with his baggage of endless court cases.

Vinny Aloi
1971-1972

Tom DiBella
1973-1980

Gerry Langella
198?-1984

Andy Russo
1984-1985

Anthony Scarpati
1985-1986

Panel
Jan 87-Summer 87
Angelino, Tomasello, Ben Aloi

Panel
Summer 87-Ap 8/88
Ben Aloi, Jo Jo Russo, Orena

Vic Orena
April 8/88-1992

Joe Tomasello
1992

Ben Aloi
1992-1993

Andy Russo
1994-January 1999

Alphonse Persico Jr.
1999-2000

John DeRoss
2001-2002

Joel Cacace
2002-2003

Thomas Gioeli
2003-2008

Panel
Ted Persico Jr., Ben Castellazo, Richie Fusco
2008-2009

Note:
An informant taped Ted Persico Jr., in 2008, stating that Castellazo was the
Acting Boss.

Other information indicated that Boston based Ralph DeLeo was the "Street Boss" between 2008 and 2009.

Andy Russo
2009-2011

ACTING BOSS PROFILES

VINCENT "VINNY" ALOI

Acting Boss
1971-1972

> May 22, 1971
> A lone, disturbed gunman severely wounded Boss Joe Colombo during the second Italian-American Civil Rights League rally. Consigliere Joseph "Joe Yac" Yacovelli took charge of the Family as per La Cosa Nostra protocol. He quickly appointed Capo Vinny Aloi as the Acting Boss.
>
> For some time, no one was sure if Colombo would recover, so the new leader's status would have to be "Acting." Powerful Capo Carmine Persico was the logical choice, but he was facing prison time. Secondly, Yacovelli's decision would have to be acceptable to Carlo Gambino and the rest of the Commission. Aloi's father, Sebastiano Aloi, was a long-time friend of Gambino. Gambino would feel that he could "control" the young Aloi, so his blessing was forthcoming.
>
> Turncoat Colombo Associate Joseph Luparelli provided some insight into Aloi. According to Luparelli, Benny was educated, dressed well, and ran some legitimate businesses. After each gathering of all the Capos, Yacovelli, Aloi, and Persico would hold a second meeting. Everyone understood that the real power in the Family lay in Persico's hands.

April 1, 1972
An FBI Agent accidentally noticed Vinny Aloi visiting an apartment in the building where the agent resided.

April 7, 1972
A group of gunmen, including Joseph Luparelli, carried out a hit on rebel Colombo Soldier Joey Gallo. This event led to a widespread investigation. Luparelli soon rolled over and asked for police protection.

April 20, 1972
FBI Agents observed Vinny Aloi make a brief visit to the Nyack apartment where Yacovelli was hold up. They saw Aloi leave in a black Caddy, which the Agents followed to an Aloi meeting in Tappan, New Jersey.

December 1972
Informer Greg Scarpa informed the FBI that veteran Capo Tom DiBella was now the Acting Boss. The belief was that Aloi's reluctance to do the job plus his legal problems led to the change.

January 1973
The feds indicted Aloi for perjury. Before a grand jury, he had denied visiting the Nyack apartment.

June 20, 1973
At Aloi's perjury trial turncoat Colombo Associate Joseph Luparelli testified that a year before Joey Gallos 1972 killing, Aloi, the then Acting Boss, ordered Gallo's death.

June 26, 1973
A jury found Aloi guilty of the Nyack perjury.

April 7, 1973
A judge sentenced Aloi up to seven years for his perjury conviction. He remained free on bail.

December 22, 1973
A jury found Aloi guilty of the stock manipulation charge from November 1970.

February 5, 1974
Judge Whitman Knapp sentenced Aloi to nine years for the stock fraud. He ruled that this term would be served consecutive to Aloi's earlier sentence of seven years for perjury.

October 13, 1978
Aloi's perjury conviction (June 1973) was thrown out in District Court. An appeal court upheld that decision later.

November 17, 1980
A judge jailed Aloi for a different perjury conviction. His sentence was two years and four months.

THOMAS DIBELLA

Acting Boss
1972-1980

DiBella was basically a non-entity before being elevated to Acting Boss. From 1925 onward he was a member of the International Longshoreman's Union but not a power in that organization. Despite being a Mafia member DiBella did not have a criminal record until 1974 and that was only for criminal contempt for refusing to testify before a federal grand jury despite being granted immunity.

The Acting Boss fought the contempt sentence all the way to the Supreme Court but lost. He served his six month sentence beginning on July 12, 1974. Capo John Brancato took his place during that period.

Perhaps DiBella's biggest claim to fame was that he presided over the induction of Michael Franzese. A more embarrassing highlight might be the fact DiBella willingly let the FBI bug his home. The old gangster thought he was getting a stolen security system!

In the mid-seventies DiBella was sitting on the throne when Underboss Tony Abbatemarco went to the Commission to complain about his rule. As explained earlier the Commission totally backed DiBella. Abbatemarco fled and an Associate was killed.

On October 24, 1984, the feds indicted DiBella and 11 other men in their StarQuest investigation. However, the courts severed DiBella from the trial due to his extremely poor health. DiBella died on June 10 1988.

GENNARO "GERRY LANG" LANGELLA

Acting Boss
1982-1984

April 5, 1972
Langella accompanied Alphonse Persico to Atlanta prison to visit
Carmine Persico. They returned to New York the same night.

April 24, 1972
The FBI and State cops arrested Langella and Alphonse Persico as
they left Carmine Persico's farm. Their vehicle had some fireworks
in it. Charles Panarella, accompanied by his girlfriend, drove the
second car. John Pate was in the backseat. They had two revolvers
in their vehicle.

May 3, 1972
Langella pled guilty to possessing fireworks, driving with
a suspended license, and illegal possession of a rifle. The judge fined
him $250 on each count. (He was seen firing the gun at the farm)

August 11, 1972
A disguised gunman killed two innocent meat dealers and wounded
two others in the Neopolitan Noodle Restaurant. The real targets
were Langella and other Colombo hoods.

August 21, 1972
Langella appeared before a grand jury investigating the Neopolitan
Noodle shooting.

December 19, 1972
A judge denied Langella's request to quash his grand jury subpoena.
The judge then gave Langella immunity. He still refused to talk.

January 18, 1973
The court indicted Langella for criminal contempt for his refusal
to testify.

June 24, 1975
A judge sentenced Langella to five months for criminal contempt.

March 4, 1976
An appeals court rejected Langella's appeal of his criminal contempt conviction.

April 3, 1976
The New York Court of Appeals refused to hear Langella's plea.

May 12, 1976
A judge refused Langella's writ of habeas corpus.

November 22, 1976
An appeals court refused Langella's appeal of the rejection of his habeas corpus writ.

1976
The Colombo Family accepted Langella as a new member.

November 5, 1980
Informer Greg Scarpa told the FBI that Langella was now Acting Consigliere.

January 7, 1981
Scarpa told the FBI that Langella was now the Underboss.

November 1, 1982
A judge accepted Langella's guilty plea of conspiring to bribe a public official. The charges were about the bribe paid to have Carmine Persico moved back to New York in 1997.

January 26, 1983
The FBI taped Langella complaining about a Commission decision that went against him.

May 1983
Frankie Ancona approached the FBI for help. He owed a lot of money to Langella.

May 15, 1984
The FBI took pictures of Langella and others, leaving a Commission meeting.

September 1984
A grand jury indicted Langella for perjury and obstruction of justice. He was trying to protect Carmine Persico.

October 24, 1984
The feds indicted Langella and other leading Colombo hoods in the StarQuest case (Colombo Family case).

January 29, 1985
A jury convicted Langella of perjury and obstruction of justice.

May 10, 1986
Joe Cantaluppo identified Langella during the Colombo Family trial.

June 13, 1986
A jury convicted Langella and other Colombo hoods in the Colombo Family trial.

November 17, 1986
Judge John Keenan sentenced Langella to 65 years for his Colombo Family convictions.

November 19, 1986
A jury convicted Langella in the Commission case.

January 13, 1987
Judge Richard Owen sentenced Langella to 100 years for his Commission case conviction.

December 15, 2013
Langella died in the Springfield, Illinois prison hospital.

ANDREW "MUSH" RUSSO

Acting Boss
1984-1985

2009-2011
Andy Russo was a long-time member of the Colombo Family and also a cousin of Boss Carmine Persico. Persico had promoted Russo to Capo then later to Acting Boss during two different periods. Persico had great trust in his cousin.

1975
Russo became a member of the Colombo Family in 1975, according to testimony from his brother-in-law Fred DeChristopher.

1984
Persico appointed Russo Acting Boss to replace the incarcerated Gerry Langella.

1985
Andy Russo's legal problems ended his brief reign as Acting Boss. The feds had indicted him in the StarQuest investigation that targeted the Colombo Family.

1985
Carmine Persico replaced Russo as Acting Boss with Anthony "Scappy" Scarpati.

April 26, 1986
Russo pleaded guilty to conspiracy to bribe IRS Agent Annicharico and obstruction of justice. As outlined in an earlier chapter Agent Annicharico was part of a ruse used against Carmine Persico and members of his Family.

June 13, 1986
A jury convicted Russo and others in the Colombo Family trial. They believed Russo was guilty of both RICO conspiracy (planning criminal acts) and substantive RICO (carrying out the criminal acts.)

September 25, 1986
The District Court rejected Russo's move to have his two convictions thrown out.

November 17, 1986
Judge John Keenan sentenced Russo to 14 years for his Colombo Family convictions.

October 27, 1987
The Second Court of Appeals gave Russo a partial victory. They confirmed his RICO conspiracy conviction but threw out the substantive RICO one due to a statute of limitation problems. The result was that Russo would serve eight years in prison rather than the original 14.

July 29, 1994
The Bureau of Prisons released Andrew Russo.

May 20, 1996
An FBI Agent observed Russo having a short meeting with Colombo member Joel Cacace. This event would come back to bite Russo.

September 11, 1996
The FBI arrested Russo and Dennis Hickey on a 31 count indictment. The charges included mail fraud, money laundering, conspiracy, and other counts. The government alleged that the two men attempted to control the Long Island garbage industry by illegal means. Judge Dennis Hurley set bail at $3 million for Russo.

Before he could post bail Russo was detained for a parole violation related to his observed meeting with Cacace on May 20, 1996. The parole rules stated that Russo was not to meet with other criminals.

The parole board decided that Russo had to do 19 months for his parole violation. That term was longer than average for the officials enhanced the time due to Russo's status as Acting Boss.

March 1997
Russo paid his $3 million bail amount but was not released, for he had to begin serving his parole violation.

May 1998
Federal Judge John Keenan refused to overrule the parole board's enhancement decision on Russo.

January 26, 1999
During the 1994 trial of Russo's son Joseph and others, the mistress of Joseph, Teresa Castronova, recognized an alternate

juror. Ironically the juror also regularly saw her old school friend in court and told Judge Sifton. He took no action, for there was no crime committed.

Before the jury began deliberations, the judge dismissed the alternate jurors. The jury convicted the men as outlined previously. At this point, Russo and Hickey hired a private detective in the hopes of talking to the juror. Presumably, they hoped to discover some wrongdoing by the jury.

The PI contacted the juror's mother, who refused to cooperate. However, she told her daughter, who then contacted Judge Sifton. He called the US Attorney, who began an investigation. The FBI wanted to talk to the spectator whom the juror had recognized but could not locate her. Russo and Hickey had her hidden.

None of this became known until 1997. During the 1994 trial, the married Russo had a mistress who was a lawyer. At Russo's urging, she carried messages to Joseph Russo, who was in prison, awaiting his 1994 trial. Russo's mistress also handled communications from Joseph Russo to his mistress Castronova. She knew all about the attempt to contact the alternate juror.

By 1997 things had changed for the young lawyer. Her relationship with Andy Russo had ended, and she grew attached to another bad boy whom she met during her prison visits. She married Larry Firoenza and was desperate to get him out of prison. At the same time, they both began to fear the reaction of Russo to her knowledge of the attempted jury tampering back in 1994. They both began to cooperate with authorities. This lead to the indictments of Andy Russo and Hickey.

January 26, 1999
A jury found both Andy Russo and Hickey guilty of jury tampering and obstruction of justice. The prosecution had used the testimony of the female lawyer and turncoat Mario Palagreco who was in prison with the Russos at the time. Also, the government presented taped conversations and video from jail during the trial.

February 1999
Russo took a plea deal in his garbage racketeering indictment.

March 1999
Judge Charles Sifton reduced Larry Fiorenza's sentence to time served plus 30 days for his cooperation in the Russo tampering investigation. The Bureau of Prison's released him in April. Both he and his lawyer wife, Dorothy, went into the witness protection program.

August 3, 1999
Russo appeared in court for sentencing on his jury tampering and garbage racket convictions. He was not a happy camper and called the jury tampering case "Mickey Mouse." Federal Judge David Trager handed out a 57-month term for the jury tampering and five years for the racketeering. He ruled that the two sentences would run consecutively.

August 22, 2002
The Second Court of Appeals confirmed the convictions of Dennis Hickey and Andy Russo.

2009
Carmine Persico appointed Russo as Acting Boss once again.

January 20, 20011
The feds in 16 indictments charged 127 members and Associates of La Cosa Nostra of a wide variety of federal offenses. The FBI arrested Russo and 109 others.

January 25, 2011
At Russo's bail, hearing a very supportive letter from actor James Caan (Sonny in the Godfather movies) was entered. In another show of support, actor Frederico Castelluccio (Furio in the Sopranos) was in the audience. A secret tape recording by an informer, Capo Paul Bevacqua, helped the prosecutors who opposed bail. Belevaqua introduced Russo to another member as "Boss." Magistrate Cheryl Pollak ruled that there was enough evidence to prove Russo was the leader of the Family and as such a danger to the community. She refused bail for Russo.

January 21, 2012
In allegations filed later, the government claimed that Russo inducted Ilario "Fat Larry" Sessa on this date despite both men

being in prison. Unfortunately for the feds, a prison official accidentally destroyed the tape showing men entering Russo's cell. Turncoat Colombo Capo Reynold Maragni provided the tip.

November 8, 2012
Russo pled guilty to conspiracy and illegal gambling.

March 21, 2013
Federal Judge Kiyo Matsumoto sentenced Russo to 33 months after he made a plea deal.

June 13, 2013
The Bureau of Prisons released Russo.

ANTHONY "SCAPPY" SCARPATI

Acting Boss
1985-1986

Like so many members of La Cosa Nostra, Scarpati was no stranger to violence as a youth. In 1950 he and his gang of South Brooklyn boys got into a scrap. Scarpati shot and killed another teenager and quickly admitted to the crime. The judge sentenced him to 15 to 30 years.

1977
Scarpati became a new member of the Colombo Family in a ceremony.

1982
Scarpati's hangout was the Nestor Social Club at 5th Avenue and President Street. He was involved in numbers, sports betting, and loansharking.

July 1982
Scarpati was reportedly a co-owner of a Staten Island bar called "On the Rocks." His co-owners were Greg Scarpa Sr. and Jr.

September 25, 1984
Greg Scarpa Sr. feared that the ex-girlfriend of Alphonse Persico might co-operate with the police. Capo Anthony Scarpati approved the hit but said, "We're going to probably go to hell for this," according to trial testimony years later.

1985
Carmine Persico appointed Scarpati as Acting Boss to replace Andy Russo.

June 13, 1986
A jury convicted Scarpati and other Colombo hoods in the StarQuest case.

November 18, 1986
A judge sentenced Scarpati to 35 years for his StarQuest conviction.

1986
Carmine Persico replaced Scarpati as Acting Boss with Jimmy Angelino.

1987
According to Greg Scarpa Jr., he made two trips to a Florida prison to get permission from Scarpati to kill Colombo soldier Joseph De Domenico. The latter was killed on September 17, 1987, by Scarpa Jr. and others.

VINCENT "JIMMY" ANGELINO

Acting Boss
1986-April 1988

January 4, 1982
Angelino and Sal Misciotta killed Joe Perraino Jr. and wounded his father in a sanctioned hit. The hitmen also accidentally killed an innocent woman.

May 6, 1983 (date uncertain)
The police found the body of Larry Carrozza in his mother's car. Later, informant Sal Misciotta told the FBI that Capo Angelino had lured Carrozza by claiming they had to do a hit. At some point, Angelino, who was driving, stopped the car and shot Carrozza once in the head.

May 20, 1983
Capo Jimmy Angelino told Soldier Michael Franzese that his married friend, Larry Carrozza, was having an affair with Michael's sister plus using cocaine. This behavior was a death sentence for Carrozza.

1986
Carmine Persico appointed Angelino as Acting Boss to replace Scarpati.

September 10, 1986
The FBI arrested Jimmy Angelino and Joseph Tomasello for conspiring to receive hijacked goods. They identified Angelino as the Acting Boss with Tomasello's status placed at Capo.

September 14, 1986
On this date, three men attempted to kill Anthony "Gaspipe" Casso but failed. Casso quickly began a search for the hitmen to determine who was behind the shooting. At some point, Angelino met with Casso and others. He relayed the news that someone heard Jimmy Hydell talking about killing Casso.

Later, corrupt Mafia cops Louie Eppolito and Stephen Caracappa captured Hydell and brought him to Casso. After questioning the hood, Casso killed him.

September 11, 1986
The feds release the sealed indictment charging Angelino and Tomasello with conspiracy. At their arraignment, both men plead not guilty.

December 1986
A jury convicted Angelino and Tomasello of conspiracy to receive hijacked goods.

January 3, 1987
A judge sentenced the two hoods to short terms.

July 1987
Informer Greg Scarpa told the FBI that Angelino was the Acting Boss.

April 3, 1988
Greg Scarpa reported that Capo Vic Orena was now Carmine Persico's choice as Acting Boss. Angelino became the Consigliere with Pasquale Amato, taking over Angelino's crew. In hindsight, it appears Angelino was oblivious to the meaning behind this demotion.

November 28, 1988
Earlier in the month, Acting Boss Vic Orena ordered the murder of Consigliere Vincent "Jimmy" Angelino. Carmine Persico either ordered the hit or gave his blessing to it. There were several men involved in the killing.

Dennis DeLuca picked up Angelino and drove him to the Kenilworth, New Jersey home of soldier Aurelio "Ray" Cagno. They were able to drive into an attached garage so that no one could see them. Angellino started up the stairs, but Carmine Sessa and Billy Cutolo were standing there. Sessa shot Angelino, who slumped against the wall at the bottom of the steps.

Jimmy LeGrano and others placed Angelino's corpse in a body bag that soldier Jimmy Randazzo had brought. Then the body was placed in the truck of Randazzo's vehicle and driven away. Rocco and Ray Cagno stayed to clean up the mess.

November 29, 1988
Informer Greg Scarpa told his FBI handler that Angelino had been ordered to step down from his Consigliere position but refused. This disobedience got him killed.

1991 or 1992
Carmine Sessa ordered Ray Cagno to change the stairs in case there was blood evidence on them.

May 17, 1993
Ray Cagno and Salvatore Lombardino shot and killed Colombo soldier James Randazzo. Rocco Cagno was also present. The three believed Randazzo might roll and reveal past murders and crimes. The shooting was an unsanctioned hit. The subsequent investigation led to information on the Angelino killing.

May 18, 1993
New Jersey State Police legally searched Ray Cagno's home.

May 20, 1993
The FBI legally searched Ray Cagno's home concerning the Randazzo murder.

September 1993
Rocco Cagno secretly begins cooperating with authorities giving them details of crimes, and he also wore a wire to tape conversations with co-conspirators.

November 9, 1993
The feds arrested Rocco Cagno and two other men for the murder of Angelino, conspiracy to murder Angelino and using firearms to commit violent crimes.

November 10, 1993
At his arraignment for the 1988 murder of Angelino, William Cutolo pled not guilty. He, Michael Spataro, and Frank Campanella pled not guilty to other charges. Four other men did the same.

February 2, 1994
The feds arrested Joseph LeGrano, Dennis DeLucia, Ray Cagno, and Rocco Cagno for the killing of Angelino in 1988.

March 18, 1994
Rocco Cagno formally pleaded guilty to RICO conspiracy. The three predicate acts were the murder of an unknown man in the 1970s, the killing of Angelino in 1988, and the whacking of Jimmy Randazzo.

May 5, 1994
Rocco Cagno made a deal to plead to three acts of conspiracy to murder, including the Angelino hit.

December 20, 1994
A jury acquitted William Cutolo of the murder of Vincent "Jimmy" Angelino. He and six others were found not guilty of a variety of other charges.

August 14, 1995
A jury convicted Dennis DeLucia and Joseph LeGrano for aiding in the killing of Angelino.

March 7, 1996
A judge sentenced Rocco Cagno to five years' probation for his role in three conspiracy to murder counts including the murder of Angelino.

December 4, 1998
Rocco Cagno appeared before a grand jury in New Jersey.

February 24, 2000
A grand jury indicted Ray Cagno for RICO conspiracy and the murder of Jimmy Randazzo. The GJ alleged Cagno was a member of the Colombo Family. The three predicate acts in the RICO conspiracy were: the killing of Angelino, the murder of Randazzo, and planning how to avoid charges.

June 28, 2002
In his New Jersey court case, the jury was unable to decide on the charges, so the judge declared a mistrial.

January 2, 2003
A New Jersey grand jury released a superseding indictment involving the same three RICO conspiracy charges as in the original from February 24, 2000.

March 5, 2004
The jury found Ray Cagno guilty of RICO conspiracy and the murder of Jimmy Randazzo. Conspiracy to murder Angelino was part of the RICO conspiracy guilty verdict.

June 4, 2004
Superior Court Judge Patricia Del Bueno Cleary sentenced Ray Cagno to an accumulated sentence of life plus 20 years. He would have to serve 40 years before becoming eligible for parole.

September 10, 2009
The Appellate Division of New Jersey's Superior Court rejected Ray Cagno's appeal and affirmed his convictions and sentences. Later the US Supreme Court refused to hear Cagno's case. Other legal petitions followed to no avail.

Note:
Ray Cagno remains in New Jersey State Prison as of October 2019. Jimmy LeGrano died in prison on October 3, 2017.

VIC ORENA

Acting Boss
April 1988-1992

Carmine Persico appointed Orena as his Acting Boss in the spring of 1988. By 1992 Orena was out of favor with Persico and replaced by Joseph Tomasello. Chapter 20 outlined Orena's rebellion.

JOSEPH "JOEY T" TOMASELLO

Acting Boss
1992

Tomasello was a veteran mobster who had briefly served as the Colombo Family's Acting Underboss in 1986. Legal difficulties ended his brief reign.

1980
Boss Carmine Persico promoted Tomasello to Capo.

September 10, 1986
The good guys arrested Tomasello and Angelino. The following day the indictment was made public. The government accused the two hoods of conspiracy to receive hijacked goods. Both pleaded not guilty.

December 1986
A jury found both men guilty of the conspiracy charge.

January 23, 1987
A judge sentenced Tomasello and Angelino to short prison terms.

July 1987
Informer Greg Scarpa told the FBI that Orena reduced Tomasello's power. This information made sense for Tomasello had started to do time in prison.

June 6, 1988
Informer Greg Scarpa told his FBI handler that Orena had demoted Tomasello from Capo to Soldier. This move was probably an early indication that Orena wanted his loyalists in place. Tomasello would have taken a big financial hit for no longer would Soldiers in the crew pass money up to him. Tomasello couldn't have been happy but was smart enough to keep his discontent quiet.

November 28, 1991
The New York Post ran a story alleging that Scarpa was an informant. It was like a bombshell went off in the Persico faction. Carmine Sessa consulted veteran mobster Joe Tomasello for advice. According to Sessa, Tomasello suggested that the best course of action would be to have Scarpa kill someone. The thinking, at the time, was that the FBI would never allow one of their informants to be involved in a killing. Oops!

1992
Boss Carmine Persico appointed Tomasello as Acting Boss.

May 13, 1993
The feds revealed a superseding indictment that accused Tomasello and other Colombo guys of a wide variety of crimes. I detailed these events in a previous chapter.

May 22, 1992

Greg Scarpa and two of his men, Larry Mazza, and Jimmy Del Masto, gunned down Larry Lampasi near the gated driveway of his home. At first, this appeared to be yet another act of violence in the Colombo war, but later evidence changed that theory.

Turncoat Carmine Sessa explained that a friend of Lampasi owed Greg Scarpa money and was being slow in making payment. Lampasi had made the introduction, so he was in the middle of the dispute. Around this same time, rumors were rampant that Scarpa was an informant. Lampasi sent the loan payment to Scarpa in an envelope, which was just fine. However, he allegedly included a note suggesting he hadn't delivered the money in person due to the questionable status of Scarpa's loyalty. Scarpa was infuriated. He was an informant and was desperate to prove otherwise.

Scarpa contacted Acting Boss Joseph Tomasello and sought permission to hit Lampasi. Tomasello granted the request. Furthermore, according to Sessa, Tomasello gave Scarpa the home address of the veteran gangster.

Whether Scarpa killed Lampasi out of anger or in an attempt to prove he was not an informer is unclear. It was probably a combination of both reasons.

Note:

At one point, Carmine Sessa told the FBI that Scarpo hit Lampasi because he was an Orena loyalist.

Late May 1993 (a guess)

Joseph Tomasello decided he'd be better off hiding than surrendering to face the May 13, 1993 indictment. Boss Carmine Persico may have ordered this strategy, but I have not been able to find any evidence to support the theory.

November 15, 1994

The Fox TV show, "America's Most Wanted" featured Tomasello. Nothing came of this effort.

July 29, 1998

In one of many efforts to catch Tomasello, the FBI put surveillance on his son. The young man was getting married on this date, and the agents hoped the father couldn't resist showing up. He didn't.

The persistent FBI agents followed Tomasello's son and daughter-in-law up into the Catskills. There they discovered Tomasello and arrested the long-time fugitive. He didn't resist.

The agents took Tomasello to New York City to face the music from the May 1993 indictment. A jury had convicted his fellow defendants, and they were rotting in prison. The future did not look bright for the mobster.

Summer 1999

Tomasello and his lawyers engaged in discussions with the prosecutors and finally reached an agreement. They agreed on an eight-year sentence. That was a long time, but compared to the life terms of the Russo Cousins, Tomasello had hit a home run.

August 15, 2005

The Bureau of Prisons released Tomasello. He would be on parole for a considerable amount of time.

November 20016

Joseph "Joe T" Tomasello passed away in Florida.

BENEDETTO "BENNY" ALOI

Acting Boss
1992-1993

Aloi was born into La Cosa Nostra for his father, Sebastiano was a long-time power in the Colombo Family with close connections to Gambino Family boss Carlo Gambino. Despite nearly endless legal problems and even a period when he was a prime target of rivals, Aloi remained in the Mafia milieu.

June 11, 1970
Aloi is one of 46 hoods indicted for refusing to testify before a Brooklyn grand jury. They all faced one year in prison, along with a $1,000 fine.

November 19, 1970
Benny Aloi was one of a group of men indicted for stock manipulation.

June 21, 1981
The Aloi brothers paid for an "In Memoriam" announcement for their father Sebastiano in the New York Daily News. It read: "Aloi-Sabastiano. (Buster). Happy Father's Day in heaven. From your sons, Frank, Vinny, Benny, and Sebastiano Jr."

Note:
I am not sure why they spelled their father's name as Sabastiano. Perhaps it was a typo, for they spelled the son's name as Sebastiano.

July 28, 1981
Informer Greg Scarpa attended a Colombo induction ceremony at the Bay Lounge. He reported that five men joined the Family, including a brother of Benny Aloi.

June 1984
A grand jury indicted Benny Aloi and 15 others on loansharking charges.

April 19, 1985
A jury acquitted Aloi and seven others of the loansharking charges from 1984. (Nine others were convicted)

November 1986
A Time magazine article stated that both Ben Aloi and his brother Vinny were both likely candidates to replace the convicted Boss, Carmine Persico.

April 3, 1988
Jailed Boss Carmine Persico appointed Capo Vic Orena as the new
Acting Boss. Orena picked Benny Aloi as his Acting Underboss.
The soon to be dead Jimmy Angelino was the Consigliere.

December 21, 1988
Informer Greg Scarpa told the FBI that Benny Aloi was now the
Consigliere in the Orena administration. Orena promoted Capo
William Cutolo as his new Underboss.

May 1990
Scarpa reported that the Orena administration remained the same
as it was in December 1988.

April 21, 1990
Benny Aloi attended the wedding of John Gotti Jr. along with Vic
Orena and Bill Cutolo. Gotti Jr. preserved their names and a long
list of other hoods in attendance. The good guys discovered the
records at a later date. The men were representing the Colombos
at the nuptials.

May 30, 1990
The feds announced an indictment, now commonly called "The
Windows Case." It involved bid-rigging and extortion in the very
lucrative window replacement projects in New York. Among the
15 men named was Benny Aloi.

August 21, 1991
Informer Greg Scarpa told the FBI that Boss Carmine Persico had
dethroned Acting Boss Vic Orena and his Underboss, Ben Aloi.
He appointed Consigliere Carmine Sessa as the new Acting Boss.

As described earlier, the Orena group ignored this edict
from Persico. For some time, the Family had two competing
administrations and Capos.

October 18, 1991
A jury convicted Benny Aloi and two other men in the "Windows"
trial. They acquitted five others, including John Gotti's brother
Peter. The judge released Aloi on bail until sentencing.

1992
Carmine Persico appointed Ben Aloi as his Acting Boss.

December 14, 1992
At a sentencing hearing for Aloi, turncoat Sammy Gravano testified about Aloi's position in the Colombo Family.

March 26, 1993
Judge Dearie sentenced Aloi to 16 years and eight months for his "Windows" conviction. This term was an upward departure from standard sentencing. The judge felt that although not found guilty of murder in the indictment, the preponderance of evidence convinced him Aloi was guilty of the killing. Dearie imposed a fine of $100,000 as well.

1994
Carmine Persico promoted Andy Russo as Acting Boss to replace Ben Aloi. It was act two for Russo.

August 26, 1996
For the second time, the Second Circuit Court of Appeal denied Aloi's appeal of his "Windows" conviction. They also affirmed the District Court Judge's increasing his sentence above the average level.

July 2004
In court testimony turncoat Bonanno Underboss Sal Vitale mentioned that at some unspecified time, Vinnie Aloi had commented that the Bonannos had inducted a former cop. Vitale revealed that Boss Joe Massino, who was also his brother-in-law, had broken La Cosa Nostra's rules by enlisting Vitale despite his having been a corrections officer in his past. (Ben Aloi was in prison at the time of this testimony.)

March 17, 2009
The Bureau of Prisons released Aloi from his "Windows" sentence.

May 11, 2011
Benedetto Aloi died. He had not been active in the Family since his release from prison.

ANDY RUSSO

Acting Boss
1994-1999

Note
See the above entry on Russo for the details of this period.

TOO MUCH!

By this point, most readers are probably totally confused by the lengthy list of Acting Bosses plus their seemingly endless court cases. Sorry. We are only halfway through. The next chapter will complete the lives of the remainder of Carmine Persico's Acting Bosses. Perhaps it's best if you put down the book and take a drive to the mall to clear your head. (Big smile)

CHAPTER TWENTY-THREE

More Acting Bosses

ALPHONSE PERSICO JR.

Acting Boss
1999-2000

By all accounts, Alphonse Persico Jr. is an intelligent man. However, he made many incredibly bad decisions that I will outline below. Alphonse probably should have stayed in college rather than follow in the footsteps of his infamous father, Carmine Persico.

> April 17, 1977
> Persico Jr. accepted induction into the Colombo Family. His uncle Alphonse Persico, then the Acting Boss, handled the ceremonies. Afterward, Al Jr. and the other four inductees celebrated at Tomasso's restaurant. Joseph Cantalupo, a Colombo Associate, accidentally crashed the party but quickly left. Later, he testified about seeing the men there along with new members from other Families.

May 12, 1981

Carmine Persico promoted his son Al Jr. to Capo around this time.

April 25, 1983

In a 13 count indictment, the feds charged Al Jr. and three other men with conspiracy and possession of a controlled substance with the intent to distribute it. Their arrests were part of a much broader federal investigation into the drug trade called "Operation Sailfish."

One of the arrested men was Antony "Tony the Gawk" Augello, He was a veteran Colombo hood who was close to Capo John "Sonny" Franzese.

Augello was extremely nervous about being connected to drugs, for it was against La Cosa Nostra's rules. Franzese's son Michael later wrote about Augello's torment. Within weeks of his arrest, Augello killed himself, fearing death at the hands of his superiors.

October 24, 1984

The feds released a 51 count indictment charging Al Jr, his father Carmine, and other leading Colombos with a host of charges involving mob control of unions, restaurants, trucking, and construction. The FBI called the three and a half year investigation "StarQuest."

June 13, 1985

The police discover the decomposed body of Steven Piazza, wrapped in plastic garbage bags in the trunk of his 1980 Caddy in the Bay Ridge section of Brooklyn. Piazza was a brother-in-law of Persico Jr.

June 13, 1986

A jury lowered the boom on the Colombos charged in Operation StarQuest, convicting all of those accused. Al Jr. went down on racketeering, conspiracy, and bribery charges. The Daily News reported that Persico Jr. was so angry at the verdict that he ripped off his gold neck chain.

November 18, 1986

Federal judge John Keenan sentenced Persico Jr. to 12 years for his StarQuest convictions. To add to Al Jr.'s misery, the judge called him "a chump" for getting involved in the criminal life. The Bureau of Prisons sent Persico Jr. to the penitentiary in Milan, Michigan.

June 1991

At the beginning of the Colombo War, Persico Jr. attempted to make peace between the warring factions. In a phone call, he told loyalist John Pate that he would try to get some of his father's Capos to attend a peace meeting. The next day Pate flew to Michigan to consult with Al Jr.

January 24, 1992

Someone killed Michael Devine, a part-owner of a Staten Island bar. The hitman shot Devine in the head as well as two times in the groin. It didn't take the good guys long to link this hit to Persico Jr.

In the spring of 1993, Assistant US Attorney George Stamboulides filed an objection to Persico's scheduled parole release in June 1993. Stamboulides claimed that evidence from turncoats such as Carmine Sessa and informers claimed that Persico Jr. ordered the Devine hit. The Parole Board did not release Persico Jr. as planned.

An unidentified law enforcement official told the New York Daily News that Devine had been having an affair with Persico's estranged wife since August of 1991. Someone warned Devine of the dangers of dating the wife of a made member, but he continued the relationship. The Daily News article stated that the two daughters of Persico Jr. informed their father about Devine and their mother. Persico Jr. had his wife followed to confirm the stories. Devine died soon afterward.

Note:

Neither the feds nor NY State authorities ever charged Persico Jr. with this murder.

May 14, 1993

The feds indicted Persico Jr. and ten other Colombo men for participation in the Colombo War. They charged Al Jr. with RICO conspiracy and six murders while he was still in prison.

August 8, 1994

In a big surprise, a federal jury acquitted Persico Jr. of RICO conspiracy. At one point, they announced that they had concluded he was involved in the 1985 murder of his brother-in-law. However, the law required at least two convictions for the RICO conspiracy to be valid. The jury returned to deliberate and decided that Persico Jr. was not guilty on all counts. He walked free and said, "I want to go home and see my kids." He had been in prison for eight years at this point.

During the trial, the testimony of John Pate greatly aided Persico Jr. Pate insisted that even though he and Al Jr. had talked during the war, Persico Jr. had no involvement in the hostilities. Another essential assist came for notorious informer Greg Scarpa. A few days before Scarpa died, he signed an affidavit that said Persico Jr. was not involved in the war.

September 1998

The US Coast Guard stopped Persico Jr. in his boat off the coast of Florida. They charged him with illegal possession of weapons after discovering a shotgun and a pistol. As a result of his 1986 conviction, the law forbade Persico Jr. from possessing guns.

May 25, 1999

Persico Jr., out on bail, flew to New York

May 26, 1999

The Persico group lured Underboss William Cutolo, a former member of the Orena rebel faction, to a meeting. Cutolo thought Alphonse Persico Jr. would be present at Soldier Dino Saracino's home. He wasn't. Dino Calabro shot Cutolo and killed him.

The leading theory behind Cutolo's murder was that the Persico group feared his ambition. Persico Jr. was probably going to do prison time for his gun possession charge, leaving a leadership vacuum that Cutolo might try to fill. The fact that Cutolo played a leading role in the Orena rebellion must have been a factor, as well.

August 1999
Boss Carmine Persico appointed his son Alphonse Jr. to be his Acting Boss. He replaced Andy Russo, who was off to prison.

October 8, 1999
The feds raided Al Jr.'s apartment while he was present. They confiscated some loanshark records that had been Cutolo's. Very early the next morning, Persico's lawyer arranged for his client to surrender.

October 10, 1999
The feds charged Persico Jr. with racketeering and loansharking. There was no mention of the Cutolo murder. US Magistrate Arlene Lindsay refused to release Persico Jr. on bail.

November 1999
A judge threw out the racketeering and loansharking charges against Al Jr.

February 10, 2000
A judge sentenced Persico Jr. to 18 months for his illegal gun possession charge stemming from a September 1998 incident. He would serve his time in a federal prison in Florida.

January 24, 2001
On the day of his scheduled release from his gun charge, the feds hit Persico Jr. with an indictment for loansharking.

January 25, 2001
In Brooklyn, federal court Judge Reena Raggi held Persico Jr.'s arraignment on loansharking. She denied his release on bail.

January 31, 2001
The feds indict Persico Jr. and ten others on RICO and RICO conspiracy charges involving loansharking, extortion, money laundering, gambling, drug dealing, and securities fraud. Most of the accused were members of Capo John DeRoss' crew. DeRoss had taken over Cutolo's men.

December 20, 2001
After lengthy negotiations, Persico agreed to plead guilty to racketeering, loansharking and money laundering.

2001
Carmine Persico appointed John DeRoss as Acting Boss to replace Al Persico Jr.

June 12, 2002
Persico unsuccessfully tried to withdraw his guilty plea. Speculation suggested he did so because the feds had decided not to use the son of Billy Cutolo as a prosecution witness.

November 21, 2003
Judge Reena Raggi tore into Persico Jr. at his sentencing hearing from his December 2001 guilty plea. She said, "There is no crime he wouldn't commit" and other insults. Raggi formally sentenced the mobster to 13 years and a $1 million fine. As part of the plea agreement, Persico had to admit to being a member of La Cosa Nostra.

October 14, 2004
The feds charged Persico Jr. and John DeRoss with the murder of William Cutolo and witness tampering.

November 3, 2006
Judge Joanne Sybert declared a mistrial in the murder case of Persico Jr. and John DeRoss. The jury deadlocked at ten for conviction with two against.

The next day two jurors told the Daily News that Persico Jr. tried to intimidate the jury during the trial by making pistol images with his hand and other antics. They also remarked that they weren't too impressed with his flirting with Sarita Kedia, his defense attorney. One of the jurors described Al Jr. as "a jerk."

November 28, 2007
A federal jury convicted Persico Jr. and DeRoss of the murder of William Cutolo in aid of racketeering as well as witness tampering. They cleared the two hoods of participation in the attempted murder of Cutolo's friend Joseph Campanella.

February 27, 2009
Judge Joanne Sybert sentenced Alphonse Persico Jr. and John DeRoss to life without parole for their murder of William Cutolo and witness tampering.

US Attorney John Buretta said, "Alphonse Persico and Jackie DeRoss are cowards who threatened a woman and children to protect themselves."

Judge Sybert's comment was, "It's sad for the defendant (Persico) and his family, but it's a choice he made."

May 3, 2011
The Second Court of Appeals upheld the convictions of Persico Jr. and DeRoss.

November 2019
As of this date, Persico Jr. is in the McKean Federal Corrections Institution at Lewis Rus, Pennsylvania. It is a medium-security facility. He is serving life without parole.

JOHN "JACKIE" DEROSS

Acting Boss
2001-2002

DeRoss is a long time Colombo member plus a brother-in-law of Boss Carmine Persico and Capo Charles Panarella. The feds believed the leaders made DeRoss around the mid-seventies in a flurry of new inductions.

March 24, 1984
The feds indicted DeRoss, Carmine Persico, and many other Colombo hoods in their StarQuest investigation. The agents didn't arrest DeRoss for his location was unknown.

October 31, 1984
DeRoss finally turned himself in to face the March 1984 indictment. There were 51 counts in the charges. His lawyer explained that DeRoss had health problems and wanted to see his

doctor before surrendering. He pled not guilty at his arraignment. He was facing loansharking and extortion charges.

The Mid-1980s
DeRoss and others complained about Charles Panarella to Boss Carmine Persico. They argued that Panarella was flamboyant, self-centered, and had an abusive style when dealing with his men. The leadership sent the veteran mobster to Las Vegas to get him out of everyone's way.

Note:
An insulted Panarella later sided with the Orena rebel faction.

June 13, 1986
In the Colombo Family trial, the jury found most of the defendants guilty as charged. However, they only hit DeRoss with one conspiracy conviction.

November 18, 1986
Judge John F. Keenan sentenced DeRoss to 14 years. He also sent a large group of Colombos to prison, as well.

October 27, 1987
The Second Circuit Court of Appeals affirmed DeRoss' sentence.

May 26, 1999
The Persico faction killed Underboss William Cutolo on this day.

May 27, 1999
John DeRoss began the first of several intimidations of Cutolo's family. He was attempting to find Cutolo's loansharking records plus ensure that the Cutolo family did not cooperate with any law enforcement investigations of Cutolo's disappearance.

January 31, 2001
The feds indicted ten Colombo men, including Acting Boss Al Persico Jr. and Capo John DeRoss. Most of the others were members of William Cutolo's crew, which DeRoss took over. The Colombos faced RICO and RICO conspiracy charges. They

involved gambling, loansharking, money laundering, drug dealing, and extortion.

2001
Carmine Persico appointed DeRoss as his new Acting Boss to replace his son Al Persico Jr.

February 2001
Judge Reena Raggi released DeRoss on a $4 million bond and restricted him to Staten Island.

Fall 2001
Unlike his with Al Persico Jr., DeRoss refused to make a plea deal due to the feds demand that he admit being a member of La Cosa Nostra. He was overheard in court, saying, "I'm not going to do it. I would if I could, but I'm not going to do it."

February 6, 2002
A jury found DeRoss not guilty of racketeering, money laundering, extortion, and conspiracy. They only convicted him of one charge of extorting money from a salad company.

2002
Carmine Persico appointed Joel Cacace as Acting Boss to replaced John DeRoss.

July 2003
Judge Reena Raggi sentenced DeRoss to 87 months. His term would have been shorter with a guilty plea, but he refused to admit being in the Mafia.

October 12, 2004
DeRoss pled guilty to one count of labor racketeering. He admitted using his union connections to provide a no-show job for a son of Joel Cacace. He faced four years in prison at sentencing.

October 14, 2004
The feds indict DeRoss and Persico Jr. for the murder of William Cutolo in aid of racketeering and witness tampering.

November 3, 2006
The judge declared a mistrial in the DeRoss and Persico murder case. The appearance of Cutolo's mistress with whom he had a child caused a lot of attention.

November 28, 2007
A jury found DeRoss and Persico Jr. guilty of the murder in aid of racketeering of William Cutolo as well as witness tampering with the Cutolo family. The jury found them not guilty of the attempted murder of William Campanella.

Witness testimony by Cutolo's widow and daughter greatly aided the prosecutor's case. Tapes made by Cutolo's son played an influential role as well. Several turncoats also testified for the feds.

February 27, 2009
Judge Joanne Sybert sentenced both DeRoss and Persico Jr. to life without parole.

May 3, 2011
The Second Circuit Court of Appeals confirmed the sentences of DeRoss and Persico Jr.

November 2019
DeRoss is doing his life sentence without parole at the Cumberland Federal Corrections Institution at Cumberland, Maryland. It is a medium level prison.

JOEL "JOE WAVERLY" CACACE

2002-2003
Acting Boss

December 21, 1976
Three men accosted Cacace as he was leaving his Waverly Florist shop in Brooklyn. They forced him into the back seat of their car, but Cacace shot the man sitting beside him and wounded the driver. The two hoods in the front opened up on Cacace, but when the vehicle crashed, they fled. The wounded mobster jumped into

the front seat and drove to the Coney Island NYPD station with the dead kidnapper still in the rear seat. Cacace recovered but had little to say to the police. Why the thugs were trying to kidnap Cacace remains unknown.

January 1987
Someone killed former police officer Carlo Antonio, an Associate of Cacace. Years later, the feds would accuse Cacace of being involved in this hit.

May 20, 1987
Administrative Judge George Aronwald was gunned down in a laundromat near his apartment. The killing was a huge mystery and a shock to his son, former prosecutor William Aronwald. It later turned out that he was the target, not his father. Hitmen Eddie and Vincent Carini and Frank Smith had picked the wrong Aronwald. The order for the murder had come from imprisoned Boss Carmine Persico.

The killing created a storm of publicity which aroused the ire of the other mob Bosses. Soon everyone was looking for who was behind the terrible mistake.

June 12, 1987
Police found the bodies of brothers Eddie and Vincent Carini in two separate vehicles. The feds later alleged that Cacace had ordered them killed to cover up his involvement in the Aronwald disaster. One of the alleged killers was Lucchese Associate Carmine Varriale.

September 3, 1987
Frank Smith gunned down Varriale and Frank Santora, allegedly on the orders of Cacace. Years later, he told the good guys that Cacace had ordered the hit on Varriale to revenge his killing of his friends, the Carini brothers. Frank Santora just happened to be with Varriale. To the feds, these killings were another attempt by Cacace to cover up his role in the death of George Aronwald.

Note:
When Smith rolled over in the fall of 2001, he explained that his father, Frank Sr. and his cousin Michael Cilone helped him with the killings of Varriale and Santora.

Note:
Frank Santora was related to Mafia Cop Louie Eppolito. Santora was the connection between killer cops Eppolito and Steve Caracappa and hood Burton Kaplan. Murderous Lucchese Underboss Antony "Gaspipe" Casso worked through Kaplan to get information from the crooked cops.
After Santora's death, Kaplan dealt directly with Eppolito and Caracappa.

March 2, 1988
Informer Greg Scarpa told the FBI that the leaders of the Family had recently promoted Cacace to Capo.

April 8, 1988
Scarpa reported that imprisoned Boss Carmine Persico had appointed Capo Vic Orena as his new Acting Boss. In turn, Cacace became the Acting Capo of Orena's crew.

May 1990
In yet another report, Greg Scarpa revealed that Persico had demoted Cacace from Capo. This demotion was one of the first indications that the Persicos feared Cacace's growing power and charisma.

October 6, 1991
The competing factions, Orena and Persico, met to try to avoid further conflict. Cacace was present with the Orena group.

January 29, 1992
Greg Scarpa and his crew opened fire on Cacace and ten other men in front of the Party Room Social Club in the Sheepshead section of Brooklyn.

February 26, 1992
The Scarpa crew made another attempt on Cacace on this date. They managed to wound him outside the Party Room Social Club in Brooklyn. Cacace was alone carrying dry cleaning when the

gunfire erupted. Although hit in the chest, Cacace returned fire at the men in the white station wagon. Greg Scarpa was the attacker firing a .22 rifle. An ambulance transported Cacace to Coney Island Hospital then to King's County Memorial. Although police found two empty holsters on Cacace, they couldn't find his weapons. Cacace slowly recovered from this latest hit attempt.

August 25, 1997

Shooters ambushed and killed police officer Ralph Dols outside his own home. This murder caused a great deal of publicity due to the fact Dols was off duty. Such events were rare. It wasn't long before the background of Dol's wife caused suspicions.

Her second ex-husband was Enrico "Eddie" Carini. Two hoods killed him for his involvement in the murder of George Aronwald back in 1987. In a surprising twist, Kim Kennaugh married Joel Cacace; the man feds figured had her ex-husband Eddie Carini murdered. A theory soon emerged that Cacace had ordered Dols killed due to the mobster feeling a cop marrying his former wife disrespected him. It would take years before this killing made its way into court.

Note:

More than a decade later, Kim Kennaugh revealed that she and Dols were not legally married even though they had gone through a church wedding. Joel Cacace, her third husband, had given her divorce papers to sign but never filed the papers.

2002

Carmine Persico appointed Cacace as Acting Boss to replace John DeRoss.

January 22, 2003

Police and federal agents arrested Cacace at his Deer Park, Long Island home. Strangely the cops let Cacace and some relatives enjoy breakfast before hauling him off to the FBI office. During this period, Cacace talked some to the federal agents. When asked if he was concerned that his neighbors might think he was involved in the Dols hit, Cacace replied: "I don't give a fuck."

January 23, 2003
The feds announced a 20 count indictment that included Cacace and 11 other hoods. They charged him with four murders, Carlo Antonino, George Aronwald, Carmine Variale, and Frank Santora. Also, the indictment identified Cacace as the Colombo Acting Boss.

February 6, 2003
A judge refused to release Cacace on bail. The presence of a loaded shotgun in his home plus witness testimony that he was the Acting Boss for the Colombos didn't help his case.

2003
Carmine Persico appointed Thomas Gioeli as Acting Boss to replace Cacace.

August 13, 2004
Cacace pled guilty to racketeering charges that included the killing of George Aronwald, conspiracy to murder Carmine Variale, and loansharking.

December 8, 2004
Judge Sterling Johnson Sr. formally sentenced Cacace to 20 years for his racketeering plea. He also suggested to the Bureau of Prisons that Cacace serve his time at the Supermax prison in Florence, Colorado.

In a victim impact statement, former prosecutor William Aronwald called Cacace a coward, a thug, and a hoodlum. Cacace sneered and chewed gum according to a New York Daily News article from the time.

2008
Joseph "Joey Caves" Competiello decided to become a cooperating witness. He had been a driver in the Ralph Dols murder. Competiello revealed the entire sordid story of that killing to the feds.

December 18, 2008
A federal indictment charged Cacace with racketeering, including the murder of police officer Ralph Dols.

The feds also accused Dino Calabro, Dino Saracino, and Thomas Gioeli of participation in the William Cutolo killing. There were other murder charges, as well.

March 25, 2010
Dino "Big Dino" Calabro rolled over and agreed to become a cooperating witness. The Acting Boss had inducted Calabro after the Cutolo hit. Later he promoted Calabro to Capo after the Dols murder.

November 26, 2013
A jury acquitted Joel Cacace of involvement in the murder of police officer Ralph Dols. Several cooperating witnesses testified, including Capo Dino Calabro. It appeared that the tribunal did not believe the former hitman.

January 1, 2015
Cacace's son, Joel "Jo Jo" Cacace Jr. died of a heart attack.

November 2019
The Bureau of Prisons presently has Cacace locked away at their Ashland, Kentucky facility. His projected release date is May 24, 2020.

THOMAS "TOMMY SHOTS" GIOELI

Acting Boss
2004-2008

Gioeli was born in 1952 and quickly took to the criminal life in his teens. At some point, he became associated with the crew of Victor Orena.

Late 1990's
Unconfirmed reports claim that Carmine Persico promoted Gioeli to Capo during this period.

March 27, 1992
Some persons ambushed Gioeli, and a chase ensued. He was shot in the stomach but survived.

2004
After Acting Boss, Joel Cacace took a plea deal, Gioeli took over as Acting Boss.

June 4, 2008
The feds arrested Thomas Gioeli and eight other Colombo men on a variety of charges, including the 1991 murder of Frank Marassa and the 1992 killings of John Minerva and Michael Imbregamo. (This was a superseding indictment meaning the prosecutor filed the original earlier but then added new charges as information became available.)

2008
Carmine Persico replaced Gioeli as his Acting Boss with a panel of three.

December 15, 2008
Defendant Joseph "Joey Caves" Competiello made a plea deal with the feds. He admitted to taking part in three murders and assorted other crimes.

December 16, 2008
The feds charged Gioeli with the additional murders of Richard Greaves (1992) and William Cutolo (1999). Turncoat Competiello had provided these details when he rolled over.

February 9, 2010
Gioeli suffered a minor stroke and spent a month in the hospital.

Spring 2009
Dino Calabro's wife signed an agreement with the feds. She scouted out Mrs. Gioeli's home, borrowed relevant photographs, provided a diagram for the officers, and did assorted other things. She later explained that she was trying to help her husband win a plea deal. Her undercover work did not become known until a court hearing in 2010.

October 13, 2009
During a court appearance, Gioeli's lawyer filed several complaints about Gioeli's incarceration. The mobster claimed he had broken his dentures, his unique mattress and shoes were lost when the

prison officials moved him into segregation, the food was terrible, and so on.

July 2010
The feds indicted Gioeli for the Ralph Dol's murder.

September 7, 2010
Magistrate Ramon Reyes told Gioeli to stop complaining about his prison conditions. A complaint about a watch set the magistrate off.

April 12, 2011
The Gioelli family canceled a deal made with the feds that permitted Gioeli to view his father's remains in the garage of the Federal Court House.

March 20, 2012
Former Bonanno Family Underboss Sal Vitale testified against Gioeli. At one point, Vitale explained that when Acting Boss Joel Cacace was feeling a lot of heat in the early 1990's Gioeli took over as Acting Boss. The turncoat confused a lot of people when he stated that Gioeli didn't want to take on the new responsibilities for he had a new bride. (This wasn't correct.)

March 22, 2012
Turncoat Capo Reynold Maragni testified about a 2007 incident where Gioeli reamed out an Associate who was pretending to be a formal member. The prosecutor also played a secret tape Maragnie had made with Colombo Soldier Vincent Manzo. The recording caught Manzo, claiming that Gioeli was involved in the murder of William Cutolo.

March 25, 2012
Turncoat Capo Dino "Big Dino" Calabro took the stand against Gioeli. He explained that the two men and their families were very close and socialized and traveled together.

Calabro claimed that Gioeli drove William Cutolo to his death at the Saracino home. "Big Dino" greeted Cutolo in the driveway and directed him into the house. Calabro then shot Cutolo in the back of the head.

The hoods placed Cutolo's jewelry in a pail, then added concrete to it. They dumped the container off some pier in Brooklyn. Cutolo was wrapped in garbage bags and driven to a grave in Farmingdale, LI. According to Calabro, Gioeli waited at a nearby Dunkin Donuts while he and others buried Cutolo. Calabro testified that the leaders inducted him into the Family in 2000, presumably as a reward for his Cutolo actions.

April 2, 2012

Turncoat Joseph Competiello testified against Gioeli. "Joey Caves" explained to the jury how he gunned down Joseph Miccio, who was driving his Jaguar. He went on to describe burying victim Carmine Gargano outside the Competiello auto chop shop. Later he moved the body to a grave he dug in Farmingdale, Long Island.

April 11, 2012

David Gorden testified about helping hog tie murder victim Richard Greaves, placing the body in garbage bags and burying him in an industrial park in Farmingdale, LI. He described how they used towels and bleach to clean up the basement of the Saracino home. Gordon went on to detail how he and the Saracinos replaced the floors and walls about one year after Calabro et al. murdered Cutolo in the house.

April 12, 2012

Turncoat Robert Ventriglia testified that he was forced to take part in the 1992 killing of John Minerva and Michael Imbregamo. He claimed to have been afraid of mobster Eric Curcio. Ventriglia stated that Anthony Colandra was the second shooter. At this date in time, Anthony was still denying taking part in the hit, but he rolled over later.

April 19, 2012

Sebastian "Sebby" Saracino was the brother of defendant Dino Saracino. In gruesome detail, "Sebby" described how Dino shot Associate Richard Greaves in the basement of the Saracino home. He went on to testify that hoods murdered Cutolo at the same residence. One detail he added was that someone ordered Dino to get rid of his prized Caddy after the Ralph Dols hit.

Sebastian's brother Dino was furious with this betrayal. If those foul deeds weren't enough, "Sebby" also confessed to helping bury the body of Carmine "The Gorilla" Gargano.

May 9, 2012
A jury convicted Gioeli and Dino Saracino of RICO conspiracy in the Colombo War. They were guilty of conspiring to kill opponents of their faction. The two hoods were found not guilty of the Cutolo, Dols, Minerva, Imbregamo, and Greaves murders.

May 12, 2012
Judge Kiyo Matsumoto accepted the plea deal of Anthony Calabro. He had admitted helping bury the bodies of Richard Greaves and William Cutolo. The judge sentenced him to 41 months.

May 23, 2013
Judge Brian Cogan postponed Gioeli's sentencing after the DEA informed him there was some evidence suggesting Gioeli wasn't involved in the 1991 murder conspiracy against Frank Marasa.

August 2013
Gioeli slipped in a puddle of water while going after an errant ping pong ball in prison. He later filed suit for his cracked knee cap.

March 19, 2014
Judge Brian Cogan sentenced Gioeli to 18 years and eight months for his RICO conspiracy convictions involving the planning of the murders of Frank Marasa and John Greaves

April 28, 2014
Judge Brian Cogan sentenced Dino Saracino to 50 years.

December 9, 2014
Judge Brian Cogan sentenced turncoat Joseph Competiello to a 12 year term for the five murders he confessed to.

November 13, 2017
Judge Brian Cogan sentenced turncoat Dino Calabro to 11 years on his RICO plea. He had already done nine years, so he had 24 months to finish. He had taken part in the killing of at least 11 men.

June 2018
Gioeli was in court over his lawsuit against the prison for his cracked knee cap.

November 29, 2018
Judge Kiyo Matsumoto found Gioeli 50% responsible for his knee injury. Any settlement he received would go to paying down his $360,000 restitution order from his March 2014 sentencing.

September 21, 2019
The feds were in court trying to confiscate Gioeli's $250,000 award for his knee injury. He had been paying $25 every three months towards his $360,000 restitution order.

WHAT NEXT?

In 2008 the feds arrested Thomas Gioeli, making it impossible for him to continue as Acting Boss. By this time, the number of men filling this slot seemed endless. A bug caught Ted Persico Jr. explaining that Carmine Persico decided that Acting Underboss Ben Castellazo would be his new stand-in.

CHAPTER TWENTY-FOUR

What's Going On?

RALPH DELEO

Street Boss
2008-2009

The feds jammed up Acting Boss Thomas Gioeli in 2008, and he won't be out of prison for a long time. It appears that Boss Carmine Persico appointed a three-person panel to run the Family at this point. Its membership was Ted Persico Jr., Acting Underboss Ben Castellazo, and Acting Consigliere Richie Fusco.

However, the evidence is not substantial on this theory. A tape exists, from 2008, in which Ted Persico Jr., was quoted as saying Ben Castellazo was the new Acting Boss. To add more confusion to the mix, a member from far away Boston suddenly appeared as the "Street Boss."

Ralph DeLeo was a low-level hood from the Boston area. During his many travels, he wound up in Ohio and got involved in a dispute between two medical doctors. According to DeLeo's later testimony, he was supposed to kidnap one doctor but lost his cool and killed the man. Convicted of the crime, DeLeo rolled over and testified against the second doctor. As a reward, he received a 15-life sentence and a promise that he would serve his time in federal prison.

In December of 1986, DeLeo shared a cell with Alphonse Persico Jr., in prison in Bastrop, Texas. From later events, it's clear that the fact DeLeo once was a cooperating witness never came up. Young Persico would have been well served to ask around about his cellmate.

By 1997 DeLeo was released from prison and returned to Boston. Three years later, in a puzzling move, Al Persico Jr. received permission to have DeLeo inducted into the Colombo Family. After the ceremony, DeLeo returned to the Boston area and continued his street crimes of loansharking, drug dealing, and the like. His membership in the Colombo Family prevented the New England members from moving in on his rackets.

When Gioeli could no longer function as Acting Boss in 2008, young Persico wrangled the promotion of his old cellmate to the position of "Street Boss." That title has always lead to confusion. Was the hood the Acting Boss, or was he just the top Capo who was still on the street? In this case, it looks like DeLeo was the latter. Whatever DeLeo was, he made a mess of it.

The scrounging around of his motley crew attempting to piece together drug deals caught the attention of the feds. In short order, they had bugged DeLeo's cell phone and were privy to just about everything he did. Included in his actions was his presence at a February 2009 Colombo induction ceremony.

In December of 2009, the feds rolled up DeLeo and his crew. Whatever role he played in the Colombo Family was over, for now, his previous cooperation with the good guys was public news. Three years later, DeLeo pleaded out, and late in the year, the judge sentenced DeLeo to 235 months. The Bureau of Prison projects his release date for October 2, 2025.

ANDY "MUSH" RUSSO

Acting Boss
2009-2011

Unbelievable as it may sound, Andy Russo agreed to take the Acting Boss hot seat one again in 2009. On June 20, 2011, he and about 100 other hoods were rounded up in a much-championed strike by the good guys. I outlined his entire profile and the outcome of this case in Chapter 21.

RICHARD "NERVES" FUSCO

Consigliere
2008-2011

Fusco was a long time Colombo Family member who periodically popped into the news due to some big event beyond his control. Back in the 1970s, he was involved in a famous bankruptcy/skimming scam at the Westchester Theater in Tarrytown, New York. These events became well known due to the presence of the infamous Los Angeles mobster Jimmy "The Weasel" Fratianno. Throw in Frank Sinatra and Dean Martin, and no media outlet could pass up on the story.

The original plan was pretty simple. The hoods would build a dinner theater on the site of an old landfill then attract top-flight entertainment. During the process, they'd skim as much money out of the joint as possible and live happily ever after. Oops!

Raising money through a stock sale seemed like a good idea, on paper at least. The problem was they didn't sell enough stock to meet their quota. That meant the principals would have to return all the investors' money. That wasn't going to work for most of it was already spent.

The new illegal idea was to have front men buy blocks of stock to meet the quota. The leading investors would pay back these people with money skimmed from the joint. This process meant that desperate skimming was required to keep up with the payments to heavy hitters like Boss Carlo Gambino. This plan worked if a Frank Sinatra show packed the theater, but many of the other performers drew poorly. The place was the Titanic waiting to sink.

By the late 1970s, the authorities had filed fraud charges against a number of the major players in the fiasco. A jury convicted many of the accused, including Richie Fusco. In the end, a judge sentenced Fusco to two and a half years. At that time, the young Fusco could do that bit standing on his head as the veteran prisoners used to say.

As far as the public was concerned, Fusco laid low until a 1993 indictment. A grand jury hit Fusco and several other Colombo hoods on counts related to the Colombo war. The indictment charged Fusco with: racketeering, racketeering conspiracy, conspiracy to murder, loansharking conspiracy, using and carrying a firearm in connection to the above-listed crimes, and illegal possession of a firearm and ammunition by a felon. Whew! If a jury convicted Fusco on all charges, he was facing life.

At the start of the Colombo members' trial, the judge ruled that Fusco's health was too fragile for him to continue. In May of 1994, the prosecutor and Fusco arranged that Fusco would plead to a racketeering conspiracy charge in return for a 14-year sentence. Meanwhile, the Bureau of Prison's had Fusco housed in several federal prison medical facilities during this period.

Meanwhile, all the alleged misdeeds of informer Greg Scarpa had become public along with allegations that an FBI agent had assisted Scarpa in his crimes. Several defendants and convicted mobsters sought to have charges dropped, or new trials ordered based on these Scarpa allegations. Fusco was no different.

There was no question that Fusco was very ill. While in prison, he underwent a triple bypass, kidney cancer surgery, and suffered from severe hypertension. With these legitimate ills, Fusco appealed to the court to throw out his plea agreement and his sentence. On January 15, 1999, the Second Circuit Court of Appeals rejected Fusco's arguments. He would have to do the 14 years.

Once released from prison, Fusco did not move south to spend the last years of his life in peace. In 2008 Carmine Persico appointed Fusco as the new Consigliere of the Family. The guy could hardly walk. The law came knocking on his door once again on January 20, 2011. The feds rounded up over 100 hoods in a massive sweep that included Fusco. It appeared he would end his days behind bars.

To the surprise of no one, Fusco played the health card once again. However, this time, the list of ailments had grown to include prostate cancer, three heart attacks, depression, and other illnesses. On September 29, 2011, Judge Kiyo Matsumoto accepted Fusco's plea to extortion. Two months later, Judge Matsumoto sentenced the old mobster to four months in a prison hospital. Fusco completed his time, and prison authorities released him on June 15, 2013. He finally died on December 19, 2013.

TOMMY FARESE

Consigliere
2011-2012

Richie Fusco was jammed up on legal problems, so Acting Boss Andy Russo appointed Florida Capo Tommy Farese as the new Acting Consigliere in 2011. The man had quite a criminal pedigree. Besides, he was married to a daughter of the late Alphonse Persico, brother of Carmine.

In the 1960s, Farese had an extensive criminal record, but it wasn't until 1973 that he faced severe prison time. A judge sentenced the young hood to ten years for the interstate transportation of forged and fraudulently made securities.

Farese hadn't wasted time while in lockup. He met veteran Colombo loanshark Nicholas "Jiggs" Forlano, and the two began a long and close friendship. The parole authorities released Forlano in 1974 and also freed Farese, although he had only finished ten months of his ten-year sentence.

Within a few years of his release, Farese controlled two restaurants, a Cayman Island bank, three ocean-going freighters, and assorted other enterprises. This new-found wealth and his continuing friendship with Forlano much interested the good guys. It wasn't long before Farese was the target of a multi-agency task force. To them, drugs were the only reasonable explanation for Farese's wealth.

Due to the money, Farese was bringing into the Family coffers, it was not a massive surprise that Carmine Persico approved the induction of Farese in 1978. The fact that he was Alphonse Persico's son-in-law didn't hurt either.

On August 21, 1978, the feds hammered Farese and others with an indictment. They charged Farese with racketeering and drug dealing. The RICO charge alleged he was carrying on drug dealing on behalf of the Colombo Family criminal enterprise. A jury found Farese guilty on December 19, 1980, of one count of racketeering and four counts of marijuana smuggling. The judge hit Farese with a 24-year sentence in March of 1981, along with six years of special parole plus a $115,000 fine. It looked like Farese was finished. Nope!

Farese filed a series of appeals against his sentences but to no avail. On July 21, 1987, the Sixth Circuit Court of Appeals affirmed the original District Court sentence. However, despite his extensive record, the parole board freed Farese in 1994 after he completed 14 1/2 years. He didn't retire to his lawn chair as most intelligent people would have.

Surprisingly, Farese convinced the feds to invest nearly $200,000 in a halfway house he controlled. Other than these bare-bone facts, I have been unable to find the whole story behind this incredible endeavor.

The feds suckered Farese again in the mid-1990s. They had learned that the veteran mobster was willing to launder money through a number of his legitimate holdings. Using agents posing as drug dealers, they conned Farese into washing some of their supposed ill-gotten wealth. On January 16, 1996, the feds indicted Farese on money laundering charges.

Two years later, Farese hammered out a deal with the prosecutor. He would plead to a RICO conspiracy charge involving money laundering. Farese claimed he took a plea so the feds would drop charges against his wife. At sentencing, Farese was unhappy with the six-year term the judge decreed. On April 6, 2001, the Eleventh Circuit Court of Appeals overturned the sentence and ordered a rehearing by the district court.

2005 was a good year for Farese. The parole board released him from prison, and a jury awarded him $13 million in a civil suit over ownership of one of his strip clubs. Unfortunately for Farese, the 11 Circuit Court of Appeals overturned that judgment in 2009.

The feds were pleased to indict new Consigliere Tommy Farese in January of 2012 for money laundering. They had once again stung Farese by using turncoat Capo Ralph Maragni against him. Maragni wore a unique watch that recorded conversations. Farese never suspected he was being set up.

On March 20, 2012, Magistrate Judge Joan M Azrack released Farese on a $2.5 million bond. The Federal Bureau of Prisons released Farese on September 9, 2012. That information seems to indicate that the parole board had Farese imprisoned for a violation, although I cannot find evidence to confirm that theory.

Farese lucked out on November 30, 2012. A jury found him not guilty of money laundering, and Judge Carol Amon ordered his release. The feds didn't use turncoat Capo Ralph Maragni as a prosecution witness as expected. A previous hearing demonstrated that Maragni continued to engage in criminal activities after his arrest, plus he was selective in his use of the watch recording device.

As of this writing, November 2019, it is unclear whether Farese has gone straight or returned to his former criminal life.

KILLING JOEY SCOPO

October 20, 1993

Joey Scopo was a son of Ralph Scopo, a key man in the Commission's Concrete Club racket. Joey was briefly vice president of Local 6A of the Cement and Concrete Workers, but the feds threw him and his brother out in one of their pushes against mob influence in unions.

In the fall of 1990, Acting Boss Vic Orena promoted Scopo to Underboss after the feds jammed Ben Aloi up in the famous Windows case. When the Orena faction moved away from the Persico orbit, Scopo remained with Orena. In hindsight, it was a fatal mistake.

As we outlined in a previous chapter, the Colombo War came to a close with multiple arrests of many of the major combatants. The net result was that the Persico faction controlled the Family. Scopo was vulnerable.

On August 18, 1993, Ted Persico Jr. received a pass to attend the wake of his grandmother. Despite being accompanied by guards, Persico was able to order a hit on Scopo right under their noses. A few months later, his crew carried out his command.

Michael Persico directed the hit team to an Associate nicknamed "Smitty" who provided a silenced Mac 10 and two pistols. The crew had a stolen Buick sedan, which they used as the hit car. Capo Anthony Russo drove that vehicle with Associate John Sparacino riding in the back with the machine gun. Associates Eric Curcio and Frank Guerra drove two crash cars. They set up near Joey Scopo's home and waited for him to appear.

When Scopo arrived, he was in the passenger seat with a driver and another person in the back. Russo pulled up just in front of the vehicle, and Sparacino jumped out and unloaded the Mac 10 into Scopo's car. Meanwhile, John Pappa had exited the front door and ended up behind a tree stunned that Russo and Sparacino had taken off without him.

Scopo's two passengers fled, but he confronted Pappa. Unarmed Scopo was helpless but defiant. Pappa walked over and emptied his gun into the forty-something gangster. Not surprisingly, Scopo died from all the gunshots.

Unbelievably Pappa, Sparacino, and Curcio talked continuously about their evil deed. It wasn't long before Pappa decided to kill Sparacino for bragging that he was the leading player in the hit. A Pappa buddy, Calvin Hennigar, lured Sparacino to his home and killed him with a shot to the back of the head (August 15, 1994). When Pappa arrived, he went nuts. He badly mutilated the corpse, then the killers put the body in a car, drove it to some location, and set it on fire.

Next up was Curcio. Pappa went to Curcio's business, walked in, and killed him (October 4, 1994.) Then, as was his usual practice, Pappa bragged about this hit as well. To make this sordid tale even more unbelievable, the good guys arrested Pappa at a wedding rehearsal for Sparacino's brother Salvatore. There was a wild chase through the church before Pappa surrendered. He was going to be the best man! The Sparacinos didn't know he had killed Joseph.

To further demonstrate what a weird life these people led, Sparacino's father had been gunned down in a bar back in 1992. At the time, the attackers wounded future victim John Sparacino, in the chest. That family didn't seem to get the message that this life was something to avoid like the plague.

JOHN PAPPA

The chickens came home to roost for Pappa on May 14, 1999. A jury found him guilty of racketeering. The murder counts included that of Scopo and three others. Also, the panel said he was guilty of drug dealing. Several co-operating witnesses sealed his fate. Joseph Iborti told the court how Pappa phoned him after killing Curcio and enthusiastically gave all the details. Ronald "Messy Marvin" Moran related how Pappa described shooting Scopo with a .38 pistol. Accomplice Hennigar went down on one murder and some drug charges. Pappa will spend the rest of his life in prison.

FRANK GUERRA

The feds charged Associate Frank Guerra with the murders of Scopo and another man. However, at trial, the jury acquitted Guerra of the two killings and extortion but found him guilty of selling some of his prescription drugs (July 11, 2012.) A year later, the judge sentenced Guerra to a stiff 14-year term for drug sales.

MICHAEL PERSICO

On June 8, 2012, Judge Sandra Townes approved a plea deal worked out between Michael Persico and the prosecutor. The feds dropped racketeering and murder charges after Persico agreed to plead guilty to a single extortion charge. It was a great deal. But, at sentencing, the judge took into account the evidence the feds had on the five other charges and decided it was strong enough to prove Persico's guilt. She then hit him with a five-year term. His projected release date is in November 2020.

TED PERSICO, JR.

Ted Persico also took a plea deal. He admitted conspiring in the murder of Joey Scopo. On May 29, 2014, Judge Townes sentenced Ted Jr. to 12 years. His projected release date is May 29, 2020. (The prison authorities credited him for time served.)

THE FUTURE

If veteran mobster Andy Russo has once again taken the reigns of the Colombo Family, that will not be the long term solution. He will be in his mid-eighties in 2020. The future belongs elsewhere.

Will Ted Persico Jr. have had enough of Mafia life when he is released? Keep in mind that he will be on parole, which will make communicating with underlings very difficult.

For those who want to keep up to date on the Colombo leadership, your best bet is to follow www.ganglandnews.com, the website of noted organized crime expert Jerry Capeci.

Appendix A

Colombo Family Membership 1962

FBI informant NY T-4 provided the following details on November 20, 1962. Greg Scarpa was the informant. His knowledge of the Family was extensive but not error-free.

The Capos had voted Joseph Magliocco as their new Boss after the death of Joe Profaci in June of 1962. However, the Commission never approved Magliocco and his administration. They deposed him in the fall of 1963.

Abbatemarco, Anthony	
Abbatemarco, Frank	Dead
Aloi, Sebastian	
Aloi, Vincent	
Amendola, Anthony	
Augello, Anthony	
Badalamenti, Sam	Capo
Bonasera, Anthony	
Botta, Nicholas	
Brancato, Joseph	

Buzzo, Sally	
Cardello, Danny	
Cardello, James	
Cardello, Joey	
Cardello, Mickey	
Carlino, Leo	
Carpenteri, Nicholas	
Catrone, John	Believe it to be Cutrone
Cerillo, Larry	
Colombo, Joe	Capo
D'Alessandro, Christopher	
D'Ambrosie, Salvatore	
De Filippo, Freddie	
De Stefano, Vincent	
DeLucia, Fred	
DiBella, Thomas	Capo
Fanale, William	
Ferigno, Bartolo	
Ferrara, Larry	
Fontana, Harry	Capo
Forlano, Nicholas	
Franzese, John	Capo
Fusco, Dick	
Gagliardi, Frank	
Gallo, Albert	Incorrect, not made
Gallo, Joey	
Gallo, Lawrence	
Genise, Eugene	
Gentile, Joseph	
Giamarino, Joseph	
Giorelli, Joseph	Dead
Guariglia, John	
Guariglia, Patsy	
Guariglia, Salvatore	
Gugliaro, Vincent	
Iacovelli, Joseph	
Illiano, Frank	Incorrect, not made

Imperiale, Salvatore	
Italiano, Stephen	
La Padura, Joseph	
La Ponzina, Anthony	
La Ponzina, Ernie	
La Ponzina, Ralph	
Leone, Joseph	
Licari, Joseph	
Liquori, Vincent	
Little Toddo	
Livoti, Joseph	
Lo Cicero, Benny	
Lo Cicero, Charles	
Lo Cicero, Charles Jr.	Proposed
Lo Cicero, Frank	
Lombardino, Salvatore	
Madeleone, Joseph	
Magliocco, Ambrose	Capo
Magliocco, Anthony	
Magliocco, Joseph	Boss
Maione, Albert	
Manelli, Vincent	
Mangano, Vincent	
Maniscalco, Abby	
Mansaselma, Sally	
Misuraca, John	Underboss
Misuraca, John	
Muce, Vincenzo	
Musameci, Joseph	
Mussachio, Frank	
Mussachio, Sally	
Nussachio, Rosario	
Oddo, John	Capo
Panarella, Charles	
Peraino, Anthony	
Peritore, Salvatore	
Profaci, Frank	

Profaci, Salvatore, Jr.	
Profaci, Sam	
Ricciardi, Anthony	
Rondosto, Joe	
Russo, Tony	
Russo, Vincent	
San Antonio, Freddie	
Santoro, Modesto	
Saponaro, John	
Saponaro, Joseph	
Scarpa, Greg	
Scarpa, Sal	
Scialo, Dominick	
Sciana, Anthony	
Sciana, Jimmy	
Scimone, John	
Serrentino, Nickolini	Capo
Simone,?	Capo
Susino, Carmelo	
Tagliagambi, Mario	
Tipa, Joseph	
Traina, Joe	
Tropiano, George	
Tropiano, Ralph	
Unknown	Capo in NJ
Ursino, Dominick	
Vitacco, Joseph	
Vitale, Mike	

Appendix B

Gallo Crew
1962

This crew was always in flux. There were only three formal Colombo Family members in 1962. The list contains the names of the "regulars" who were usually around President Street.

Bongiovi, Robert "Bobby Darrow"	
Abbatemarco, Anthony "Abby"	
Balsamo, Salvatore, "Tough Sally"	
Basciano, Gennaro "Chitoz"	
Bernardo, Tony	
Bianco, Nicky	
Cardiello, Joe "Bats"	
Carna, Joseph "Little Lollipop"	
Carna, Larry "Big Lollipop"	
Cutrone, John "Mooney"	Colombo soldier
D'Antuano, Joseph "Smokey"	
Dello, Leonard "Lenny Dell"	
Diapoulos, Pete "Pete the Greek"	

DiCarlo, Tony	
DiMatteo, Ricky	
Gallo, Al "Blast"	
Gallo, Joey "Crazy Joey"	Colombo soldier
Gallo, Larry	Colombo soldier
Garguilo, Anthony "Tony"	
Gioelli, Joe "Joe Jelly"	
Hubella, Louie "The Syrian"	
Illiano, Armando "The Dwarf"	
Illiano, Frank "Punchy"	
Lusterino, John "Tarzan"	
Magnasco, Joe	Killed Oct 1961
Mangiamelli, Salvatore "Sally Boy"	
Mariani, Louie "Cadillac"	
Moreli, Marco	
Muscio, Roy "Roy Roy"	
Musemeci, Joseph "Cockeyed Butch"	
Parfumi, Angelo	
Regina, Vincent "Chico"	
Serratino, Al	
Waffa, Ali	
Zahralbam, Sammy "The Syrian"	

Appendix C

Author Charles Brandt Gets Conned by the Irishman

Charles Brandt's bestselling book, *I Heard You Paint Houses*, is the basis for Martin Scorsese's acclaimed film *The Irishman*. Brandt conducted many interviews with long-time Teamster Frank Sheeran, who claimed he killed Jimmy Hoffa. Among many other crimes that Sheeran took ownership of was the 1972 murder of notorious Mafioso Joseph "Crazy Joe" Gallo. Sheeran lied to Brandt about this event, which brings all his other statements into question.

Most experts agree that the Colombo Family put out a contract on Joey Gallo. Sheeran's story was that he was ordered to carry out the hit after running into Gallo at the Copacabana night club in the early hours of April 7, 1972. According to Sheeran, someone told him that Gallo would be in Umbertos restaurant and gave him a seating plan of the joint. These latter two points are outright lies.

On that fateful night, Gallo was accompanied to the restaurant by his new wife, Sina Essary, her young daughter Lisa, Gallo's recently widowed sister Carmella Fiorello, Associate Peter "Pete the Greek" Diapoulos, and his date Edith Russo. After the shooting, Sina Gallo and Carmella explained to the police and FBI that they had initially planned to go to Luna's restaurant but found it closed. They then accidentally came across Umbertos and decided to go in to eat. (April 10, NY FBI report to the Director)

Peter Diapoulos later confirmed this version in his book *The Sixth Family* on page 143. After seeing a show at the Copacabana, Greek wished to call it a night but, "he (Gallo) …wanted to go to Su Lings. It was closed. Then he decided on Luna's….but it was shut and dark when we drove up." Diapoulos then explained how they turned a corner and came upon the still open Umbertos. The Gallo party went in much to their later regret. They ended up there by chance. The versions of Carmella, Sina, and Diapoulos are in accord. There was no way Sheeran would know beforehand they would be in Umbertos, let alone have a seating plan of the place.

Brandt either didn't check the FBI files on the shooting or chose to ignore them. Instead, he believed Sheeran's version. This error would lead him into more mistakes.

A NY FBI communique sent to FBI Director Hoover at 10:10 AM April 7/72, includes Gallo's sister's description of the shooter to the NYPD. "Lone assailant described by sister as white, male, five feet seven inches, Italian, age early forties."

According to an April 12/72 FBI report, "top echelon informants…the participants in the gang killing of Joey Gallo were Carmine DiBiase, also known as Sonny Pinto and his close Associate (Phil Gambino) …"

An April 13/72 FBI summary contains this information, "NYPD has a witness (Carmella Gallo) who stated photo of (the brother) of Vincent Aloi, Acting Boss, Colombo Family, resembles individual who killed Gallo. It is noted that the photo of Carmine DiBiase closely resembles photo of (Benny Aloi)…." Carmella has picked the wrong guy, but this person looks like Italian and NOT Irishman Sheeran.

Peter Diapoulos recognized DiBiase as the lead shooter. On page 144 of *The Sixth Family*, the Greek states, "Just then, at the side door, I saw Sonny Pinto. ….Sonny firing shots right for our faces." Diapoulos knew DiBiase and recognized him immediately. This person was NOT Frank Sheeran shooting.

Diapoulos goes on to describe how he saw the three gunmen fleeing, "I made Sonny Pinto and two other guys (they were fleeing at this point). I had the piece (gun) out and threw the bolt, a shell flipping out ….I emptied and had nothing left." Sheeran makes NO mention of being shot at as he fled.

Another direct participant in the shooting was Colombo Associate Joseph Luparelli. Not long after the Gallo hit, Luparelli fled to Los Angeles, fearing for his life. He turned himself into the Santa Anna FBI office. An April 18/72 FBI report contained the whole story.

"On early morning April six or April seven seventy-two he (Luparelli) observed Joey Gallo and (Diapoulos) entering Umberto's restaurant… (Luparelli) contacted Carmine Di Biasee and (Phil Fungy Gambino). (Luparelli) and (Fungy) returned to Umbertos restaurant in (Luparelli's) car while Di Biase arrived in his own car with two unknown subjects. Di Biase, accompanied by the two unknown subjects entered Umbertos where Di Biase shot and killed Gallo."

According to an April 13/72 FBI report, "..witnesses reported a tan or brown color vehicle speeding from the scene." It goes on to say that the Motor Vehicle Bureau reported that DiBiase, "had tags…for use on a one nine seven one Pontiac sedan, color brown." As Luparelli said, DiBiase drove his vehicle during the Gallo hit.

Two direct participants in the shooting were familiar with DiBiase and said he was the lead gunman in the Gallo hit. Gallo's sister didn't know DiBiase but described him to a "t" and picked out a picture of another hood that looked remarkably like that of Di Biase. What does Brandt have in terms of eyewitnesses besides Sheeran?

After *I Heard You Paint Houses* was released (2004) and criticisms of the Gallo account began, a female involved with the media happened to be talking to an associate about Brandt's book. She stated that she was present at the Gallo hit. The woman identified a picture of Sheeran as the man she saw that night. Brandt jumped all over this "collaboration" and used it to defend Sheeran's account. The eye witness accounts above, and the physical evidence contradicts her story.

We are fortunate that the NYPD did a thorough examination of the shooting scene. I included an enlarged, simplified print to ease your understanding of the events plus the original NYPD copy.

The side door from which Diapoulos, Luparelli, and Carmella Gallo stated the shots came from is in the lower left of the diagram. Just inside the door is an unfired bullet from Diapoulos' .25 Titan semi-automatic pistol. (Labelled S10) That bullet confirms Diapoulos' account of firing at the fleeing three hitmen. Nearby is a .32 round (S8). This bullet is the same caliber slugs that killed Gallo. The presumption is that DiBiase was firing this gun for his Associates, all acknowledged that DiBiase killed Gallo plus Diapoulos stated DiBiase was the first one who came in shooting. It makes sense that this slug ended up in that location, for that is where Gallo and Diapoulos and the others were sitting.

Along the right side of the diagram is the bar. You can see the slugs the NYPD located along there. The three men were shooting as Gallo fled towards the front door at the top of the diagram. Near the front door is yet another .32 slug fired at Gallo just as he reached the exit.

The ballistic evidence shows that the participants fired four weapons, a .32, a Smith and Wesson .38, a Colt .38, and Diapoulos' .25 Titan. Sheeran claimed he used two weapons. He also boasted that he was a precision shot. As you can see from the spray of bullets along the counter, it's clear the shooters were anything but proficient. Then there is the final blow to Brandt. Sheeran said he fired at Gallo from the counter/bar. Oops—all the bullets were going the other way!

It's unreal to me that Brandt's female witness didn't describe in great detail all the slugs roaring across the restaurant. She must have accepted Sheeran's account of deliberately wounding Diapoulos from the bar then killing Gallo after following him out into the street. (NONE of the witnesses reported anyone shooting at Gallo out in the street)

The eyewitness identification of DiBiase by Diapoulos and Luparelli is rock solid. Carmella fingered a picture of an Italian guy who looked remarkably like DiBiase as the lead shooter. None of the three identified anyone even remotely resembling Sheeran. Their accounts are backed up by irrefutable crime scene evidence. The bottom line is that Sheeran was not there, which means he conned Brandt about the Gallo killing. This fact alone severely weakens Sheeran's other claims, for Brandt accepted that Sheeran was telling the truth about everything since he was dying and wanted to make peace. Sheeran went to his grave a liar. Brandt gained fame and financial reward, but mob followers will remember him as the naive writer who was conned by a veteran hood.

Appendix D

A shooting diagram of the Joey Gallo killing on April 9, 1972, at Umbertos Clam House in Little Italy in Manhattan.

The three shooters entered the restaurant by the side door on the lower left. They wounded Peter Diapoulos and hit Joey Gallo three times as he fled toward the front door. Gallo made it to Hester Street, where he collapsed.

The location of the bullets along the bar indicates the shooters were firing at Gallo as he fled. It also pins down their position near the side door.

Also, by the side door was a .25 cartridge that Diapoulos discharged from his Titan pistol before firing at the fleeing trio.

The diagram proves that Frank Sheeran's claim that he initially fired at the Gallo party from the bar is a lie.

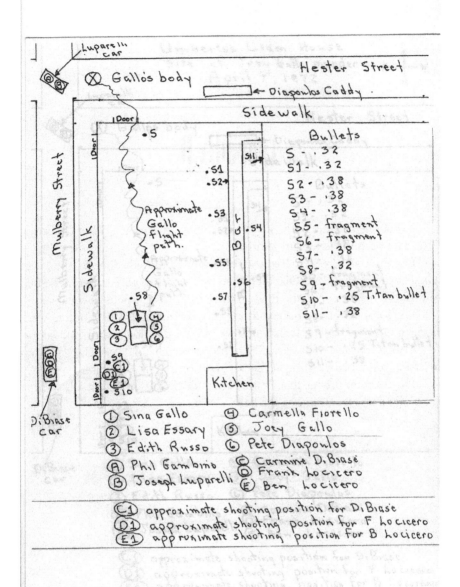

Luparelli car

⊗ Gallo's body

Hester Street

◻ ← Diapoulos Caddy

Sidewalk

Door

•S

Bullets

S - .32
S1 - .32
S2 - .38
S3 - .38
S4 - .38
S5 - fragment
S6 - fragment
S7 - .38
S8 - .32
S9 - fragment
S10 - .25 Titan bullet
S11 - .38

Door

Mulberry Street

Sidewalk

Approximate Gallo flight path.

•S1
•S2→
•S3
•S4
•S5
•S6
•S7
•S8

S11

Bar

①②③ ④⑤⑥

•S9
Ⓒ1
Ⓓ1
Ⓔ1
•S10

Door

Kitchen

DiBiase car

① Sina Gallo   ④ Carmella Fiorello
② Lisa Essary   ⑤ Joey Gallo
③ Edith Russo   ⑥ Pete Diapoulos
Ⓐ Phil Gambino   Ⓒ Carmine DiBiase
Ⓑ Joseph Luparelli   Ⓓ Frank Locicero
                      Ⓔ Ben Locicero

Ⓒ1 approximate shooting position for DiBiase
Ⓓ1 approximate shooting position for F Locicero
Ⓔ1 approximate shooting position for B Locicero

224

Appendix E

This picture is the NYPD shooting diagram from the Joey Gallo murder. It is too small to read, so I enlarged and added to it on the chart in Appendix D. I've included the original to demonstrate I didn't merely make up my document.

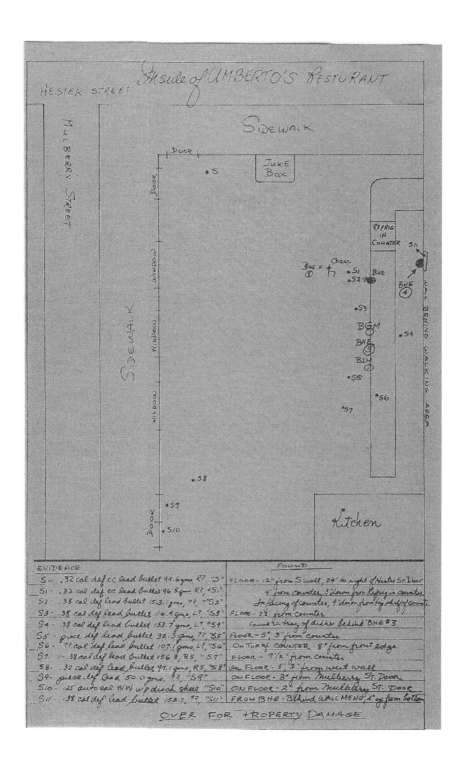

Appendix F

Colombo Family Leaders 1968 (FBI)

III. LEADERSHIP
COLOMBO "FAMILY" (New York City)

LEADERSHIP

      The leadership of the COLOMBO "family" remains the same.

JOSEPH COLOMBO	"Boss"
SALVATORE MINEO	"Underboss"
BENEDETTO D'ALESSANDRO	"Consiglieri"
VINCENT ALOI	"Capodecina"
SIMONE ANDOLINO	"Capodecina"
HARRY FONTANA	"Capodecina"
NICHOLAS FORLANO	"Capodecina"
JOHN FRANZESE	"Capodecina"
FRANK RICHARD FUSCO	"Capodecina"
JOHN MISURACA	"Capodecina"
SALVATORE MUSACCHIO	"Capodecina"
JOHN ODDO	"Capodecina"
CARMINE PERSICO, Jr.	"Capodecina"
NICHOLINE SORRENTINO	"Capodecina"
JOSEPH YACCOVELLI	"Capodecina"

- 20 -

Appendix G

July 27, 1964
FBI bug in the office of Magaddino's funeral home in Niagara Falls, NY.

The illegal FBI bug overheard Buffalo Boss Stefano Magaddino discussing the 1963 leadership problem in the Colombo Family. AL T-1 is the bug, but the report tries to make it look as if a person has overheard the conversation.

The relevant parts are near the bottom. Magaddino is relating that he told Magliocco not to try and deny attempting to kill "them." The "them" is Carlo Gambino and Tommy Lucchese. Magliocco admitted the plot.

AL T-1 further advised that in this conversation with DE STEFANO, MAGADDINO was overheard to state he had been on the table for seven years (possibly indicating he was a "commission" member). AL T-1 further advised FALCONE was overheard to participate in this conversation and was heard to address MAGADDINO as "compare", telling MAGADDINO he had to congratulate him, FALCONE, as they had stated that he, FALCONE, had 87 men in Utica. AL T-1 advised that MAGADDINO, in reply to this comment of FALCONE, stated that they had first said that "we," apparently referring to the family in Buffalo, New York, had 22 and now have 125.

AL T-1 then advised that MAGADDINO and FALCONE then held a conversation pertaining to the MAGLIOCCO family and that in this conversation, MAGADDINO indicated he had visited New York City to handle the "situation" in the "MAGLIOCCO family". AL T-1 stated that MAGADDINO mentioned CARLO GAMBINO had told him to let MAGLIOCCO remain as he was at the present time.

AL T-1 then advised he overheard MAGADDINO tell FALCONE that MAGLIOCCO was trying to use FALCONE. AL T-1 stated that he heard FALCONE tell MAGADDINO not to worry, indicating MAGLIOCCO would not use him.

AL T-1 then advised that MAGADDINO continued his discussion with FALCONE, telling FALCONE he had to wait many days in New York City for JOHN BURNS and BONANNO to show up. AL T-1 stated he overheard MAGADDINO tell FALCONE there were many "stool pidgeons" in the MAGLIOCCO family.

AL T-1 further advised he overheard MAGADDINO tell FALCONE that MAGLIOCCO could not deny giving the orders for the "shooting" because he, MAGADDINO, had several persons present and available who could readily attest to the fact that MAGLIOCCO had issued "these orders". AL T-1 then advised MAGADDINO indicated that MAGLIOCCO had admitted to him, MAGADDINO, that he, MAGLIOCCO, had condemned them to death. (This could refer to the PROFACI - GALLO Gang killings.)

-3-

Appendix H

July 27, 1964
FBI summary of conversations overheard by an FBI bug in the office of Magaddino's funeral home office in Niagara Falls, NY.

Buffalo Boss Stefano Magaddino is relating to underlings how he castigated Joseph Magliocco telling him that the Commission never approved his election as Boss of the Colombo Family.

Magaddino also states that they were going to force Magliocco to pay $100,000 for the Commission investigation costs but settled on $43,000.

In another segment, Magaddino revealed that Joe Bonanno wanted to put his son Bill on top of the Los Angeles Family. Whether that was a gross exaggeration by Magaddino or the truth, I have not been able to determine.

the meeting, MAGADDINO denounced MAGLIOCCO as a "dishonorable disgrace" and that he should know that a person who makes a mistake is going to die.

MAGADDINO then proceeded to castigate MAGLIOCCO, pointing out that the "Commission" has never recognized him as a "Boss" and as far as MAGADDINO is concerned MAGLIOCCO is a "Nobody." He informed MAGLIOCCO that from this time on he, MAGLIOCCO, is nothing, the boss of nothing, and that MAGLIOCCO should understand this.

BU T-1 advised that MAGADDINO informed MAGLIOCCO that he owes $100,000 to the "Commission," however, a figure of $43,000 was agreed upon as the amount to be paid. This debt represents the cost of airplane trips and other travel expenses. MAGADDINO further charged MAGLIOCCO with becoming a millionaire and not giving anything to those who have been risking their lives for him during the past three years. After, MAGLIOCCO came up and paid $10,000 on this debt. The "Commission" decided that the GALLO-PROFACI feud should be settled peacefully. Those involved in this fight were ordered to meet in one place together with or without the GALLOs to settle this dispute. At the meeting they should themselves select the person they want to be their "reppresentante." MAGADDINO pointed out that the "Commission" would not involve itself with the selection of this leader.

According to BU T-1, this peaceful handling of the trouble in New York City would be made without any killing anyone, however, MAGADDINO seems to think JOSEPH BONANNO prefers to settle such affairs as they did in the old days.

BU T-1 stated that another matter was considered by the "Commission" at these meetings. BU T-1 reported that JOSEPH BONANNO of Phoenix, Arizona had told the "Commission" that his son was to take over the "Borgata" and to be "reppresentante" at Los Angeles, California.

MAGADDINO complained that BONANNO had not mentioned this before and opposed the selection. MAGADDINO was then approached by "TOMMY BROWN" LUCHESE about this appointment because BONANNO is related to MAGADDINO.

MAGADDINO immediately informed LUCHESE that their relationship should not enter into the matter since relationship means nothing in Cosa Nostra.

-22-